THE LITERARY LANGUAGE OF SHAKESPEARE

The literary language of Shakespeare

S. S. Hussey

Longman
London and New York

Longman Group Limited
Longman House
Burnt Mill, Harlow, Essex, UK

Published in the United States of America
by Longman Inc., New York

© Longman Group Limited 1982

First published 1982

British Library Cataloguing in Publication Data

Hussey, S.S.
The literary language of Shakespeare.
1. Shakespeare, William – Language
I. Title
822.3'3   PR3072

ISBN 0-582-49228-9

Library of Congress Cataloguing in Publication Data

Hussey, S. S., 1925–
The literary language of Shakespeare.
Bibliography: p. 203
Includes index.
1. Shakespeare, William, 1564–1616 – Language.
2. Shakespeare, William, 1564–1616 – Style. I. Title.
PR3072.H86   822.3'3   81-20889
ISBN 0–582–49228–9   AACR2

Set in 10/12 pt Linotron 202 Bembo
Printed in Great Britain by
William Clowes (Beccles) Ltd, Beccles and London

Contents

For Joyce

Preface

'Please,' a despairing sixth-former asked her teacher after her first inconclusive encounter with Shakespeare, 'haven't you got any plays in *proper* English?' It would be folly to deny that understanding what Shakespeare says is yearly becoming more difficult for the beginner and equally naive to suppose that one short book will put everything right. Yet a proper appreciation of any great writer must begin with his language. Why does he put it in that particular way at that particular point in the play? To say that a writer is great because he exploits the linguistic conventions of his age is to risk a truism. Yet the further back we go, the greater the risk of partial or unsound literary judgements, simply because those conventions may be unfamiliar or even unrecognised. Although we cannot be sure what Shakespeare's own speech was like (any more than we can Chaucer's), we can distinguish, from his own work and that of his fellow Elizabethans, a number of accepted styles in use around the turn of the century. From these Shakespeare selects to achieve a range of characterisation, description or conversation far beyond that of even the best of his contemporaries. Since they are norms, he can also deliberately deviate from these styles to produce a type of language remarkable simply because it is so unexpected in that particular context.

There are, of course, books on Shakespeare's language which illustrate in detail the main features of his vocabulary, grammar, syntax and phonology. What they do not attempt is to demonstrate how these same features achieve the stylistic effects they do. Several articles, often limited to individual plays, have recently begun to make this approach to Shakespeare, but, so far as I know, no one book has yet taken it as its subject. Naturally I have been able to illustrate only some of these effects, and certain plays perhaps receive less attention than they merit. It is virtually certain, too, that from the vast albatross of Shakespearean criticism (even criticism of his style) I shall have failed to pluck some of the choicest feathers. But I have tried to acknowledge the work of those writers whom I have found most helpful. I have profited too from the stimulus of sharing courses in Early Modern English Language with my colleague, Dr A. J. Gilbert. Messrs Longman have shown a care and courtesy beyond that which any author has a right to expect.

Some of these ideas were set out in an inaugural lecture given in the University of Lancaster in December 1976. I am grateful to those who listened on that occasion.

List of abbreviations

Shakespeare is quoted from the New Penguin edition where available at present (September 1981), otherwise from the Signet edition (for *TA, LLL, MWW, TC, TNK, Hen VIII*) and from *Elizabethan Verse Romances*, ed. M. M. Reese (1968), Routledge, for *VA*.

In the list of abbreviated titles below, I have also added approximate dates. These are conservative in that they sometimes represent the first known production rather than the possible date of composition. It is the probable order of the plays rather than the date of any one or two of them that is important for my argument.

1 Hen VI	*1 Henry VI*	1591		*MND*	*A Midsummer*	
2 Hen VI	*2 Henry VI*	1591–2			*Night's Dream*	
3 Hen VI	*3 Henry VI*			*MV*	*The Merchant*	1596
R III	*Richard III*	1592			*of Venice*	
VA	*Venus and Adonis*	1593		*1 Hen IV*	*1 Henry IV*	1597
TS	*The Taming of*	1593–4		*2 Hen IV*	*2 Henry IV*	1598
	the Shrew			*MA*	*Much Ado*	
TA	*Titus Andronicus*				*About Nothing*	
CE	*The Comedy of*			*JC*	*Julius Caesar*	1599
	Errors			*Hen V*	*Henry V*	
TGV	*The Two*			*AYLI*	*As You Like It*	
	Gentlemen of			*MWW*	*The Merry*	1600
	Verona				*Wives of*	
RL	*The Rape of*	1594			*Windsor*	
	Lucrece			*TC*	*Troilus and*	
LLL	*Love's Labour's*				*Cressida*	
	Lost			*Ham*	*Hamlet*	1601
KJ	*King John*			*TN*	*Twelfth Night*	1602
RII	*Richard II*	1595		*AW*	*All's Well That*	1604
RJ	*Romeo and*				*Ends Well*	
	Juliet			*MM*	*Measure for Measure*	

List of abbreviations

Oth	Othello	
KL	King Lear	1605
Mac	Macbeth	1606
AC	Antony and Cleopatra	1607
Cor	Coriolanus	
Tim	Timon of Athens	

Per	Pericles	1608
Cym	Cymbeline	1610
WT	The Winter's Tale	1611
Temp	The Tempest	
TNK	The Two Noble Kinsmen	1613
Hen VIII	Henry VIII	

CHAPTER ONE
Is this Shakespeare's language?

What the 'real' language of Shakespeare – his own language – was like, we will probably never completely know. He came to London from Stratford before 1592, in which year he was sufficiently established for his fellow writer Robert Greene, embittered by poverty and ill-health, to attack him in print:

> . . . an upstart Crow, beautified with our feathers, that with his *Tygers heart wrapt in a Players hide*, supposes he is as well able to bumbast out a blanke verse as the best of you: and being an absolute *Iohannes fac totum*, is in his owne conceit the onely Shake-scene in a countrie.[1]

In the middle of a long speech in *3 Henry VI* (possibly performed the year before) York calls the Queen a 'tiger's heart wrapped in a *women's* hide!' (I.iv.137). There is no firm evidence for dating any of his plays before 1590–1. He was not a university man, as were many of his contemporaries: Marlowe, Greene and Nashe, for instance. His father, indeed, although a prominent Stratford citizen and merchant, was perhaps illiterate – at least, he signed documents with his mark. There is a tradition that, in his earlier years, William was a schoolmaster 'in the country'. From a literary point of view this is so much more attractive, if less romantic, than the other story which has him holding horses outside the theatre. Certainly his first plays already exhibit a close knowledge of rhetorical devices of the kind found in contemporary school textbooks, but this of course is not proof. It is possible to make informed guesses at many of the circumstances of Shakespeare's career,[2] but several tantalising questions must remain unanswered. Did his wife and children stay at Stratford? If so, perhaps he visited them fairly regularly; he certainly retained some business connections in the town. Yet he lived in London, close to the theatres in which he worked, first in Bishopsgate near the Theatre and later on the Bankside near the Globe in Southwark. He acted in plays as well as wrote them (Greene's attack is on both the player and the playwright). Tradition has it that he played Adam in *As You Like It* and the Ghost in *Hamlet*; he certainly appeared in at least two of Ben Jonson's plays. So, whatever Warwickshire may have contributed to his own language, he was presumably understood on the London stage.

We might have hoped for more from Christopher Sly, the drunken Warwickshire tinker who, in the Induction to *The Taming of the Shrew*, is persuaded that he is a 'lord indeed' and, in the country house, 'wrapped in sweet clothes', surrounded by attentive servants, 'wanton pictures' and music sweeter than that of Apollo or caged nightingales, dreams he sees a play, 'a kind of history', performed by the sort of strolling players who might have captivated the young Shakespeare. But although the local names are present (Wincot was four miles from Stratford and a Sara Hacket was baptised there in 1591):

> What, would you make me mad? Am not I Christoper Sly, old Sly's son
> of Burton-heath, by birth a pedlar, by education a cardmaker, by
> transmutation a bear-herd, and now by present profession a tinker? Ask
> Marian Hacket, the fat ale-wife of Wincot, if she know me not. If she say
> I am not fourteen pence on the score for sheer ale, score me up for the
> lyingest knave in Christendom.   (Ind. II.16–23)

indications of specifically Warwickshire language are disappointingly absent, as they are from the further Sly scenes found in *The Taming of A Shrew*.

The large *Oxford English Dictionary* (OED) is compiled almost entirely from printed accounts for Shakespeare's time and its localisations for dialect words are usually very tentative. We lack a Tudor and Stuart dictionary of the kind which might provide more extensive (and more recently documented) coverage over a more limited period. We can, however, get a little help from Warwickshire documents, such as the parish accounts recording the detailed spending by public officers. These are valuable because they are clearly localised and dated, and for most of the seventeenth century they are not influenced by the spread of standard English which reduces their linguistic usefulness later. Two examples quoted by Dr Hilda Hulme, who has made a special study of these records,[3] will illustrate the kind of help they can give in appreciating Shakespearean usage. In *The Merry Wives of Windsor* (IV.iii.8), the retainers of a suspicious-sounding German duke wish to hire horses from the Host of the Garter inn. The Host replies

> They shall have my horses, but I'll make them pay; I'll sauce them. They have had my house a week at command. I have turned away my other guests. They must come off. I'll sauce them. Come.

The *OED* interprets *to pay sauce* as 'to pay dearly', but can only date this usage between 1678 and 1718. Even if we turn to *As You Like It* (III.v.67) where Rosalind says

> If it be so, as fast as she answers thee with frowning looks, I'll sauce her with bitter words.

we still only perceive the metaphor of an unexpectedly hot seasoning. The parish accounts of Solihull (Warwickshire) for 1666, however, contain the following record:

> Thomas Palmer & my selfe went before to vew the timber & caused sawers to look on it. 0–0–4
> Another time I took 2 Carpenters to looke on it and to saw it & I found ye sauce worse then the meat. 0–0–8

Surely, as Dr Hulme remarks, one would expect to pay less for the sauce than for the meat, just as the churchwardens expected to pay less (not more) to the carpenters than to the real wood cutters, the *sawers*. Hence the meaning can be elaborated from 'to pay dearly' to 'to pay more than you expected'. The furious Host of the Garter is determined to obtain his revenge by deliberate overcharging. Again, the accounts of the Stratford Corporation for 1582–3 read

> Payd to davi Jones and his companye for his pastyme at Whitsontyde xii s iii d.

where *pastyme* is clearly not merely 'entertainment' but some kind of dramatic entertainment. When Gertrude, worried about Hamlet's melancholia, asks (III.i.15):

> Did you assay him/To any pastime?

it is natural that Rosencrantz and Guildenstern should at once think of actors:

> Madam, it so fell out that certain *players*/We o'er-raught on the way.

This is fascinating, and shows how quite usual words could acquire a special use so that a joke or an extra layer of meaning becomes apparent. Yet it is inevitably limited in its extent, nor do we know how widespread these dialectal usages were. Did they seem, to London au-

diences, simply 'country' as opposed to 'normal' usage and not Warwickshire dialect at all?

In one way, however, the Elizabethan play-text may come between Shakespeare's own language and the modern reader. It is natural for the latter to assume that the text he reads is in all respects – act
and scene division, lineation, spelling and punctuation – what
Shakespeare wrote. An author today will correct his own proofs (or
at least designate a responsible person to do it for him) so that the
published version of the work will represent what author and editor
have agreed should appear. But we have no fair copies of the plays
which are demonstrably in Shakespeare's own hand. The first collected edition, the First Folio, was published in 1623, seven years
after Shakespeare's death, and was compiled by two of his fellow-
actors and business associates, John Heminges and Henry Condell. A
volume of 'collected works' by the author himself was a rarity at that
time, and drama was perhaps not thought of as sufficient of a literary
form to justify such care and exactness. Ben Jonson, whose interest
in language is shown by his English-Latin grammar (covering pronunciation, morphology and syntax) and whose reputation was very
dear to him, is the exception in issuing in 1616 the first volume of the
Workes of Beniamin Jonson. When a playwright sold his play to a company he ceased to be responsible for it. The company in turn tended
not to publish unless they needed the money or unless the play was
no longer a box-office success, for publication might mean a production by a rival company.

The First Folio (F1) contains thirty-six of Shakespeare's plays, sixteen of them appearing in print for the first time. The Sonnets, *Venus
and Adonis* and *The Rape of Lucrece* are not included, and *Pericles* was
added in the 1664 copy of the Folio. But during Shakespeare's life-
time, seventeen plays were published in quarto and a quarto text of
Othello appeared in 1622. The sheets of a quarto are printed on both
sides and folded twice to give eight pages per gathering (or quire); in
a folio each sheet is folded only once. The quarto versions which are
reasonably accurate are known as 'good' quartos and the six which
are seriously corrupt, textually, are called 'bad' quartos. *Hamlet* and
Romeo and Juliet exist in both good and bad quartos, as well as in F1. In
their address 'To the great Variety of Readers', Heminges and
Condell claim that their texts are greatly superior to previous bad
quartos and indeed represent Shakespeare's own version:

> where (before) you were abus'd with diuerse stolne, and surreptitious
> copies, maimed, and deformed by the frauds and stealthes of iniurious

imposters, that expos'd them; euen those, are now offer'd to your view
cur'd, and perfect of their limbes; and all the rest, absolute in their
numbers, as he conceiued them.

This is frankly advertising copy; in fact the quality of a text available
to the printer, whether of F1 or of any quarto, varied considerably.
Shakespeare, no doubt, had his original rough copy (or 'foul papers')
and this sometimes seems to lie not far below some of the good
quartos. In these, the stage directions are often of a 'literary' nature,
of the kind which might assist the author's memory rather than be of
great use to the producer, and the designation of minor characters
shows that Shakespeare was thinking of the type of character rather
than of an individual. The stage-direction at I.i.69 of *Titus Andronicus*, for example, after listing the characters who actually enter at that
point, concludes 'and others as many as can be'; just how many can
be decided later by the producer. *All's Well* (II.iii.182) has 'Exeunt all
but Parolles and Lafew, *who stay behind, commenting on this wedding.*'
The succeeding lines make the last part of this direction, which I
have italicised, perfectly obvious. An author, perhaps breaking off at
this point, might need a reminder of what he had intended; the
prompter would almost certainly delete it. In the stage-directions of
the quarto of *Much Ado*, Dogberry and Verges are sometimes given
their proper names, sometimes called 'Constable' and 'Headbor-
ough', and sometimes (IV.ii) 'Kemp' and 'Cowley', the actors for
whom the parts were written. The printer might at best receive a fair
copy of the authorial manuscript, like those made for some of the
plays in F1 by Ralph Crane, a professional scribe, who probably produced the copy for *The Tempest*, the first play in F1 and which is well
set out, and others such as *The Winter's Tale* and *The Two Gentlemen
of Verona*. His copies have full division into acts and scenes, although
few stage directions, and one of his identifying features is his extensive use of brackets and hyphens.

   The other source of printer's copy was the theatre prompt-book.
The prompter (or book-keeper), as well as tidying up the stage-
directions, especially marking entrances and exits, might himself
make interpolations or cuts, perhaps for a particular performance or
to reduce the size of a travelling company through the elimination of
minor characters. The Folio text of *Richard II*, for example, was
printed from a quarto that had been checked against a theatre copy.
Its stage-directions are therefore businesslike, indicating entrances
and exits clearly. One of the most uncompromising (yet perfectly
adequate) stage directions in Shakespeare is that which begins Act II

of *Pericles*: 'Enter Pericles, wet.' The F1 text of *King John*, on the other hand, has infrequent stage-directions and these are not conspicuously theatrical in character; it was probably set up from a copy of an authorial manuscript.

Where we are fortunate enough to possess both the Folio and a quarto text, we can use one to throw light on the other, but even so they may vary considerably. The quarto of *Henry V* omits the prologue, choruses and epilogue; the F1 text of *Hamlet* omits one of the soliloquies, 'How all occasions . . .' Some bad quartos were probably put together illegally ('stolne and surreptitious copies') by one or two of the actors. Their attempts at memorial reconstruction of the whole play show a good recollection of the parts these actors themselves played but a tendency to fill out the lines less clearly remembered. Here is the opening of the best-known of all Hamlet's soliloquies as it appears in the bad Q1:

> To be, or not to be, I there's the point,
> To Die, to sleepe, is that all? I all:
> No, to sleepe, to dreame, I mary there it goes,
> For in that dreame of death, when wee awake,
> And borne before an euerlasting Iudge,
> From whence no passenger euer retur'nd,
> The vndiscouered country, at whose sight
> The happy smile, and the accursed damn'd.

If an actor was responsible for this, it was probably not Hamlet himself who would have remembered better.

The bad quarto of *2 Henry VI* is entitled 'The First part of the Contention betwixt the two famous Houses of Yorke and Lancaster, with the death of the good Duke Humphrey: And the banishment and death of the Duke of Suffolke, and the Tragicall end of the proud Cardinall of Winchester, with the notable Rebellion of Iacke Cade: And the Duke of Yorkes first claime vnto the Crowne', and it contains echoes of Marlowe's *Edward II* and *Arden of Feversham*.

But what about a situation in which the comparative textual value of Folio and quarto(s) is unclear? The 1608 quarto of *King Lear* contains about 300 lines not in F1 which in its turn includes some 100 lines not in the quarto. These differences go far beyond mere variations in phraseology. Did Lear die believing Cordelia was still alive? The Folio suggests he did:

> Why should a Dog, a Horse, a Rat haue life,
> And thou no breath at all? Thou'lt come no more,
> Neuer, neuer, neuer, neuer, neuer.
> Pray you vndo this Button. Thanke you Sir,

Do you see this? Looke on her. Looke her lips,
Looke there, looke there.   (V.iii.306–11)

But the quarto (which, incidentally, prints the speech as prose) omits the last two lines of the Folio text:

Why should a dog, a horse, a rat of life and thou no breath at all. O thou wilt come no more, neuer, neuer, neuer, pray you vndo this button, thank you sir, O, o, o, o.

The *O, o, o, o* is the usual indication of a long-drawn out death-cry on stage. So this is probably an actor's interpolation. But of what? Lear's own dying groans or a realisation that Cordelia is in fact dead (in which latter case he would of course be looking at Cordelia)? If our modern stage direction (at 256) reads 'Enter Lear with Cordelia dead in his arms', this does not solve the puzzle, for the *dead* was added by the eighteenth–century editor Nicholas Rowe. Of the two surviving versions of Marlowe's *Dr Faustus* (both published some years after Marlowe's death) the 1604 text almost certainly represents memorial reconstruction by a group of actors. The 1616 text is longer and more coherent, but this will not do either for it seems to be based on a prompt-book which has been subject to a good deal of revision and perhaps some augmentation by other hands. In such cases today's editor is faced with a dilemma and must simply select on the best textual, linguistic and dramatic principles he can.

Even if the printer received good copy, he might himself contribute some errors, either through carelessness, or through a desire to correct apparent nonsense, or to achieve a typographically tidy page. The first kind is comparatively easy to spot and rectify, the second and third more difficult to detect because they may produce a plausible reading. Not only writing but also spelling was a personal matter (as may be seen from the quotations and titles above) and contracted forms, not marked by punctuation as now, were frequent. Furthermore, the printing of a text may have been divided between two or more compositors working simultaneously and each with his own idiosyncracies. Clearly a knowledge of the palaeographical and linguistic habits of Shakespeare's age is an indispensible part of the modern editor's equipment. We have some knowledge of a few typically Shakespearean spellings, largely from his contribution to the play of Sir Thomas More. This play, in a unique manuscript and originally written in one hand, perhaps in the mid 1590s, was augmented and corrected by five other hands, one of which is thought to be Shakespeare's. He contributed the early part of Act II, scene iii, in which More pacifies the citizens, and, less certainly, More's soliloquy which opens Act III, scene i.

Where F1 is printed from a good quarto, textual criticism is correspondingly easier, but in any event the task of reconstructing what Shakespeare actually wrote is far less hopeless than some of the above remarks may have suggested. Printers, prompters, scribes and unauthorised actors may all have helped to obscure what Shakespeare intended, but we now have a far better knowledge of Elizabethan handwriting, stage conditions, the whole printing process (even to the extent of identifying scribes such as Ralph Crane and individual compositors from their linguistic mannerisms and minor damage to their typefaces) and, finally, contemporary language than our predecessors had. The editor will supply act and scene division where these are either not marked or demonstrably erroneous, silently regularise speech prefixes (Lady Macbeth for 'Lady' and Armado for 'Braggart'), correct mislineation and verse printed as prose, supply stage-directions and indicate locale. He will almost always use modern punctuation. Elizabethan punctuation, especially in the quartos, is less than today's reader is accustomed to and frequently rhetorical in its aim (as an aid to the actor speaking the lines) rather than grammatical (for the convenience of the reader). The amount and the style of modern punctuation is important, for punctuation is itself a form of interpretation; the editor is himself contributing here to the way we understand the text. In his aim of reconstructing as closely as possible what Shakespeare wrote, the editor should remember that Shakespeare at times wrote below his best and should resist any temptation to remove every awkwardness of expression. He must always give his reasons for his choice between variant but possible readings. In this book I quote from the New Penguin texts where these are available and from the Signet texts otherwise, not only because these are easily accessible but because they provide (the New Penguin especially) a sound text and the evidence on which that text is based.

Our modern texts, therefore, represent a reasonable approximation to what Shakespeare wrote. In most cases it will no doubt be what he actually wrote, although we cannot always be sure just what the words sounded like on stage (there was certainly a good deal of punning, for example) or how closely drama recaptured the spoken idiom. Drama selects from the language of its time, and although at times it may approach colloquial English more than other kinds of writing, it has also of necessity to concentrate its material more than, say, the narrative poem or the novel. And the essence of drama is to sound spontaneous, to be spoken as if it were *not* written. The features of the spoken language it contains will be partly deliberate and partly unconscious. For all these reasons this book perforce deals with the *literary* language of Shakespeare.

NOTES AND REFERENCES

1. *A Groats-worth of Wit, Life and Complete Works of Robert Greene*, ed. A. B. Grosart (edn of 1964), Russell and Russell, New York, Ch. XII, p. 144.
2. A recent attempt at biography is Bradbrook (1978).
3. Hulme (1962), pp. 45–6, 337–8. For *sauce*, compare *Dr Faustus*, I.iv. 11–12.

CHAPTER TWO
The expanding vocabulary

By the final quarter of the sixteenth century (Shakespeare was born in 1564), English had been vindicated as a language able to produce good writing in both prose and verse. It was still occasionally felt to be 'rough', 'unpolished', 'uneloquent' (the standard of comparison, expressed or implied, always being Latin) but not so often as hitherto. Yet it was still considered incapable of expressing much by way of abstract, philosophical or scientific ideas. More had composed *Utopia* in Latin in 1516. It was translated into German in 1524, into Italian by 1548 and into French by 1550, but not into English (by Ralph Robinson) until 1551 – by which time More was dead. Erasmus, More's friend and arguably the most learned European man of his day, visited England but never bothered to learn English; were their conversations in Latin? English was not yet a subject in grammar schools, Latin emphatically was. Harvey, who demonstrated the circulation of the blood in the early seventeenth century, lectured to the Royal College of Physicians on his discovery in English but recorded his results in Latin. Isaac Newton (died 1727) wrote all his scientific works in Latin. The first description of a game of cricket (early eighteenth century) is also in Latin.

But by the middle of the sixteenth century it was becoming possible to view things rather differently, and it is easy to see some of the reasons why. Firstly, to write in English becomes one more manifestation of a growing patriotism. Although Roger Ascham had lamented in his preface to *Toxophilus* ('the archer') in 1545:

> . . . as for the Latin or greke tonge, euery thyng is so excellently done in them, that none can do better: In the Englysh tonge contrary, euery thinge in a manner so meanly, bothe for the matter and handelynge, that no man can do worse.[1]

he nevertheless writes his book 'on this English matter, in the English tongue, for Englishmen'. By 1582, in the *Elementarie* of Richard Mulcaster (Spenser's schoolmaster), this had become:

> For is it not in dede a mervellous bondage, to becom servants to one tung for learning sake, the most of our time, with losse of most time, whereas we maie have the verie same treasur in our own tung, with the gain of most time? our own bearing the joyfull title of our libertie and fredom, the Latin tung remembring us of our thraldom and bondage? I love Rome, but London better, I favor Italie, but England more, I honor the Latin, but I worship the English.

and again:

> But why not all in English, a tung of it self both depe in conceit and frank in deliverie? I do not think that anie language, be it whatsoever, is better able to utter all arguments, either with more pith, or greater planesse, then our English tung is, if the English utterer be as skilfull in the matter, which he is to utter: as the foren utterer is.[2]

Puttenham's *Arte of English Poesie* was published in 1589. This is essentially a rhetorical textbook, but Puttenham was a patriot too. His second chapter has the heading 'That there may be an Art of our English Poesie as well as there is of the Latine and Greeke', and he gives English definitions (which often sound amusing to us) of the Latin and Greek names for the figures of rhetoric. Even in *Utopia* More had advocated that children 'be taught learning in their own native tongue'.

Secondly, there was a demand from an increasingly literate public to share in the fruits of the Renaissance. London was a large city by European standards (although Paris, Naples and Constantinople were larger) with a population between 150,000 and 200,000. It has been estimated that between one-third and one-half of the population of Shakespeare's London could read. Noblemen's sons were now going to university, and the study of the liberal arts was no longer simply a training in scholastic method (with a career in the church in mind) but had been restored to its original connection with public affairs.[3] It aimed to make a man more able and more cultured, a rounded personality:

> . . . though I lacke Authoritie to give counsell, yet I lacke not good will to wisshe, that the yougthe in England, speciallie Ientlemen, and namelie nobilitie, shold be by good bringing up, so grounded in judgement of learninge, so founded in love of honestie, as, whan they shold be called forthe to the execution of great affaires, in service of their Prince and contrie, they might be hable, to use and to order, all experiences, were

they good were they bad, and that, according to the square, rule and line
of wisdom, learning and vertue.   (Acham, *The Schoolmaster*)[4]

As Ophelia saw Hamlet:

> O what a noble mind is here o'erthrown!
> The courtier's, soldier's, scholar's, eye, tongue, sword,
> Th'expectancy and rose of the fair state,
> The glass of fashion and the mould of form,
> Th'observed of all observers, quite, quite down!   (III.i. 151–5)

or as Sir Philip Sidney must have seemed to his contemporaries: aristocrat, statesman, parliamentarian, traveller in Europe, friend of the
Queen, author, and finally soldier, dying heroically on a foreign field
at the age of thirty-two.

   Printing, brought to England by Caxton in 1476, had so far developed by the end of the sixteenth century that middlemen begin to
appear in the publishing trade. Printing, too, was not simply a great
economic factor in the spread of books; since all copies of a printed
text were substantially the same, it acted as a great stabiliser of the
forms of the language, especially the grammar. Something similar to
the rapid spread of books in Renaissance England we have ourselves
seen (although on a considerably larger scale) in the 'paperback explosion' following the Second World War. We should, however, remember that the Elizabethans valued the classics not only – not even
mainly – for their style but for their subject-matter: they wanted to
know what earlier writers had had to say about government, ethics
or warfare. So the rush of translations in the later sixteenth and the
earlier seventeenth century is not surprising: Caesar, Cicero, Livy,
Tacitus, Seneca, Virgil, Horace, Ovid, Sallust, Plutarch, Aristotle,
and, above all, the struggle over the translation of the Bible into English which culminated in the Authorised Version of 1611. Some of
these translations, such as North's Plutarch (1579) or Golding's Ovid
(1565), we know that Shakespeare used.

   Yet as translations increase in number and the monopoly of Latin
for learning begins to be broken, so the deficiencies in English stand
out more. Ralph Lever, in his *Art of Reason* (1573) expressed the
situation succinctly; for him there were 'more things than there are
words to express things by'. The act of translation, indeed, focuses
the problem. If English is deficient – or even thought to be deficient – in words for a particular concept, what can the translator do?
Not surprisingly he often borrowed from the language of the book
he was translating and so added to the enormous number of foreign

words (especially Latin words) coming into English at this time. Since so many of these words enter English through writing, it is natural that they frequently seem more learned and unusual than earlier medieval borrowings from Old Norse and from French which had made their way into English via the spoken word.

Not everyone welcomed this influx of foreign words with enthusiasm. Extreme opposition to loan-words is seen in Sir John Cheke's translation of St Matthew's gospel where he uses such coinages as *hundreder* (centurion in the Authorised Version), *biwordes* (parables), *foresayer* (prophet), *uprising* or *gainrising* (resurrection) and *crossed* (crucified) to avoid the introduction of a Latin-derived word. But although Cheke (an excellent Latin scholar himself) wanted an English 'unmixt and vnmangeled with borrowing of other tunges', even he allowed for a minimum of necessary borrowing. Cheke's Cambridge circle included Ascham, Sir Thomas Smith, Sir Walter Haddon and Thomas Wilson whose *Art of Rhetoric* (first published 1553 but revised 1560) was in all probability known to Shakespeare. Wilson lamented:

> And thus we see that poore simple men are much troubled, and talke oftentimes they know not what for lacke of wit, and want of Latine and French, whereof many of our strange wordes full often are deriued. Those therefore that will eschue this folly, and acquaint themselues with the best kind of speech, must seeke from time to time such wordes as are commonly receiued, and such as properly may expresse in plaine maner, the whole conceipt of their minds.[5]

George Gascoigne (1542–77) went still further:

> . . . the most auncient English wordes are of one sillable, so that the more monasyllables that you use, the truer Englishman you shall seeme, and the lesse you shall smell of the Inkehorne.

and later in the same work, *Certayne notes of Instruction concerning the making of verse or ryme in English*:

> . . . asmuche as may be, eschew straunge words, or obsoleta & inusitata, unless the Theame do give just occasion; marie in some places a straunge worde doth drawe attentive reading, but yet I woulde have you therein use discretion.[6]

The opponents of these Latin newcomers dubbed them 'inkhorn' or 'inkpot' terms[7] and often made their point through parody, such as the frequently quoted plea for preferment to a benefice in Wilson's

Art of Rhetoric, or this extract from Samuel Rowland's *Signior Word-Monger, the Ape of Eloquence*:

> As on the way I itinerated,
> A rural person I obviated,
> Interrogating time's transition
> And of the passage demonstration.
> My apprehension did ingenious scan
> That he was merely a simplician;
> So when I saw he was extravagant,
> Unto the obscure vulgar consonant,
> I bade him vanish most promiscuously,
> And not contaminate my company.

The parody, however, is sometimes not so very much more preposterous than the actual. Andrew Borde began the preface to his *Breuiary of Healthe* (1552)

> Egregious Doctors and masters of the eximious and Archane Science of Physicke, of your Urbanitie exasperate not your selues against mee, for making of this little volume of Physick. Considering that my pretense is for an vtilitie and a common wealth. And this is not only, but also I doe it for no detriment but for a preferment of your laudable science, that euery man shuld esteeme, repute and regard the excellent faculty. And also you to be extolled and highly preferred, that hath and doth studie, practise and labor this said Archane Science, to the which none inartious persons, can nor shal attaine to the knowledge: yet notwithstanding fooles and insipient persons, yea and many the which doth think themselues wise (the which in this faculty be fools indeed) wil enterprise to smatter. . .

Naturally there was a compromise, and the more thoughtful critics advocated a kind of controlled borrowing where words are adopted only if they fill a gap in the native language and not merely because they *sound* impressive.[8] George Pettie argues that English has always borrowed words:

> And though for my part I vse those[borrowed] words as litle as any, yet I know no reason why I should not vse them, and I finde it a fault in my selfe that I do not vse them: for it is in deed the ready way to inrich our tongue, and make it copious, and it is the way which all tongues haue taken to inrich them selues: For take the Latine woordes from the *Spanish* tongue, and it shall be as barren as most part of their Countrey; take them from the *Italian*, and you take away in a manner the whole tongue; take them from the *Frenche*, and you marre the grace of it: yea take from the Latine it selfe the woordes deriued from the *Greeke*, and it shall not be so flowing and flourishing as it is. Wherefore I marueile how our english tongue hath cracke it[s] credite, that it may not borrow of the Latine as well as other tongues: and if it haue broken, it is but of late, for it is not vnknowen to all men how many woordes we haue fetcht from thence within these few yeeres, which if they should be all counted inkepot

termes, I know not how we should speake any thing without blacking
our mouthes with inke: for what woord can be more plaine then this
word *plaine* and yet what can come more neere to the Latine? what more
manifest then *manifest*? and yet in a manner Latine: What more commune
then *rare* or less rare then *commune*, and yet both of them coming of the
Latine? But you wyll say, long vse hath made these woords curraunt: and
why may not vse doo as much for these woords which we shall now
deriue? Why should not we doo as much for the posteritie, as we haue
receiued of the antiquitie? and yet if a thing be of it selfe ill, I see not how
the oldnesse of it can make it good, and if it be of it selfe good, I see not
how the newnesse of it can make it naught: Wherevpon I infer, that those
woords which your selues confesse, by vse to be made good, are good
the first time they are vttered, and therefore not to be iested at, nor to be
misliked.

(Preface to *The Civile Conuersation of M. Steeuen Guazzo*, 1581)[9]

Puttenham makes the same point:

> . . . seruing aptly, when a man wanteth to expresse so much vnles it be in
> two words, which surplussage to auoide, we are allowed to draw in other
> words single, and asmuch significatiue: this word *significatiue* is borrowed
> of the Latine and French, but to vs brought in first by some Noble-mans
> Secretarie, as I thinke, yet doth so well serue the turne, as it could not
> now be spared: and many more like vsurped Latine and French words: as,
> *Methode, methodicall, placation, function, assubtiling, refining, compendious,
> prolixe, figuratiue, inueigle.* A terme borrowed of our common Lawyers,
> *impression,* also a new terme, but well expressing the matter, and more
> than our English word. These words, *Numerous, numerositee, metricall,
> harmonicall,* but they cannot be refused, specially in this place for
> description of the arte. Also ye finde these words, *penetrate, penetrable,
> indignitie,* which I cannot see how we may spare them, whatsoeuer fault
> wee finde with Ink-horne termes: for our speach wanteth wordes to such
> sense so well to be vsed: yet in steade of *indignitie,* yee haue
> vnworthinesse: and for *penetrate,* we may say *peerce,* and that a French
> terme also, or *broche,* or enter into with violence, but not so well
> sounding as *penetrate.* Item, *sauage,* for wilde: *obscure,* for darke. Item
> these words, *declination, delineation, dimention,* are scholasticall termes in
> deede, and yet very proper. But peraduenture (& I could bring a reason for
> it) many other like words borrowed out of the Latin and French, were
> not so well to be allowed by vs, as these words, *audacious,* for bold:
> *facunditie,* for eloquence: *egregious,* for great or notable: *implete,* for
> replenished: *attemptat,* for attempt: *compatible,* for agreeable in nature, and
> many more.[10]

Puttenham's list of indispensable words, however, contains a few
(*placation, assubtiling, numerositee, implete*) which we seem no longer
to need, and he objects to *audacious, egregious,* and *compatible,* all of
which we have kept. Time itself has shown which are necessary, but
'necessary' (as Puttenham saw) must be allowed to include

synonyms, for it is this extensive Renaissance borrowing (following the considerable influx of French words into Middle English) that has given English so many groups of words, the first native English, the second borrowed French, and the third borrowed Latin:

end	finish	conclude
rise	mount	ascend
goodness	virtue	probity
ask	question	interrogate
two	second	dual
fire	flame	conflagration
fear	terror	trepidation

In some cases the French and the Latin borrowings are from the same root but entered English at different times:

| sicker | sure | secure |
| kingly | royal | regal |

This greatly increases the semantic *density*, although only in the case of a loan-word that has no real synonym in current English does it do much to increase semantic *range*. It is easy for native speakers of present-day English to discover contexts in which one of the group of three would be more likely to occur than either of the other two, but difficult sometimes to be sure of such semantic shading in earlier periods. Pettie called borrowing 'the ready way to inrich our tongue, and make it copious' and *copious* is the favourite Elizabethan description of a style whose lexis draws considerably on such synonyms or near-synonyms, often in doublets or triplets, to help provide dignity and sonority. (In the same way, copious syntax is balanced, complex, but, above all, controlled.) Examples abound in Elizabethan prose:

> But now that we may lift up our eyes (as it were) from the footstool to the throne of God, and leaving these natural, consider a little the state of heavenly and divine creatures; touching Angels which are spirits immaterial and intellectual, the glorious inhabitants of those sacred palaces, where nothing but light and blessed immortality, no shadow of matter for tears, discontentments, griefs, and uncomfortable passions to work upon, but all joy, tranquillity, and peace, even for ever and ever doth dwell; as in number and order they are huge, mighty, and royal armies: so likewise in perfection of obedience unto that law, which the Highest, whom they adore, love, and imitate, hath imposed upon them, such observants they are thereof, that our Saviour himself being to set down the perfect idea of that which we are to pray and wish for on earth, did not teach to pray or wish for more than only that here it might be with us, as with them it is in heaven.
>
> (Hooker, *Laws of Ecclesiastical Policy* (1593), Book I)[11]

Let me wither and wear out mine age in a discomfortable, in an unwholesome, in a penurious prison, and so pay my debts with my bones, and recompense the wastefulness of my youth, with the beggary of mine age; let me wither in a spital under sharp, and foul, and infamous diseases, and so recompense the wantonness of my youth, with that loathsomeness in mine age: yet, if God withdraw not his spiritual blessings, his grace, his patience, if I can call my suffering his doing, my passion his action, all this that is temporal, is but a caterpillar got into one corner of my garden, but a mildew fallen upon one acre of my corn; the body of all, the substance of all is safe, as long as the soul is safe. But when I shall trust to that, which we call a good spirit, and God shall deject, and impoverish, and evacuate that spirit, when I shall rely upon a moral constancy, and God shall shake, and enfeeble, and enervate, destroy and demolish that constancy; when I shall think to refresh myself in the serenity and sweet air of a good conscience, and God shall call up the damps and vapours of hell itself, and spread a cloud of diffidence, and an impenetrable crust of desperation upon my conscience; when health shall fly from me, and I shall lay hold upon riches to succour me, and comfort me in my sickness, and riches shall fly from me, and I shall snatch after favour, and good opinion, to comfort me in my poverty; when even this good opinion shall leave me, and calumnies and misinformations shall prevail against me; when I shall need peace, because there is none but thou, O Lord, that should stand for me, and then shall find, that all the wounds that I have, come from thy hand, all the arrows that stick in me, from thy quiver; when I shall see, that because I have given myself to my corrupt nature, thou hast changed thine; and because I am all evil towards thee, therefore thou hast given over being good towards me; when it comes to this height, that the fever is not in the humours, but in the spirits, that mine enemy is not an imaginary enemy, fortune, nor a transitory enemy, malice in great persons, but a real, and an irresistible, and an inexorable, and an everlasting enemy, the Lord of hosts himself, the Almighty God himself, the Almighty God himself only knows the weight of this affliction, and except he put in that *pondus gloriæ*, that exceeding weight of an eternal glory, with his own hand, into the other scale, we are weighed down, we are swallowed up, irreparably, irrevocably, irrecoverably, irremediably.[12]

(Donne, Sermon preached at St Paul's, 29 Jan. 1626)

Hooker's sentence (there is only a single sentence in the Hooker extract and only two in the longer Donne passage) contains, for example, the groups *heavenly and divine; tears, discontentments, griefs and uncomfortable passions; joy, tranquillity and peace; adore, love and imitate.* Donne, whose approach is even more expansive (more copious) not only has such groups as *discomfortable . . . unwholesome . . . penurious; sharp and foul and infamous; deject and impoverish and evacuate; shake and enfeeble, and enervate, destroy and demolish,* but is able to balance the groups against one another: *my suffering his doing, my passion his action; wounds . . . from thy hand . . . arrows . . . from thy quiver,* until the

17

whole reaches its climax with those four adverbs which come crashing down at the end of the paragraph. Yet in one of the passages previously held up to ridicule, Borde groups *eximious and Archane; esteeme, repute and regard; extolled and highly preferred; studie, practise and labour; fooles and insipient persons*. But Borde simply elaborates because three words are more impressive than one, and heaps one elaboration upon another. Hooker and Donne write of great matters in an appropriately dignified style. Their doublets (especially Hooker's) are not so much difficult words needing elucidation as a means of adding weight to the sentence. Their examples are better spaced within the passage. They are also not merely synonyms, since frequently the last member adds a new dimension to the group: 'huge, mighty and *royal*'; 'sharp and foul and *infamous* diseases'.

The debate over the *amount* of borrowing into the English vocabulary is perhaps the first extensive critique of the language by its native speakers. Yet the problem itself was not a new one. In the morality play *Mankind*, dated 1465–70, Mercy rhymes *denomynacyon* and *communycacyon*, to which New Gyse immediately retorts 'Ey, ey! Your body ys full of Englysch Laten.'[13] Choice of an appropriate vocabulary for his translations had exercised Caxton at the end of the fifteenth century:

> And that comyn Englysshe that is spoken in one shyre varyeth from another.... Certaynly it is harde to playse every man bycause of dyversite and chaunge of langage. For in these dayes every man that is in ony reputaycon in his countre, wyll utter his commynycacyon and matters in suche maners and termes that fewe men shall understoode theym. And som honest and grete clerkes have been wyth me, and desired me to wryte the moste curyous termes that I coude fyne. And thus bytwene playn rude and curyous I stande abasshed.   (*Preface to Eneydos*, 1490)[14]

Caxton had been worried about two things: variation between regional dialects and the intelligibility of both *curious* and *playn rude* terms. The first was, by the Renaissance, no longer such a problem, for, by the mid sixteenth century it is evident that some form of southern speech (later defined by Puttenham as 'the usual speech of the Court, and that of London and the shires lying about London within 60 miles and not much above') was a mark of good birth and good education. Even in the north and 'far west', men might be sufficiently educated to *write* good southern English even if they spoke in dialect (as Sir Walter Raleigh is supposed to have done in 'broad Devonshire'). Caxton's second problem, the number of 'curious' terms to be used, was essentially the same as that facing Renaissance writers; indeed, Caxton has his own doublets within this short passage (*dyversite and chaunge; commynycacyon and maters; maners and termes*). The 'aureate' language of one particular fifteenth-century literary style had, in all probability, paved the way for more extensive – and more Latinate – borrowing later. Lydgate (c. 1370–c. 1450), who wrote twice as much as Shakespeare and three times as much as Chaucer, and whose all-inclusive mind demonstrates a real talent for elaboration, seems to have been the first to use in English such words as *abuse, adjacent, capacity, circumspect, combine, credulity, delude, depend, disappear, equivalent, equipollent, excel, facundious* ('eloquent'), *fructyf* ('fertile'), *obumbred* ('overshadowed'). Even this short list shows the same mixture of necessary and merely outlandish terms.[15]

It is not always realised how widespread are the effects of wholesale borrowing of words in the Renaissance. It might be fanciful, yet not altogether wrong, to view it as another aspect of their willingness to experiment, the spirit that sent them exploring across half the world. Another manifestation of borrowing, especially from the classical languages, is the enormous growth of scientific and medical terminology in English. (Before the sixteenth century most scientific works were written in Latin.) One could have *smallpox* by 1518, *scurvy* by 1565, *mumps* by 1598 and *rheumatism* by 1601. (Shakespeare uses *rheum* which had been in the language from 1377 and which meant a cold in the head – compare French *enrhumé*.) Scientific borrowings are found more extensively in the seventeenth century: *acid* (1626), *apparatus* (1628), *calculus* (1672), *electric* (1646, but *electrical* from 1635), *focus* (1656), *laboratory* (1605), *logarithm* (1616), *microscope* (1656), *specimen* (1610). Also in the early seventeenth century appear the first English dictionaries, although Latin/English, French/English, Italian/English and Spanish/English dictionaries were all in existence by 1600. The first purely English dictionaries were of *hard* words, principally those which had been borrowed into English in the last generation and were therefore most in need of elucidation. This is clear from the title-page of what is usually recognised as the first real English dictionary, *A Table Alphabeticall*, by Robert Cawdrey, a schoolmaster, in 1604:

A Table Alphabeticall, conteyning and teaching the true writing, and
understanding of hard usuall English wordes, borrowed from the
Hebrew, Greeke, Latin or French, etc.
With the interpretation therof by plaine English words gathered for the
benefit and helpe of Ladies, Gentlewomen, or any other unskilful
persons. Whereby they may the more easilie and better understand many

> hard English wordes, which they shall heare or read in Scriptures, Sermons, or elsewhere, and also be made able to use the same aptly themselves. . .

or that of Henry Cockerham's *The English Dictionarie* (1623, which had its twelfth and final edition in 1670 and was the first to include the word 'dictionary' in its title):

> The English Dictionarie: or, An Interpreter of hard English Words. Enabling as well Ladies and Gentlewomen, young Schollers, Clarkes, Merchants, as also Strangers of any Nation, to the vnderstanding of the more difficult Authors already printed in our Language, and the more speedy attaining of an elegant perfection of the English tongue, both in reading, speaking and writing. Being a Collection of some thousands of words, neuer published by any heretofore.[16]

How to impress your friends.

One classical word in a passage of mainly native diction may outweigh every other word in the passage because of its rarity, specialised sense, or sheer incongruity in that context. Etymological statistics, based on the sheer number of words borrowed, are therefore of only limited value. Shakespeare is far from being the only Elizabethan to realise the value of a strategically-placed borrowing:

> Whenas in silks my Julia goes,
> Then, then (methinks) how sweetly flows
> That *liquefaction* of her clothes.   (Herrick, *Upon Julia's Clothes*)

> When love, with one another so
> *Interinanimates* two souls . . .   (Donne, *The Ecstasy*)

> *Annihilating* all that's made
> To a green thought in a green shade.   (Marvell, *The Garden*)

> Sweet spring, full of sweet days and roses,
> A box where sweets *compacted* lie . . .   (Herbert, *Virtue*)

but he perhaps realised it more often than most. He is careful to position such borrowed Latinate words within the line where they coincide with heavy stress and thus achieve maximum emphasis. In practice this often means near the beginning of the line:

> Wouldst thou be windowed in great Rome and see
> Thy master thus: with pleached arms, bending down
> His *corrigible* neck, his face subdued
> To *penetrative* shame?   (*AC* IV.xiv.72–5)

> This hand of yours requires
> A *sequester* from liberty, fasting and prayer,
> Much *castigation*, exercise devout.   (*Oth* III.iv.39–41)

> By *decimation* and a tithed death –
> If thy revenges hunger for that food
> Which nature loathes – take thou the destined tenth,
> (*Tim* V.iv.31–3)

(where *decimation* is glossed by 'tithed' and 'destined tenth') or at the end of the line:

> Holla your name to the *reverberate* hills   (*TN* I.v.261)

> Requickened what in flesh was *fatigate*   (*Cor* II.ii. 115)

> With thy sharp teeth this knot *intrinsicate*
> Of life at once untie.   (*AC* V.ii.303–4)

> The multitudinous seas *incarnadine*   (*Mac* II.ii.62)

(a word which Davenant, in his version of the play, was insensitive enough to replace by 'add a tincture to').

If there is a heavy mid-line pause, the Latinate word sometimes immediately precedes that:

> Of all these bounds, even from this line to this,
> With shadowy forests, and with champains riched,
> With plenteous rivers, and wide-skirted meads,
> We make thee lady. To thine and Albany's issues
> Be this *perpetual*.   (*KL* I.i.63–7)

> Which, when I know that boasting is an honour
> I shall *provulgate*. (F reads *promulgate*)   (*Oth* I.ii.20–1)

> Now boast thee, death, in thy possession lies
> A lass *unparallelled*.   (*AC* V.ii.314–15)

or, less often, immediately follows it:

> Whilst I awhile *obsequiously* lament
> Th' untimely fall of virtuous Lancaster.   (*R III* I.ii.3–4)

> which imports at full,
> By letters *congruing* to that effect,
> The present death of Hamlet.   (*Ham* IV.iii.65–7)

My point about the single Latinate word standing out from a passage whose diction is otherwise not especially remarkable may be illustrated from the best-known soliloquy in *Hamlet* where the hero is considering the consequences of suicide. He asks who would bear the trials and tribulations of public life

> When he himself might his *quietus* make
> With a bare bodkin. (III.i.75–6)

Quietus is a technical word from accountancy; in the concluding couplet of Sonnet 126 it collocates with *audit*. And this Latin loan in *Hamlet* achieves something not only of the mystery but also of the finality of death: the red line is ruled across the page and the account is closed.[17] But with a bare *bodkin*, a word possibly of Celtic origin and as far removed from Latin as you can get. Or take *Pericles*, which has been described as 'a text full of confusion and with a clumsiness and poverty of language unrivalled in the Shakespeare canon'[18]. Critics now seem to agree that Acts I and II are, with the possible exception of a very few passages, unlikely to represent Shakespeare's work but that Acts III, IV and V show a marked improvement in dramatic style. And there, although the language still seems below Shakespeare's best, the Latinisms increase. At the beginning of Act V, in which Pericles is to be restored to Marina, it is appropriate that the diction should become more elevated:

> Helicanus   Our vessel is of Tyre; in it the King
> A man who for this three months hath not spoken
> To anyone, nor taken sustenance
> But to *prorogue* his grief.
> Lysimachus   Upon what ground is his *distemperature*? (*Per* V.i.21–5)

As with sorrows in *Hamlet*, or as in the passages from Hooker and Donne cited earlier, Shakespeare's Latin borrowings sometimes come not singly but in battalions. They are frequently doublets:

> That all the treasons for these eighteen years
> *Complotted and contrived* in this land
> Fetch from false Mowbray. (*R II* I.i.95–7)

>   if any here
> By *false intelligence or wrong surmise*
> Hold me a foe. (*R III* II.i.54–6)

> He hath deserved worthily of his country; and his ascent is not by such easy degrees as those who, having been *supple and courteous* to the people, bonneted, without any further deed to have them at all, into their *estimation and report*. (*Cor* II.ii.23–7)

Th' *extravagant and erring* spirit hies   (*Ham* I.i.155–6)
To his confine.

           Exchange me for a goat
When I shall turn the business of my soul   (*Oth* III.iii.178–80)
To such *exsufflicate and blown* surmises.

         Be *aidant and remediate*   (*KL* IV.iv.17–18)
In the good man's distress.

Often they appear in groups of near-synonyms, 'copious' diction:

Brutus is noble, wise, valiant, and honest;
Caesar was mighty, bold, royal, and loving.   (*JC* III.i.126–7)

How weary, stale, flat, and unprofitable
Seem to me all the uses of this world!   (*Ham* I.ii.133–4)

If I be not by her fair influence
Fostered, illumined, cherished, kept alive.   (*TGV* III.i.183–4)

Be opposite all planets of good luck
To my proceeding if, with dear heart's love,
Immaculate devotion, holy thoughts,
I tender not thy beauteous princely daughter!
In her consists my happiness and thine;
Without her, follows to myself and thee,
Herself, the land, and many a Christian soul,
Death, desolation, ruin, and decay.   (*R III* IV.iv.402–9)

Though sometimes it show greatness, courage, blood –
And that's the dearest grace it renders you –
Yet oftentimes it doth present harsh rage,
Defect of manners, want of government,
Pride, haughtiness, opinion, and disdain.   (*1 Hen IV* III.i.175–9)

Since his addiction was to courses vain,
His companies unlettered, rude, and shallow,
His hours filled up with riots, banquets, sports,
And never noted in him any study,
Any retirement, any sequestration,
From open haunts and popularity.   (*Hen V* I.i.54–9)

The bonds of heaven are slipped, dissolved, and loosed,
And with another knot, five-finger-tied,
The fractions of her faith, orts of her love,
The fragments, scraps, the bits, and greasy relics
Of her o'er-eaten faith, are given to Diomed.   (*TC* V.ii.153–7)

Not every member of such lexical 'sets' is a polysyllabic Latin borrowing, of course, although most groups contain one or more ('Fostered, *illumined*, cherished, kept alive', 'Death, *desolation*, ruin, and decay'). Furthermore, these examples are almost all from 'serious' plays. Comedy rarely lends itself to such deliberate parallelisms of vocabulary, although parallel syntactic structures are another thing altogether.

Not everybody understood all of these borrowed words by any means, and, if dictionaries were in short supply until the later seventeenth century, doublets might still arise in the search for efficient communication. But clowns can always be sure of a laugh by misunderstanding hard words; it is good stage business. Both Armado and Berowne use Costard as a messenger-boy:

Armado   Bear this significant to the country maid Jaquenetta. There is
remuneration; for the best ward of mine honour is rewarding
my dependants . . .
Costard   Now will I look to his remuneration. Remuneration? O
that's the Latin word for three farthings.

Berowne, the aristocrat, is, however, more generous:

Berowne   And Rosaline they call her. Ask for her,
And to her white hand see thou do commend
This sealed-up counsel. There's thy guerdon. Go.
Costard   Gardon, O sweet gardon ! Better than remuneration – a
'leven-pence farthing better.   (*LLL* III.i.131–8, 168–72)

The obvious examples are, I suppose, Dogberry and Verges in *Much Ado* whose inability to distinguish between *sensible* and *senseless, apprehend* and *comprehend, odious* and *odorous, auspicious* and *suspicious* or to grasp the meaning of *tolerable, tedious, malefactors* or *verify* is part of their general muddleheadedness. But Mistress Quickly and Elbow (another constable) in *Measure for Measure*, each of whom is capable of confusing *protest* and *detest* are little better; nor indeed is Bottom ('we may rehearse most *obscenely* and courageously'; 'I have an *exposition* of sleep come upon me'). Mistress Quickly (whose outstanding lexical confusion is perhaps *honeysuckle* and *homicidal*, *2 Henry IV*, II.i.48) later manages to combine her failure to understand Latin grammar with an indecent pun on *genitive case* ('pudendum'):

Evans   What is your genitive case plural, William?
William   Genitive case?
Evans   Ay.
William   Genitive – *horum, harum, horum.*

24

Quickly	Vengeance of Jenny's case! Fie on her! Never name her, child, if she be a whore.
Evans	For shame, 'oman.
Quickly	You do ill to teach the child such words. He teaches him to hick and to hack, which they'll do fast enough of themselves, and to call 'horum'. Fie upon you!

(MWW IV.i.55–65)

Elbow uses *respected* when he means *suspected*, Dogberry the other way round. Perhaps some of these pairs *were* confused, it is difficult to be sure, since malapropisms by clowns are rare before Shakespeare.

Somewhat higher up the social scale is Ancient Pistol, but with him Latinate diction is part of his bravado. Falstaff's heart is *fracted and corroborate (Hen V* II.i.119). *Fracted* is perhaps acceptable for 'broken', but *corroborate*, literally 'made strong', is clearly absurd as a doublet. Yet somehow this does not detract from the melancholy at the imminent death of Falstaff, any more than does Mistress Quickly's failure not long afterwards to understand women as *devils incarnate* ("A could never abide carnation, 'twas a colour he never liked'. II.iii.30–1). Sir Andrew Aguecheek demonstrates a variant on the game of misapprehension: he is honest and simple enough to admit that he does not understand:

By my troth, I would not undertake her in this company. Is that the meaning of 'accost'?   *(TN* I.iii.55)

What is *pourquoi?* Do or not do?   (I.iii.88)

(a reminder that Latin was not the only source of linguistic difficulty)

Sir Toby	Approach, Sir Andrew. Not to be abed after midnight, is to be up betimes, and *diluculo surgere*, thou knowest –
Sir Andrew	Nay, by my troth, I know not; but I know to be up late is to be up late. (II.iii.1–5)

Diluculo surgere, 'to rise at daybreak (is most healthy)', was a Latin phrase from an Elizabethan school-book which Sir Andrew had evidently never studied. But he stores up three fine-sounding words, perhaps in his commonplace book:

Odours, pregnant, and *vouchsafed*. I'll get 'em all three ready   (III.i.87)[19]

As late as *The Winter's Tale*, the Clown is sure that 'Advocate's the court-word for a pheasant' (IV.iv.737). He probably confuses it with

25

avocet, a bird of the snipe family. The first *OED* entry is 1674, but *advocate* was earlier spelt *avocat* before it became Latinised in spelling (a 'court word'?) during the Renaissance. By 1613, however, the Induction of *Bartholomew Fair* attacks the stage-practice of 'mistaking words'. Had it by that time become old-fashioned, or simply too unsophisticated for Ben Jonson? Whichever it was, Shakespeare had long since realised its appeal to an audience:

> *Speed* How now, Signior Launce? What news with your mastership?
> *Launce* With my master's ship? Why, it is at sea.
> *Speed* Well, your old vice still: mistake the word.
>
> (*TGV* III.i.276–9)

Old vice perhaps, but good for several more laughs yet.

Another aspect of Latin loan-words in the Renaissance is that the *form* of Shakespeare's word will often be easily recognisable to us but its *sense* may not correspond to our present-day meaning. Since the borrowings were often comparatively recent, the word's signification will still be close to that which it had in Latin. The problem of semantic change is not in fact quite so serious a problem as has sometimes been suggested. Any moderately attentive reader of Shakespeare will be aware when the modern meaning of a word will not fit the Elizabethan context. For instance, when Old Capulet says that Romeo 'bears him like a *portly* gentleman' (I.v.66), the word seems inapplicable to a youth so agile in climbing up to Juliet's balcony. Even less likely is Marlowe's Zenocrate being described as *portly* (*1 Tamburlaine* I.ii.187). On the other hand, when Hector says that Achilles can be recognised by his *large and portly* size (*TC* IV.v.161), we do not feel the need for explanation because we have the gloss *large* to guide us: we expect the two words to be at least partly synonymous. Even so, the etymological meaning (from Latin *portare*) of 'dignified', one who *carries* himself well, may apply to Achilles almost as much as it obviously applies to Romeo and Zenocrate. Again, in *As You Like It*, the *humorous* Duke is the villainous one, anything but a comic character. When Hamlet welcomes the players, the *humorous* man (II.ii.322) is not the comedian but the character actor, especially the man who played unusual, 'fantastical' characters, like Jaques or Lucio in *Measure for Measure*. Here we need to know something about the medical idea of humours, which were originally thought of as fluids so that the *humorous* night (*RJ* II.i.31) simply means 'humid', 'damp'. In a complete, well-balanced man no one humour predominates, but in most of us one quality or another will be especially prominent and will largely determine our disposition. Jonson used this as a theory of comedy (*Every Man in His Humour*). For the Elizabethans, then, a man whose humours often changed was temperamental or capricious.

So there are several aids we can summon to our assistance. The etymological meaning will often help and this will be especially so with Latin borrowings. Hence *prevented* ('forestalled), *admire* ('marvel at'), *secure* ('free from suspicion'), *luxury* ('lust'), *accident* ('something which happens', not necessarily unpleasant), *err* ('wander') and *extravagant* ('out of bounds') – the Ghost in *Hamlet* is *th'extravagant and erring spirit* – *honest* ('honourable', or, of women, 'chaste'), *pregnant* ('significant'), *modern* ('commonplace'), *vulgar* ('ordinary'), and several others.[20] Secondly there is our general, 'background' knowledge of the age, such as the theory of humours or the acceptance that in both the English and the Roman histories *policy* (now a neutral word) and *politician* have a distinct flavour of underhand dealing. Thirdly, and most important, the context will frequently guide us to the Elizabethan meaning or at least put us on the alert to look for a meaning other than the twentieth-century one. If the word in question appears in the same phrase as another word, the same part of speech and apparently synonymous, we are doubly fortunate. Take the word *rank*. One of its Middle English meanings was 'luxuriant' (of growth): the late fourteenth-century romance *Sir Gawain and the Green Knight* speaks of *rawez* (hedgerows) *rych and ronk*. The sense of 'grossly rich', 'overblown' was, however, already possible in the fourteenth century, although the use suggesting an excessively strong *smell* did not apparently arise before the sixteenth century. In *Hamlet, rank* means 'gross': the world is an unweeded garden, 'things *rank and gross* in nature/Possess it merely.' (I.ii.136). Hamlet advises his mother 'do not spread the compost on the weeds/ To make them *ranker*' (III.iv.152). Earlier, Claudius, trying in vain to pray, cries out 'O, my offence is *rank*, It smells to heaven' (III.iii.36). But *rank and gross* or something rank which smells stands oddly against the Authorised Version (1611, and therefore later than *Hamlet*) where one lot of ears of corn in Pharaoh's dream were *rank and good*. The language of the Authorised Version is, however, conservative, like most religious register: it seldom reminds us of Shakespeare so much as of the English of half a century before. But here we can, exceptionally, catch a word in the course of change, so that the unpleasant connotation of *rank* is clearly now the usual one and the favourable sense will shortly disappear.[21]

Sometimes the difficulty is just a matter of interpreting the prefix or suffix: *questionable* means 'able to be questioned', *deceivable* 'deceit-

ful', *comfortable* 'comforting', *sensible* 'sensitive', *unexpressive* 'inex-
pressible', *unvalued* 'priceless' and *timorous* 'frightening', not 'fright-
ened'. But the most difficult cases of semantic change are those
where the modern meaning of the word might just fit the immediate
Elizabethan context, although, a wider context will often show it to
be inappropriate. *Hamlet* will once more provide a useful example. In
response to Ophelia's explanation to her father of Hamlet's ab-
stracted behaviour towards her, Polonius asserts (II.i.102) 'this is the
very *ecstasy* of love'. Similarly Hamlet, outraged that Gertrude
should claim to love Claudius after that paragon her first husband,
blurts out:

> Nor sense to *ecstasy* was ne'er so thralled
> But it reserved some quantity of choice
> To serve in such a difference.   (III.iv.75–7)

Now we may quite naturally associate ecstasy with love, but I have
not been quite fair here, because even a cursory reading of the surrounding lines of either quotation would suggest 'madness' (and a
self-induced madness at that) as a better equivalent. This would be
confirmed when, on another occasion (III.i.161), Ophelia speaks of
Hamlet's mind as 'blasted with ecstasy', and when Gertrude, who
has not been able to see the Ghost which has been clearly visible to
Hamlet, dismisses the whole episode:

> This is the very coinage of your brain.
> This bodiless creation ecstasy
> Is very cunning in.   (III.iv.138–40)

Ecstasy in *Hamlet*, then, clearly means madness, unreasonably extravagant behaviour.

In a similar way, careful reading *in context* will show that
Shakespeare usually meant 'absolute', 'complete', by his use of *mere*
(*Ham* I.ii.136, above) and 'wicked', 'malicious' by *shrewd* (from Old
English *screawa*, 'shrewmouse', thought to have a poisonous bite) –
Cassius (II.i.158) adjudges Antony a *shrewd contriver* and argues that
he should be killed with Caesar. Cymbeline (V.v.47) calls the Queen
most *delicate* fiend, that is, 'subtle'. *Advertisement* means 'information'
at *1 Henry IV* III.ii.172 but 'exhortation' (closer to the modern sense)
at IV.i.36. Edmund (*KL* II.i.72) speaks of '*suggestion*, plot and damned
practice'; the other two terms imply a pejorative meaning for *suggestion* which it does not have now (although the adjective *suggestive*
sometimes does). *Obsequious* (e.g. *3 Hen VI* II.v.118, *R III* I.ii.3,

Ham I.ii.92) should be interpreted as 'dutiful', not 'sycophantic': all three contexts refer to mourning and our own use of *obsequies* should guide us here. *Ostentation* (*Cor* I.vi.86) has no sense of showing *off*, merely of show. Of the two instances of *sanctimonious* in Shakespeare, one (*MM* I.ii.7) has the present meaning, but the other (*Temp* IV.i.16) is simply equivalent to 'holy'. *Officious* usually carries the implication of interfering, but *tenderly officious* (*WT* II.iii.158) can hardly bear this interpretation. When her father calls Juliet *a peevish, self-willed harlotry* (IV.ii.14), it is our equivalent of 'silly, obstinate girl'. In these last few examples we have become involved with the tone of the word and the expected response to it, and such matters of semantic shading are difficult to establish exactly for earlier periods. Perhaps the best example is still the one F. P. Wilson quoted some years ago[22]:

> When you shall these unlucky deeds relate,
> Speak of me as I am: nothing extenuate,
> Nor set down aught in malice. Then must you speak
> Of one that loved not wisely, but too well;
> Of one, not easily jealous but, being wrought,
> Perplexed in the extreme. (*Oth* V.ii.337–42)

These lines, from Othello's dying speech, are not, as we might at first think, an example of understatement. *Unlucky* and *perplexed* were much stronger words then than now, and together with *wrought* ('overwrought') suggest Othello's unbearable mental agony.

Loan-words are the easiest way of enriching the word-stock of a language, especially if circumstances bring that language into contact with one that is much more prestigious in particular fields (as Latin was in philosophy, science or medicine, for example). But alternatives do exist. Old English (c. 700–c. 1100) borrowed comparatively few words and those chiefly from Latin to express new concepts resulting from the coming of Christianity. Instead it employed its own resources to make compounds (where no part of the two words is lost in the process of joining them together and where they continue to exist individually, as in Modern English *gas-stove, dark-blue, over-turn*) or to engage in *affixation* (the addition of a prefix or suffix to an existing word or root, as in Modern English *postgraduate, bitterness, motherhood*). The two processes are essentially the same and it does not seem worthwhile separating them in general discussion. Compounding and affixation can, of course, involve earlier loan-words which have become part of the English lexicon; in the examples above *gas* is borrowed from Dutch (perhaps based on Greek *chaos*) and *post–* from Latin. Equally the status of a word may change: Old English *had* meant 'rank', 'position', but it is now simply the suffix *–hood*, having passed from full lexical to grammatical status. Middle English (c.1100–c. 1500), however, borrowed extensively from French, and the proportion of compounds therefore drops considerably. In the Renaissance compounding was seen by some writers as an alternative to borrowing 'inkhorn' terms from Latin, and an alternative worth cultivating, for native compounds might be more intelligible than foreign-sounding loans. Sir Philip Sidney believed English to be especially rich in compounds:

> But for the uttering sweetly and properly the conceits of the mind, which is the end of speech, that hath it [English] equally with any other tongue in the world; and is particulary happy in compositions of two or three words together, near the Greek, far beyond the Latin: which is one of the greatest beauties can be in a language.[23]

Another possibility was to venture outside standard English and to introduce (especially into poetry) dialect words or words which had been used by the great national writers of the fairly recent past.

The most important Elizabethan writer to examine these last two possibilities of extending the lexicon is Spenser, and it is worth delaying a moment to consider his success in this. His poetic and stylistic credo is best expressed in the Dedicatory Epistle (to Gabriel Harvey) at the beginning of *The Shepherd's Calendar*, 1579. This shows the work to be a conscious linguistic experiment within the traditional poetic form of the pastoral which aims, as Puttenham said, 'under the veil of homely persons, and in rude speeches, to insinuate and glance at greater matters'. Spenser's choice of diction would commend itself to nationalistic critics of overmuch borrowing such as Cheke, Ascham and Wilson[24], but his occasional defensive attitude in the Epistle reminds us that he had his opponents too. Sidney blamed him for 'framing of his style to an old rustick language' and Ben Jonson believed that 'Spenser, in affecting the ancients, writ no language'. The Epistle is allegedly composed by E. K. who points out the contribution made to Spenser's diction by native English words:

> For in my opinion it is one special prayse, of many whych are dew to this Poete, that he hath laboured to restore, as to theyr rightfull heritage such good and naturall English words, as haue ben long time out of vse and almost cleane disherited. Which is the onely cause, that our Mother tonge, which truely of it self is both ful enough for prose and stately enough for verse, hath long time ben counted most bare and barrein of both. Which default when some endeuoured to salue and recure, they patched vp the holes with peces and rags of other languages, borrowing

here of the french, there of the Italian, euery where of the Latine, not
weighing how il those tongues accorde with themselues, but much worse
with ours. So now they haue made our English tongue, a gallimaufray or
hodgepodge of al other speches. Other some not so wel seene in the
English tonge as perhaps in other languages, if them happen to here an
olde word albeit very naturall and significant, crye out streight way, that
we speak no English, but gibbrish.[25]

This approach is in part carried over to *The Faerie Queene* (1590),
although there are perhaps fewer archaisms and certainly more compounds than in *The Shepherd's Calendar*. It seems to have been these
compounds that attracted later poets so that Spenser became 'the
poet's poet'. Spenser's archaisms were chiefly from Chaucer but also
from fifteenth-century writers such as Malory and Lydgate.
Although *The Faerie Queene* was set in a remote and romantic past,
there was for Spenser no necessary connection between archaism and
artificiality. Some of the most common Spenserian archaisms are
algates ('at least'), *dight, doom, eke, forthy* ('therefore'),
hent ('carried off'), *hight, stour* ('time'), *vnnethes* ('scarcely'),
whylome ('formerly') and *yore*. But possibly as important in determin-
ing the tone of Spenser's poetry are some of his grammatical forms.
The endings –*est* and –*eth* were still living forms in the sixteenth century but became less common as the seventeenth century progressed;
as did the use of *do* or *did* as empty tense markers. On the other
hand, *gan* with following infinitive to represent a past tense (*gan
call* + 'called') and the prefix *y*– on past participles were decidedly
obsolescent, if not already obsolete, as were the –*ght* and *wh*– spellings (*spight* for *spite* and *whott* for *hot*). One or more of his variant
forms – *before/afore/tofore; astonished/astonied; dreariness/drearihead/
dreariment* – are usually also obsolete, although if the word were con-
nected with another word in more general use (e.g. *embracement,
avengement*) it would not give readers undue difficulty. Several of
these practices, together with Spenser's frequent alliteration, are
illustrated in these three typical stanzas:

> One day nigh wearie of the yrkesome way,
> From her vnhastie beast she *did alight*,
> And on the grasse her daintie limbes *did lay*
> In *s*ecret *s*hadow, farre from all mens *s*ight:
> From her *f*aire head her *f*illet she *vndight*,
> And laid her stole aside. Her angels face
> As the great eye of heaven shyned bright,
> And made a *s*unshine in the *s*hadie place;
> *Did* never mortall eye *behold* such heauenly grace.
>
> *It fortuned* out of the thickest wood

A *n*amping Lyon *r*ushed suddainly,
Hunting full greedie after *saluage* blood;
Soone as the royall virgin he *did spy*,
With *g*aping mouth at her ran *g*reedily,
To have *attonce* deuour'd her tender corse:
But to the pray *when as* he drew *more ny*,
His bloudie rage asswaged with remorse,
And with the sight amazd, *f*orgat his *f*urious *f*orse.

In stead thereof he kist her wearie feet,
And *l*ickt her *l*illy hands with fawning tong,
As he her wronged innocence *did weet*.
O how can beautie maister the most strong,
And simple truth subdue auenging wrong?
Whose yeelded pride and proud submission,
Still *d*reading *d*eath, when she had marked long,
Her hart *gan melt* in great compassion,
And drizling teares *did shed* for pure affection.
                    (*Faerie Queene*, Book I, canto 3, stanzas 4–6)

But by 1600, much of this must have seemed very old-fashioned
indeed; to employ deliberate archaisms is to invite the law of dimin-
ishing returns. Shakespeare does not often use archaisms, but in the
mechanicals' own play of Pyramus and Thisbe they clearly represent
the attempt by the uneducated to supply the appropriate poetic
heightening:

            For if you will know
By moonshine *did* these lovers *think* no scorn
To meet at Ninus' tomb, there, there to woo.
The grisly beast – which Lion *hight* by name –
The *t*rusty *T*hisbe, coming first by night,
Did scare away, or rather *did affright*.
And as she fled, her mantle she *did fall*,
Which *Lion vile* with bloody mouth *did stain*.
Anon comes Pyramus – sweet youth, and tall –
And finds his *t*rusty *T*hisbe's mantle slain.
Whereat with blade – with *b*loody, *b*lameful *b*lade –
He *b*ravely *b*roached his *b*oiling *b*loody *b*reast.   (*MND* V.i.135–46)

By the time of *Pericles* (? 1608), archaisms are the mark of the first
three Gower choruses which are further set apart from the play proper by their octosyllabic couplets, the metre which Gower had himself
used. *Did provoke, did begin, did die, do testify* all occur in the first
chorus; *iwis, speken, forthy* and *escapend* in the second; *yslacked* in the
opening line of the third. This may be the language of 'ancient Gower' but hardly of modern Shakespeare. Compounds, however, are a
different matter, and to these I shall return.

NOTES AND REFERENCES

1. *English Works of Roger Ascham*, ed. W. A. Wright, CUP (1904), p.xiv.
2. Peroration to the *First Part of the Elementarie*, ed. Manston, Scolar Press (1970), pp. 254, 258, spelling modernised.
3. Cook (1974).
4. Ascham, *ibid.* (note 1), p.215.
5. T. Wilson, *Arte of Rhetorique*, ed. G. H. Mair, Clarendon Press, Oxford (1909), pp. 164–5.
6. *The Complete Works of George Gascoigne*, ed. J. W. Cunliffe, CUP (1907), I, pp. 465–73.
7. In *1 Hen VI*, III.i.99, the Bishop of Winchester is called *an inkhorn mate*, i.e. a pedant.
8. Mulcaster spoke of the latest terms borrowed into English 'either of pure necessitie in new matters, or of mere brauerie, to garnish it self withall' (quoted by Barber, p.81).
9. The fullest account of the fortunes of English in the Renaissance is Jones (1953) from which I take the quotations from Borde and Pettie. Rowland is quoted from *The Knave of Clubbes* (1609), spelling modernised. See also Hall (1977).
10. *The Arte of English Poesie*, ed. G. D. Willcock and A. Walker, CUP (1936), p.147.
11. *Ecclesiastical Polity*, ed. E. Rhys, Dent (1907), p.161.
12. *Seventeenth Century Prose*, ed. B. Vickers, Longman (1969), pp. 102–3.
13. *The Macro Plays*, ed. M. Eccles, Early English Text Society (1969), 262 lines 122–4.
14. Blake (1973), pp. 10–11.
15. Pearsall (1970). Ebin (1977) suggests that Lydgate adapted existing terminology to create a new critical language.
16. For early dictionaries, see Starnes and Noyes (1946).
17. Compare *Duchess of Malfi* I.i.64 and III.ii.187.
18. Bullough (1966), Ch. 6, p.350.
19. Rather similar is Balduro's repetition of fashionable words in Marston's *Antonio's Revenge*.
20. The largest *OED* gives the etymology of words in English since 1100 and dated contexts for their use; it is the prime source of evidence for semantic change. The best general work is Waldron (1967). Copley (1961) discusses key words from this period in their contexts and Brook (1976) has a section on semantic change.
21. Outside *Hamlet*, in which *rank(er)* is used more often than in any other play, the word is applied to people five times, to animals twice, to weeds five times, and otherwise collocates with *offence, opinion, thought, speeches, jests, feud* and *riots*.
22. Wilson (1969), pp. 100–29.
23. *An Apology for Poetry*, ed. G. Shepherd, Nelson (1965), p.140. Shepherd's note, p.232, gives examples of Sidney's compounds.
24. Sherbo (1975), pp. 60–2 remarks on Spenser's limited use of Latinisms.
25. Quotations from *The Works of Edmund Spenser: A Variorum Edition*, ed. E. Greenlaw *et al.*, Baltimore, Johns Hopkins Press, for *The Shepherd's Calendar*; and from *The Faerie Queene*, ed. A. C. Hamilton, Longman (1977).

CHAPTER THREE
The uses of vocabulary

If we go searching for indications of how his immediate predecessors
in the drama might have contributed to Shakespeare's growing ability to vary and exploit the lexical resources available to him, the
results are meagre, just as the whole quest for influences is disappointing:

> He was not only the greatest of the Elizabethan dramatists, but he did far
> more than any other man to create the drama and establish it. This was
> possible because he had the most complete facility for assimilation and
> rejection. He learnt and built on the work of his predecessors, yet the
> influence is generally so indirectly perceptible that we cannot often say
> with confidence 'Here is a trace of Marlowe: here of Spenser: here of
> Kyd'. Just as it is very difficult to pin down any passage in Shakespeare to
> a particular source (apart from the obvious ones like Holinshed and
> North), so there is nothing of the notebook method in his attitude to
> other poets.[1]

If we consider the best-known of these plays, those most often
anthologised (as in the Everyman collection by T. W. Craik), the
language does not often remind us of Shakespeare. Norton and
Sackville's *Gorboduc*, the first play to be written in blank verse, was
performed in 1562: 'A play in the quen hall at Westmynster by the
gentyll-men of the Tempull', a learned audience of the sort
Shakespeare was sometimes to cultivate later (in *Troilus and Cressida*, for example). It is uncompromisingly Senecan, with lengthy
speeches full of impeccable advice to counsellors, as in I.ii or the final
speeches of Arostus and Eubulus in V.ii. Each character holds the
stage in turn, speaking not to one another but to the audience. Oratory is the order of the day, and it is easy to imagine that, after its
first production, *Gorboduc* might well have been read more often

than performed. The play contains several doublets, for the characters are, after all, courtiers and speak courtiers' language, but hardly
any of them are remarkable. There are few compounds (did these
come in later, with Spenser?) and virtually no Latinate vocabulary.
But the syntax is often Latinate: perhaps another mark of courtliness,
perhaps the result of regular reading of the classics. *Cambises*, by
Thomas Preston and perhaps even earlier than *Gorboduc*, is more pronounced in its Latin diction, but, unattractive as this may be, it is
almost always used in speeches by, to, or about, courtly characters:

Counsellor	Behold, I see him now *aggress* and enter into place.
Sisamnes	O puissant prince and mighty king, the gods preserve your grace.
	Your grace's message came to me, your will *purporting* forth;
	With grateful mind I it receiv'd, according to mine oath,
	Erecting then myself with speed, before your grace's eyes,
	The tenor of your princely will from you for to *agnise*.
	(75–80)

The morality tradition, which sits somewhat uneasily side by side with
the Senecan influences, is responsible for the colloquialisms and irregular
short lines of the comic characters and one (too lengthy) attempt at stage
Zummerset (754–826). With all its faults, the style is more varied than
that of *Gorboduc*. The domestic tragedy *Arden of Feversham* (published
1592) is more promising material and carries further the variations in
style evidently by this time becoming more common in Elizabethan
drama. It contains several compounds and doublets (although of no
great distinction) and its occasional Latinisms do not seem to be employed for any special reason. But the colloquialisms, the braggadocio that was later to become the fustian of Pistol, and an occasional
venture into a deliberately high style for the 'Ovid-like' lovers, all
suggest that the author was alert to the possibilities of varying his
style with a change of character or of situation, even if he was as yet
incapable of doing this very often.

No reader of *The Spanish Tragedy* can fail to see its effect on
Shakespeare, especially in the feigned madness of Hamlet and the
final holocaust where the stage is littered with corpses. But it is more
difficult to pinpoint much linguistic influence. Doublets, compounds
and Latinate diction are evidently by this time (1592) an accepted part
of Elizabethan drama, especially in a play with strong Senecan pretensions. The drama of Marlowe is another thing altogether. There
is, first of all, much more of it than of any one of his predecessors
and a far greater range within the canon. Some two months older

than Shakespeare, secret-service agent and freethinker, in 1593, Marlowe was stabbed to death in a tavern brawl, not yet thirty and at a time when, in all probability, Shakespeare had written little more than the *Henry VI* trilogy. Yet, apart from *The Spanish Tragedy*, his is the only work before 1600 fit to set beside Shakespeare's. The opening of *Tamburlaine* (published 1590 but possibly composed 1587) immediately announces Marlowe's dramatic and poetic credo:

> Threat'ning the world with *high astounding terms*,
> And scourging kingdoms with his conquering sword.
>
> (1 *Tam* Prol. 5–6)[2]

Tamburlaine is the self-made man, the Scythian shepherd who comes to rule half the world, whose own hand turns Fortune's wheel about. He is orator as well as conquerer, and since his conquests occur off-stage, the oratory is doubly important. 'You see, my lord, what working words he hath' says his lieutenant Theridamas at II.iii.25, the same Theridamas who had been 'won with thy words and conquered with thy looks' (I.ii.228). The pitiful Mycetes cannot compete:

> Brother Cosroe, I find myself aggriev'd,
> Yet insufficient to express the same,
> For it requires a great and thund'ring speech   (1 *Tam* I.i.1–3)

Perhaps Joseph Hall (*Virgidamiarum*, 1597) was thinking of Marlowe when he spoke of drama as containing 'terms Italianate, Big-sounding sentences, and words of state'. Ben Jonson was more outspoken still: 'the Tamerlanes, and Tamer-Chams of the late Age, which had nothing in them but the scenicall strutting, and furious vociferation, to warrant them to the ignorant gapers'.[3] The devices for making Elizabethan English sound impressive are certainly there in *Tamburlaine*: Latinate diction, doublets, compounds. Yet the Latinate diction compares poorly with Shakespeare's. In fact there is not so very much of it. Nor are the compounds as remarkable as might be expected. Doublets are rather more numerous yet not very suggestive, and copious language appears seldom. The continuation of *Tamburlaine* relies more on classical references and polysyllabic, exotic-sounding names; Marlowe had so far extended the bounds of Tamburlaine's conquests and his megalomania in Part I that only the death of Zenocrate and finally of Tamburlaine himself remained to make Part II really memorable. Shakespeare could, no doubt, appreciate all these features, although he would soon equal or surpass them. What was perhaps more impressive to him in *Tamburlaine* was the sheer amount of rhetoric, not simple verbal figures at line length but rhetoric on a grander scale, *amplificatio*. Tamburlaine *declaims* (Alleyn became famous in the part): he does not change his style throughout the two plays. D. Peet, in a discussion of the rhetoric of *Tamburlaine*[4], aptly quotes Puttenham:

> and then we lay on such load and so go to it by heapes as if we would winne the game by multitude of words and speaches. (*Arte*, p.236)

We do not need to analyse these speeches in detail: the general effect is easily communicated.

After *Tamburlaine* the chronology of Marlowe's plays becomes uncertain. *The Jew of Malta* was performed in 1592 but may well have been composed about 1590; *Dr Faustus* and *Edward II* were both written about 1592. The syntax of these two plays shows a greater experimentation, but this does not seem to be true of the vocabulary. *Faustus* still exhibits something of Marlowe's fascination with man's superhuman aspirations, although our initial sympathy with the hero is lessened by his increasing arrogance and his refusal to heed one warning after another. Surprisingly, neither compounds nor doublets are very many or very remarkable. The speeches of Chorus might be expected to produce some Latinate diction and elaborate syntax, but although Chorus 2 contains words like *gratulate* and a pair like *admired and wondered*, the Epilogue (also spoken by Chorus) relies on the hackneyed metaphor of Apollo's laurel bough and the alliteration of *fiendful fortune*. I do not mean to detract from the magnificent feeling of mounting terror in the concluding scene, if I say that the diction of *Faustus* is, finally, disappointing. In *The Jew of Malta*, and to some extent in *Edward II*, intrigue becomes all-important and the diction and syntax consequently plainer. There are rather more compounds and doublets in *Edward II*, but apart from one or two examples (*overwoo*, II.v.87, *counterbuff'd*, III.ii.19) they are mostly rather ordinary. There is not much obvious Latinate diction in either play: *refluence* (*Jew*, III.v.18) is the only really unusual word. The speech of the Herald (*Edward II*, III.iii.156–71) with its complex syntax, its Latinate terminology (*effusion, putrefying, empale, consecrate*) and its image of the vine is perhaps something of an exception, but it is really only a gesture showing Marlowe's ability to use the appropriate style for affairs of state.

Shakespeare, therefore, probably learned little about the vocabulary of drama from his fellow-playwrights, but when he began to write Spenser was the major narrative poet. As a supporter of those who advocated a greater use of the resources of native English, Spenser will not be expected to provide much by way of Latinate vocabulary. *Ingenerate* (*The Faerie Queene* III.vi.3), *degendered* (5.Prol.2), *arrogate* (*Mutability Cantos* 16) are examples, but one has to look quite hard in *The Faerie Queene* to find them. The doublets and triplets, such as *wearie and fordonne* ('tired out', I.x.47), *An vncouth, saluage and vnciuile wight/Of griesly hew, and fowle ill fauour'd sight* (ii.vii.3), *Strife and debate, bloudshed, and bitternesse* (II.vii.12), *Immortall and vnchangeable* (*Mutability Cantos*, 54), *rule and raigne* (*Mutability Cantos*, 58) are neither especially distinguished nor especially Latinate. Compounds, however, are a different matter. *True-seeming* (lyes), *euer-drizling* (raine), *rosy-fingred* (Morning), *sun-bright* (armes), *foole-happie, bloudie-mouthed, fruitfull-headed* (beast), *deaw-burning* (blade), *raw-bone* (cheekes), *fire-mouthed* (Dragon), *newly-budded* (pineons), *fire-spitting* (forge), *eye-glutting* (gaine), *counterfeisance* ('deception'), *vp-standing* (heares), *wingyheeld, hartfretting* (payne), *Lion-like, sky-ruling* (Jove) form a fairly typical list which, even so, does not include any of the numerous examples of affixation. Almost all these compounds are, perhaps not surprisingly in such descriptive writing, adjectival, and their construction is frequently noun (or adjective) plus participle. The concentration of verbal energy into the participle is useful not only to the descriptive poet but also to the poetic dramatist, and it was a habit Shakespeare never lost.

Compounds come thickest and fastest in Shakespeare's early plays. In English, verb compounds are far less common than noun compounds, and in poetry I suspect that we notice noun compounds far less than adjectival ones. The kind of appositional compounds Shakespeare uses occasionally:

You are too senseless-obstinate, my lord.   (*R III* III.i.44)

To undergo with me an enterprise
Of honourable-dangerous consequence.   (*JC* I.iii.124)

Be not so holy-cruel. Love is holy.   (*AW* IV.ii.32)

are, I imagine, not much to our taste now. Shakespeare's favourite type of compound seems to have been the adjective whose second element is a participle. In the early plays these tend to be rather self-consciously poetical and often too obviously transparent, perhaps still under the influence of Spenser whose narrative poetry gave him time for embellishment which the dramatist could not always spare. Take a relatively early play like *Romeo and Juliet* where almost two-thirds of the compounds are of this grammatical type:

Gallop apace, you fiery-footed steeds.   (III.ii.1)

(Spenser himself had used *fiery-footed team.*)

> Come, civil night,
> Thou sober-suited matron, all in black.   (III.ii.10–11)

> Dove-feathered raven! Wolvish-ravening lamb!   (III.ii.76)

and contrast it with a relatively late play like *Antony and Cleopatra*: (a handsome man) *loose-wived* I.ii.73; (these three) *world-sharers* II.vii.70; *high-battled* (Caesar) III.xiii.29. These do not merely luxuriate in description; they make us think. It is rare to find a line like '*New lighted* on a *heaven-kissing* hill' so late as *Hamlet* (III.iv.60). The line is part of a high-style speech meant to convey a general impression of the excellence of old Hamlet. It may be beautiful poetry, but in itself it has little or no particularising force. How, on the contrary, do you expand an encapsulated phrase like *summer–seeming lust* (*Macbeth* IV.iii.86)?

Romeo and Juliet, however, has a direct source which is a poem, Arthur Brooke's *The Tragicall Historye of Romeus and Juliet* (1562), in fourteen-syllable lines[5]. It is often poor stuff, perhaps because the very length of the lines invites expansion. It contains some alliteration but little or no Latinate language, and its compounds and doublets are distressingly obvious. At its worst it can descend to lines like this:

> On Wensday next, (quod Juliet) so doth my father say:
> I must give my consent, but (as I do remember)
> The solemne day of marriage is, the tenth day of September.

> (2070–2)

Our immediate reaction may be to marvel at what Shakespeare could make of such bare bones. Yet it may serve to remind us that Shakespeare was a narrative poet as well as a dramatist. *Venus and Adonis* and *The Rape of Lucrece* were almost certainly written during 1592–4 when the London companies were on tour because of a particularly bad outbreak of plague in the capital. They should be placed side by side, not only with Spenser but more particularly with poems like Lodge's *Scylla's Metamorphosis* (printed 1589 but possibly composed earlier), Marlowe's *Hero and Leander* (1598, completed by Chapman), and Drayton's *Endymion and Phoebe* (1595).[6] They are all in the mode of the then fashionable Ovidian erotic poetry, although it should be remembered that *Lucrece* is history and not myth. They include some doublets and copious language and Drayton has rather more by way of Latinate language (though the words are not really unusual). But they all contain several compounds and are essentially exercises in decorative and rhetorical embellishment. The opening stanza of *Venus and Adonis* contains four adjectival compounds, each with a past participle in second position:

> Even as the sun with purple-colour'd face
> Had ta'en his last leave of the weeping morn,
> Rose-cheek'd Adonis hied him to the chase,
> Hunting he lov'd, but love he laugh'd to scorn:
>> Sick-thoughted Venus makes amain unto him,
>> And like a bold-fac'd suitor 'gins to woo him.

The descriptions of the amorous and over-powering heroine and the somewhat petulant hero give scope for many more similar compounds such as *time-beguiling* (sport), *flint-hearted* (boy), *blue-vein'd* (violets), *strong-neck'd* (seed), *round-hoof'd, short-jointed, deep-sweet* (music), *bate-breeding* (spy), *earth-delving* (conies), *life-poisoning* (pestilence), *cold-pale* (weakness), *deep-dark* (cabins), *green-dropping* (sap). These sometimes take their place as part of the copious language of description:

> Were I hard-favour'd, foul, or wrinkled-old,
> Ill-nurtur'd, crooked, churlish, harsh in voice,
> O'erworn, despised, rheumatic and cold,
> Thick-sighted, barren, lean, and lacking juice,
> Then mightst thou pause . . .   (133–37)

> But this foul, grim and urchin-snouted boar.   (1105)

> Hard-favoured tyrant, ugly, meagre, lean.   (931)

The Rape of Lucrece is half as long again, and this is all the more remarkable in that Shakespeare does not describe Tarquin's first visit to Collatine's palace and merely mentions his eventual banishment. Most readers nowadays feel that Lucrece is far too articulate and that the long stretches of monologue alienate rather than retain our sympathy, but the poem had nevertheless gone through nine editions by 1655. The declamatory, rhetorical style gives ample scope for embellishment by doublets, copious language, alliteration and above all, compounds, one to every nineteen or so lines. Most of the latter are of the now familiar adjectival kind, such as *lust-breathed* (Tarquin), *death-boding* (cries), *hot-burning* (will), *night-wandering* (weasels), *night-waking* (cat), *pity-pleading* (eyes), *surfeit-taking* (Tarquin), *all-hiding* (cloak), *fleet-winged* (duty), *salt-waved* (ocean), *cloud-kissing* (Ilion), *Tarquin-stained*. The copious lexis is fairly obviously decorative:

> A dream, a breath, a froth of fleeting joy.   (212)

> Be moved with my tears, my sighs, my groans.   (588)

> For princes are the glass, the school, the book,
> Where subjects' eyes do learn, do read, do look.   (615–6)

Her sacred temple spotted, spoiled, corrupted,
Grossly engirt with daring infamy.   (1172–3)

Another characteristic of Spenser's descriptive style is the generalised and sometimes generic adjective which was to pass via Milton
into much eighteenth-century 'occasional' poetry. The pattern is frequently disyllabic adjective plus monosyllabic noun: *wandring sheepe,
fertile land, grassie plaine, cloudie storme* and *bitter showre*. There are
fewer examples in Shakespeare than in Spenser, but the trick does
occur occasionally, as in *Venus and Adonis*:

He burns with *bashful shame*, she with her tears
Doth quench the *maiden burning* of his cheeks;
Then with her *windy sighs* and *golden hairs*
To fan and blow them dry again she seeks.   (49–52)

His *louring brows* o'erwhelming his fair sight,
Like *misty vapours* when they blot the sky.   (183–4)

All this has been a long prologue to the play, but it is important to
realise that by the mid-1590's other writers besides Shakespeare were
experimenting with Latinate diction, poetic compounds and copious
lexis. It would, too, have been scarcely possible for Shakespeare, in
Love's Labour's Lost, to satirise the prevailing attitudes towards language if these had not been sufficiently widespread. Instances of
Latinate borrowing should by now be easy enough for the reader to
discover in the group of Shakespeare's earliest plays to which I now
turn. The exact order of the *Henry VI* trilogy, *Richard III* and *Titus
Andronicus* may be uncertain, but it is likely that all five were composed between 1591 and 1594.

There are not too many Latin loans in *Titus Andronicus*, except in
the long scene which takes up the whole of Act I and which deals
with imperial affairs. There are more examples in the three parts of
Henry VI in which Shakespeare, unhistorically, suggests that the
Wars of the Roses began through a quarrel between young aristocrats in the Temple Garden: II.iv. of *1 Henry VI*, consequently shows
a good deal of legal (i.e. Latinate) terminology, such as *quillets, signi-
ficants, subscribe, attached, attainted, apprehension, cognizance*. Not surprisingly, the three plays are frequently involved with questions of
succession and justice; even the demagogue Jack Cade has heard of
jurisdiction regal. Latinate adjective sometimes qualifies Latinate noun
and the result becomes doubly impressive: *factious emulations* (*1 Hen
VI* IV.i.113); *vehement instigation* (*Richard III* III.vii.138). Even better
is the hypocritical reluctance of Richard III to accept the crown:

> But if black scandal or foul-faced reproach
> Attend the sequel of your imposition,
> Your mere enforcement shall acquittance me
> From all the impure blots and stains thereof.   (III.vii.230–3)

Moral abstractions, carried over from the morality plays, can produce their own Latinate diction:

> Virtue is choked with foul ambition,
> And charity chased hence by rancour's hand;
> Foul subornation is predominant,
> And equity exiled your highness' land.   (*2 Hen VI* III.i.143–6)

The adroit 'placing' of a word so as to secure maximum stress is already evident:

> Wounds will I lend the French instead of eyes,
> To weep their *intermissive* miseries.   (*1 Hen VI* I.i.87–8)

> The presence of a king engenders love
> Amongst his subjects and his loyal friends,
> As it *disanimates* his enemies.   (*1 Hen VI* III.i.183–5)

Two polysyllabic Latin words sometimes occur within the line (as at *2 Henry VI* III.i.145 above) or an impressive-sounding line is achieved by a Latin-derived word followed by a compound ('As cognizance of my blood-drinking hate', *1 Hen VI* II.iv.108). What is noteworthy in these plays, and especially in *1 Henry VI*, are the uncommon Latinate words, as if Shakespeare, like some of his contemporaries, was savouring the ability of Elizabethan English to borrow such terms. *Attainture* first entered English in 1538, but was always unusual and occurs only here in Shakespeare; the two instances of *reguerdon*, rare both as noun and as verb although appearing in Gower and in Chaucer's *Boethius*, are the only two in the canon. *Proditor, periapts* (first recorded in 1584) and *immanity* (defined in Cawdrey's 1604 dictionary as 'beastlie crueltie or hugenesse and greatnes' and glossed as 'bloody strife' in *1 Henry VI*) are similarly unique within Shakespeare's plays. *Contusions* occurs from c. 1400 in the medical sense but was apparently never frequent in general use. *Corrosive* likewise had a medical and scientific sense from the late fourteenth century, but the metaphorical use ('destructive', 'wasting') was evidently becoming more common in the Elizabethan period; the *OED* has examples from Elyot, Mulcaster, Hooker, Lyly and Greene, but the word occurs only twice in Shakespeare, once at

1 Henry VI III.iii.3 and once at *2 Henry VI* III.ii.403. Other forms, rare in themselves, might be easily understood by reference to a more common word with the same root: *embassade* occurs only at *3 Henry VI*, IV.iii.3, but *embassador* was a common Tudor spelling; *extraught* was perhaps a variant of *extracted* (cf. *distraught*); *neglection* ('neglect') and *guardant* ('guard') are other examples of unusual affixes. The number of such words is greatest in *Henry VI* (especially in Part 1) but one might add *enacts* from *Titus Andronicus* IV.ii.118, the only example of the noun from Shakespeare (although *Hamlet* III.ii.207 has *enactures*). *Richard III*, too contributes its quota of unusual Latinate diction. *Inductions*, I.i.32, is the first *OED* entry for the sense 'initial step' (cf. *1 Hen IV* III.i.2), but 'preface', 'preamble' (to a book) dates from 1533 (More) and the dramatic sense ('opening scene') is found at IV.iv.5 *Recomforture*, IV.iv.425, is the only occurrence in Shakespeare and in the *OED*. *Diffused* ('shapeless', I.ii.78) and *expiate* ('fully come', III.iii.23 – changed to *expir'd* in Folios 2–4) are rare as past participles.

Doublets are fairly numerous in all five plays, but not all are Latinate by any means, and on the whole they are fairly straightforward, suggesting that the reason for their use was not intelligibility but a desire to add weight to the line. Almost half of those in *Titus Andronicus* occur in Act V where the enormity of Titus's revenge becomes evident. 'Linked' doublets occasionally appear:

Her valiant courage and undaunted spirit   (*1 Hen VI* V.v.70)

By false intelligence or wrong surmise   (*R III* II.i.55)

Compounds, similarly, are numerous, but rarely innovatory or otherwise remarkable. *2 Henry VI* III.i.335 ('Let pale-faced fear keep with the mean-born man.') is fairly typical. *Church-like* humours (I.i.245), *silken-coated* slaves (IV.ii.120) and *chair-days* ('old age', V.ii.48), all from the same play, are more imaginative, but other passages show in their choice of compounds a sense of strain rare in Shakespeare but more common in some of his contemporaries:

And for myself, foe as he was to me,
Might liquid tears or heart-offending groans
Or blood-consuming sighs recall his life,
I would be blind with weeping, sick with groans,
Look pale as primrose with blood-drinking sighs,
And all to have the noble Duke alive.   (2 Hen VIII.ii.59–64)

Weeping-ripe (*3 Hen VI* I.iv.172) and *water-standing* eye (*3 Hen VI*

V.vi.40) are little better. In this play *clear-shining* and *fair-shining* occur within a few lines of one another in II.i, and elsewhere *hard-hearted, gentle-hearted, soft-hearted, sad-hearted, proud-hearted* suggest that Shakespeare's imagination was scarcely at fever pitch. *Richard III* contains *key-cold, numb-cold* and *icy-cold. Titus Andronicus* is a play with comparatively few compounds, but it introduces the three-member type which Shakespeare used occasionally later: *worse-than-killing* lust (II.iii.175), *never-heard-of* torturing pain (II.iii.285). On the other hand, this play has several alliterative phrases – analagous to compounds – a device which Shakespeare came to associate with an outmoded style. *Ling'ring languishment* (II.i.110) and *dainty doe* (II.i.117, later on to become Bottom's 'O dainty duck, O dear!') are satirical – they occur in the same speech of Aaron – but *the fields are fragrant* (II.ii.2) and *dawning day* (II.ii.10) are part of an early attempt, not wholly successful, at the high 'prologue' style. *Brinish bowels* (III.i.97), however it appeared to the Elizabethans, strikes us as simply unfortunate. In *Richard III* there is a high incidence of compounds. Few are arresting ('I will converse with iron-witted fools/And unrespective boys', IV.ii.28, and 'impotent and snail-paced beggary', IV.iii.53, both link a compound with a Latinate term) but there are few tired examples either; most suggest careful, encapsulated thought. Richard is variously referred to as *hell-governed, elvish-marked, bunch-backed* (twice), *villain-slave, stone-hard, self-misused* and *hell-hound.*

Aaron in *Titus Andronicus* is perhaps the first major Shakespearean character to use deliberate colloquialisms. It is difficult to be completely sure of what was colloquial for the Elizabethan audience; all one can do is to check one's impression from the context against the *OED* and a Shakespeare concordance. *Brabble* (*Titus Andronicus* II.i.62) was not common, although it was increasing in frequency in the later sixteenth century; it seems to imply an undignified quarrel – Aaron's is a *petty brabble* and in *Twelfth Night* Antonio is 'desperate of shame and state / In private brabble' (v.i.61). *Jet*, in the same speech, looks colloquial and was fairly common in the sixteenth century, but more often with the meaning 'strut', 'swagger' than 'encroach' which the context here seems to suggest. *Pack*, 'conspire' (IV.ii.156) is not very usual, although there are examples from the early sixteenth century. The sense of 'suffer for it' for *smoke* (IV.ii.111) seems clear, but whether there is any more direct reference to burning is not obvious. *Some certain snatch* (II.i.95) occurs in the middle of a passage of bawdy word-play and one meaning is pretty obviously sexual, but other instances outside Shakespeare suggest a quick movement (compare modern *snatch*). Aaron is fond of racy epithets, as when he describes Tamora's two sons who ravished Lavinia:

> That codding spirit had they from their mother,
> *As sure a card as ever won the set.*
> That bloody mind, I think, they learned of me,
> *As true a dog as ever fought at head.*   (*TA* V.i.98–101)

In one of the rhetorically-pointed laments of the noble women characters in *Richard III*, the Duchess of York asks

> Why should calamity be full of words?

Queen Elizabeth replies, in a style itself expansionist:

> Windy attorneys to their client's woes,
> Airy succeeders of intestate joys,
> Poor breathing orators of miseries,
> Let them have scope! Though what they will impart
> Help nothing else, yet they do ease the heart.

and the Duchess, evidently convinced, continues

> If so, then be not tongue-tied: go with me
> And in the breath of bitter words let's smother
> My damned son that thy two sweet sons smothered.
> The trumpet sounds. Be copious in exclaims.   (IV.iv.126–35)

'Be copious in exclaims': the play does exactly that. There are several examples of simple lexical parallelism:

> No doubt, no doubt. O, 'tis a parlous boy,
> Bold, quick, ingenious, forward, capable.   (III.i.154–5)

> And yet within these five hours Hastings lived,
> Untainted, unexamined, free, at liberty.   (III.vi.8–9)

and more extended instances at III.vii.116–21 and IV.iv.168–73 where it is noticeable that Shakespeare manages both variation in word-order and syntactical balance.

This, however, is only one of the styles of *Richard III*. The hero himself dominates the play, the longest of the histories, and his exuberance, vitality and individualism are characteristic of Marlovian heroes. The other characters are distanced from the audience by rhetorical speech-patterns, and Richard can employ these too, most obviously in the two extended examples of *stichomythia*, first with Anne (I.ii) and later with Elizabeth (IV.iv). In each of these he achieves the apparently impossible: to marry the woman whose husband and father-in-law he had killed, and to persuade a mother to give her daughter's hand to the man 'who slew her brothers and her uncle'. The extreme formal expression emphasises the outrageous nature of his requests. But our feeling that Richard is simply 'more real' than the other characters[7] is largely because of his ability to change style from rhetorical to colloquial. 'I would I knew thy heart', says Anne; ''Tis figured in my tongue', Richard replies. His language is indeed often *figured*, but in his deliberate use of colloquialisms to reveal to the audience his true feelings about both people and events he is a truer Machiavel than Aaron:

> Which done, God take King Edward to His mercy
> And leave the world for me to bustle in! (I.i.151–2)

The sanctimonious 'take King Edward to His mercy' gives way to the *bustle* of further plotting.

> Amen! And make me die a good old man!
> That is the *butt-end* of a mother's blessing;
> I marvel that her grace did leave it out. (II.ii.109–11)

> Marry, as for Clarence, he is well repaid;
> He is *franked up to fatting* for his pains –
> God pardon them that are the cause thereof! (I.iii.312–4)

The verb *bustle* is recorded once only in Middle English, but although it is used reflexively in later sixteenth-century English, it apparently occurs first as a phrasal verb (*bustle in*) in North's *Plutarch*. *Butt-end*, the sole instance in Shakespeare, is also in North (was Shakespeare already reading for the later Roman plays?). This instance of *franked up*, and another in *Richard III* (IV.v.3), are the only two examples in the canon, although the noun *frank* occurs in *2 Henry IV* II.ii.140. *Cog* (I.iii.48) and *costard* (I.iv.156) are found rather more often. *Cog* seems to have developed from its original sense of 'cheat at dice' to 'cheat' (generally) and by the end of the century to 'wheedle" or 'flatter' as here. The other Shakespearean examples closest to *Richard III* are 'I'll mountebank their loves, / *Cog* their hearts from them and come home beloved' (*Cor* III.ii.132–3, where Coriolanus sarcastically chooses the terms *mountebank* and *cog* to describe his appeal to the plebs for their votes) and 'Ay, and you hear him *cog*, see him dissemble' (*Timon of Athens* V.i.93).

Two plays especially, Jonson's *Poetaster* (acted 1601) and Shakespeare's *Love's Labour's Lost* (1593–4) satirise the attitudes towards language which have been our concern in the previous chapter. Jonson was criticising not only inkhornism but also, in the character of Tucca the military parasite, the 'realistic' (but in its own way copious) language which we shall examine later in the *Henry IV* plays. But most of Jonson's ridicule is reserved for Crispinus the poetaster (hack-writer) who, in V.iii.[8], is given by Horace an emetic which makes him vomit words such as *retrograde, reciprocal incubus, glibbery, lubricall, defunct, magnificate, spurious snotteries, chilbrained, clumsy* ('benumed'), *barmy froth, puffy, inflate, turgidous, ventositous, oblatrant, furibund, fatuate, strenuous, conscious dampe, prorumped, clutcht, snarling gusts, quaking custard, obstupefact.* Caesar's comment on all this is 'Here be words, Horace, able to bastinado a man's ears' (V.iii.390, just as the Bastard in *King John* complains that Hubert of Angers 'gives the *bastinado* with his tongue'). Not all these words have been identified in the works of Marston whom Horace (i.e. Jonson) satirises under the name of Crispinus, nor are these the only inkhorn terms in the play: *gratulate, ornatures, extrude*, and *acceptive* might also qualify. Furthermore, linguistic condemnation is (as elsewhere in Jonson) allied to condemnation of the moral laxity of some of the characters, whether from the Court or from the City. Renaissance educationalists like Elyot or Ascham saw appropriate language as one of the marks of a good man.

Love's Labour's Lost is much more comprehensive and subtle in its satire. It opens with the King of Navarre and his three attendant lords (chief of whom is Berowne) vowing to live apart from society for three years and to pass their time in study and contemplation:

> Our court shall be a little academe,
> Still and contemplative in living art. (I.i.13–14)

When, in Act II, this same court of Navarre is visited by the Princess of France and her three attendant ladies, the outcome would seem inevitable. The interest, then, is less in plot than in attitudes to life, and these will be mirrored in the language employed. There is a third set of characters: Armado, a fantastical Spaniard – the name, as well as in all probability his costume, would be a give-way; Holofernes, a schoolmaster; Nathaniel, a parish priest; Costard, the clown; and Dull, the parish constable. These are not quite a group since Holofernes and Nathaniel do not appear until Act IV, scene ii (to enliven a possibly flagging interest?) and Armado and Holofernes do not in fact meet until V.i., but they are developed from stock comic types with immediately recognisable linguistic attitudes (The Folio text calls Armado simply 'Braggart', Holofernes 'Pedant' and Nathaniel 'Curate').

We may begin with Armado since he appears first. The men from Navarre regard him as comic relaxation for their high-minded existence. He is prepared for before he actually appears:

> *Berowne* But is there no quick recreation granted?
> *King*   Ay, that there is. Our court, you know, is haunted
>   With a refined traveller of Spain,
>   A man in all the world's new fashion planted,
>   That hath a mint of phrases in his brain . . .
> *Berowne* Armado is a most illustrious wight,
>   A man of fire-new words, fashion's own knight.
> (I.i.160–4, 176–7)

and immediately the connection is made between *new fashion* and *fire-new words*, those Latinate terms which were still in process of acclimatisation. Next, a letter from Armado is delivered to the King:

> So it is, besieged with sable-coloured melancholy, I did commend the black-oppressing humour to the most wholesome physic of thy health-giving air; and, as I am a gentleman, betook myself to walk. The time When? About the sixth hour; when beasts most graze, birds best peck, and men sit down to that nourishment which is called supper. So much for the time When. Now for the ground Which? Which, I mean, I walked upon. It is ycleped thy park. Then for the place Where? Where, I mean, I did encounter that obscene and most preposterous event, that draweth from my snow-white pen the ebon-coloured ink, which here thou viewest, beholdest, surveyest or seest. But to the place Where? It standeth north-north-east and by east from the west corner of thy curious-knotted garden.   (I.i.229–45)

There is some order and method about this (*When? . . . Which? . . . Where?*) and indeed balance: 'beasts most graze, birds best peck, and men sit down to that nourishment which is called supper'. But in these last words we see Armado addicted to the vices of rhetoric. First of all he offends against decorum, just as Berowne had previously forecast: 'How low soever the matter, I hope in God for high words.' He cannot simply say *supper* but *that nourishment which is called supper*. In the quotation as a whole, most of the nouns have their accompanying adjectives, either Latinate (*obscene and most preposterous*) or compound (*sable-coloured, black-oppressing, health-giving, snow-white, ebon-coloured, curious-knotted*). Not satisfied with a doublet, Armado produces no fewer than four synonyms (*viewest, beholdest, surveyest* or *seest*) and the last three add nothing further to the meaning. His method is simply to elaborate in language which *sounds* impressive either etymologically or in sheer weight of words. He is 'the *varnish* of a complete man', a variation on the more regular Elizabethan metaphor, *painted* (which is in fact used in the play at II.i.14, IV.i.16 and IV.iii.238); as we might say, he has a *veneer* of good manners.

And so he goes on. There is a second letter in IV.i. At III.i.125 he releases Costard from custody ('Thou wert immured, restrained, captivated, bound') and at V.i.87 he tells Holofernes

> Sir, it is the king's most sweet pleasure and affection to congratulate the princess at her pavilion in the posteriors of this day, which the rude multitude call the afternoon.

He even produces a neologism, a coinage of his own, but typically a Latin-sounding one, in *repasture* (IV.i.95) a blend of *repast* and *pasture*. On his first appearance in I.ii (by which time we have already been asking ourselves if the man can really be as ridiculous as has been alleged) he is provided with a diminutive page, Moth, in the tradition of the boys in Lyly's plays. Moth's function is to prick the bubble of Armado's inflated language, and so of his own view of himself, sometimes by parody, sometimes by a deliberate mono-syllabic reply:

Armado	How canst thou part sadness and melancholy, my tender juvenal?
Moth	By a familiar demonstration of the working, my tough signor.
Armado	Why tough signor? Why tough signor?
Moth	Why tender juvenal? Why tender juvenal?
Armado	I spoke it, tender juvenal, as a congruent epitheton appertaining to thy young days, which we may nominate tender.
Moth	And I, tough signor, as an appertinent title to your old time, which we may name tough. (I.ii.7–17)

Holofernes also uses an abundance of synonyms, and cannot, in the real world outside his classroom, forget his pedagogical methods. Like many Elizabethan schoolmasters, he teaches translation by trying out the various English equivalents of a Latin word:

Holofernes	The deer was, as you know, *sanguis*, in blood; ripe as the pomewater, who now hangeth like a jewel in the ear of *coelo*, the sky, the welkin, the heaven; and anon falleth like a crab on the face of *terra*, the soil, the land, the earth.
Nathaniel	Truly, Master Holofernes, the epithets are sweetly varied, like a scholar at the least. (IV.ii.3–9)

Nathaniel not only admires but echoes him:

> Nathaniel I praise God for you sir. Your reasons at dinner have been sharp and sententious, pleasant without scurrility, witty without affection, audacious without impudency, learned without opinion, and strange without heresy. I did converse this quondam day with a companion of the king's, who is intituled, nominated, or called, Don Adriano de Armado.
>
> Holofernes *Novi hominem tanquam te.* His humour is lofty, his discourse peremptory, his tongue filed, his eye ambitious, his gait majestical, and his general behaviour vain, ridiculous, and thrasonical. He is too picked, too spruce, too affected, too odd, as it were, too peregrinate, as I may call it.
>
> Nathaniel A most singular and choice epithet.   (V.i.2–17)

No doubt Nathaniel writes down the 'most singular and choice epithet' *peregrinate* for use on a future occasion, and this is surely how many of these fashionable new words must have achieved some currency. The rhetorician John Hoskins, writing in 1599, advises his pupil to compile a list of synonyms but to use them selectively, not like a *schoolmaster*. He says that *accumulation* (one of the sub-divisions of Amplification):

> hath his due season after some argument or proof. Otherwise it is like a schoolmaster foaming out synonymies, or words of one meaning, and will sooner yield a conjecture of superfluity of words than of sufficiency of matter . . . You will be well stored for this purpose when you have made up your *synonyma* book after my direction.[9]

The admiration for book-learning appears in Nathaniel's patronising remark about the constable Dull (IV.ii.24): 'Sir, he hath never fed of the dainties that are bred in a *book*'. But if this is Armado over again, it is Armado with a difference. Armado doesn't get things wrong, only far more complicated than necessary. Holofernes occasionally gets the spellings fashionably wrong because he gets the etymology wrong:

> I abhor such fanatical phantasimes, such insociable and point–devise companions; such rackers of orthography as to speak 'dout' fine when he should say 'doubt', 'det' when he should pronounce 'debt' – d,e,b,t, not d,e,t. He clepeth a calf 'cauf', half 'hauf', neighbour *vocatur* 'nebour', neigh abbreviated 'ne'. This is abhominable, which he would call 'abominable'.   (V.i.19–7)

Doubt and *debt* appear in Middle English as *doute* and *dette* (without the *b*) because they had been borrowed immediately from French and not from the original Latin *dubitum* and *debitum*. But such was their veneration for Latin that the Elizabethans restored the *b* (together

with the *d* in *advantage* and *adventure*, the *l* in *false*, the *c* in *verdict* and
the *p* in *receipt*). Purists expected pronunciation to follow the spelling. In medieval Latin and in earlier English, *abominable* was often
wrongly etymologised as *ab* + *homo* ('away from man' and hence 'in-
human') instead of from Old French *abominable*, in turn from Latin
abominabilis, and therefore 'deserving of imprecation' because it was
an ill *omen*.

Dull is beyond the linguistic pale; like those later Shakespearean
constables he misunderstands ('I myself *reprehend* his own person, for
I am his Grace's farborough.'), but Costard is rather more complex.
In part he is simple peasant who cannot understand the newly
fashionable words like *enfranchise, remuneration* and *guerdon*, and com-
ically and stupidly mixes up letters from Armado to Jaquenetta (with
whom he is himself in love) and from Berowne to Rosaline. Yet
Armado calls him *rational hind*, 'intelligent yokel' (I.ii.117) and to
Holofernes one of Costard's puns is 'A good lustre of conceit in a turf
of earth'. He is therefore also semantic juggler, as he shows in puns
with the King towards the end of I.i and by taking his part with
Boyet, Rosaline and Maria in a series of sexual innuendos on archery
and courtship in IV.i. which Maria ends by accusing him of talking
greasily. Does Costard later in Shakespeare's career become two characters: on the one hand the country bumpkin and mistaker of words,
on the other the clever clown – perhaps Touchstone (who after all
loves Audrey, a country girl like Jaquenetta) rather than Feste? Laun-
celot Gobbo in *The Merchant of Venice* is another example of this early uncertainty in characterisation. Initially he is only marginally
cleverer than his father and similarly addicted to malapropisms.
When he returns in III.v. (he has been off stage since II.v.) he still
confuses *agitation* and *cogitation* but is sufficient of a punster to de-
serve Lorenzo's retort 'How every fool can play upon the word!' It is
Costard, together with Moth, who makes what must surely be
Shakespeare's own comment on the exaggerations of the whole trio,
Armado, Holofernes and Nathaniel:

Moth   They have been at a great feast of languages and stol'n the
scraps.
Costard   O, they have lived long on the alms-basket of words.

(V.i.39–42)

Yet, towards the end of the final and very long scene, the tone of
Love's Labour's Lost suddenly changes. At V.ii.720 the messenger
Marcáde brings news of the death of the King of France, and the
ladies must return home. The speech of sympathy of the King of

Navarre is made in the old style, now to be discredited, as the Princess replies 'I understand you not.' It is Berowne who perceives that

> Honest plain words best pierce the ear of grief.

although it must be admitted that the rest of his speech (V.ii.755–77) is hardly so straightforward. Berowne had, from the beginning, been sceptical of the possibility of living such an eremetical life and of renouncing women's company altogether. Yet he *will* couch almost every speech so as to reveal his brilliance and ingenuity. This linguistic irresponsibility is noticed by Rosaline, the very lady with whom he is in love:

> Oft have I heard of you, my Lord Berowne,
> Before I saw you, and the world's large tongue
> Proclaims you for a man replete with mocks,
> Full of comparisons and wounding flouts,
> Which you on all estates will execute
> That lie within the mercy of your wit. (V.ii.842–7)

The ladies are, quite simply, kinder than the men. They are high-spirited too, but they realise that life has a serious side. The reason for the Princess's visit to Navarre, we are told, was 'serious business, craving quick dispatch' (II.i.31). When Holofernes, Armado, Nathaniel, Costard and Moth ('The pedant, the braggart, the hedge-priest, the fool, and the boy', as Berowne slightingly calls them) present their play of the Nine Worthies, it is the ladies who are encouraging and the men whose witty comments disconcert the actors (just as the courtiers in *A Midsummer Night's Dream* make fun of the mechanicals' play), so much so that Holofernes blurts out

> This is not generous, not gentle, not humble. (V.ii.630)

So it is appropriate that the play does not end with a multiple wedding. Jack hath not Jill – or, at least, not yet, for the men are put on probation for twelve months to prove their love by devoted service. Berowne's therapy, as prescribed by Rosaline, is the strictest:

> To weed this wormwood from your fructful brain,
> And therewithal to win me, if you please,
> Without the which I am not to be won,
> You shall this twelvemonth term from day to day
> Visit the speechless sick, and still converse
> With groaning wretches; and your task shall be
> With all the fierce endeavour of your wit
> To enforce the pained impotent to smile. (V.ii.848–55)

and it involves the direction of his linguistic ability towards a new and more serious purpose. There is, however, some hope for him, as revealed by a return, in the last scene, to the imagery of language and fashion which had begun the play. The four men plan to woo the ladies by an elaborate masquerade in which they disguise themselves as Russians. The ladies, privy to the plot, dress up as one another and make their partners' protestations of love ridiculous. Berowne is the first to realise that the men's elaborate style has been its own disguise:

> Taffeta phrases, silken terms precise,
> Three-piled hyperboles, spruce affectation,
> Figures pedantical – these summer flies
> Have blown me full of maggot ostentation.
> I do forswear them; and I here protest
> By this white glove (how white the hand, God knows!)
> Henceforth my wooing mind shall be expressed
> In russet yeas and honest kersey noes.   (V.ii.407–14)

Taffeta was used for expensive lining; three-piled velvet was the best weight. But russet was the characteristic reddish-brown colour of lower-class clothing, and kersey was a plain wool cloth. The contrast between (French) three-piled velvet and English kersey is made over again in *Measure for Measure* (I.ii.32–5). It has been argued that to see this image in *Love's Labour's Lost* as a way of rejecting art for nature, is far too simple. It really only changes one kind of affectation for another: the silk, taffeta and velvet of the high style for the kersey of an assumed low style.[10] There is some truth in this at the time Berowne makes the remark, but he is *beginning* the process of rejecting artificiality which is to be continued in his sojourn among the groaning wretches and pained impotents. The two songs which conclude the play are similarly contrasted in style. Spring is idealised and generalised; we hear of shepherds, ploughmen, married men and maidens. The harshness of winter is realistic and individualised; its inhabitants are Dick, Tom, Marian and greasy Joan. Each stanza is delineated by *When . . . then . . .*; the rhetoric both gives shape to the lyrics and helps to point the contrast.

The entrance of Marcade with his news of the King of France's death provides the catalyst which forces *Love's Labour's Lost* to come to terms with real life. This does not happen – or not nearly so demonstrably – in a play which might be thought to be somewhat similar, *The Two Gentlemen of Verona*. Already Launce is capable of criticising the fashionable Petrarchan attitude to love:

> Why, man, if the river were dry, I am able to fill it with my tears. If the
> wind were down, I could drive the boat with my sighs.   (II.iii.49–51)

There is some realisation in *The Two Gentlemen of Verona* that 'words
may substitute for or falsify experience'[11], but the devices which
might force a dramatic confrontation of viewpoints remain undeveloped. The lovers seldom meet, the outlaws and Eglamour are
comic-opera figures, Launce and Speed disappear in act IV, and
Valentine is too readily satisfied with Proteus's repentance. *Love's
Labour's Lost*, the most linguistically-pointed of Shakespeare's plays,
testifies to the general interest the new usages had aroused, even if, as
seems possible, the play was designed for the private theatre. Yet in
its final refusal to divorce language from life, it cannot be just 'mere
verbal promiscuity' or 'linguistically narcissistic'.[12] The extreme
view of the uselessness of language – 'Vows are but breath, and
breath a vapour is' – comes some time before the end of the play.
The play is, then, not a repudiation of language, even of elaborate
language which will take its proper place in the development of
Shakespeare's stylistic repertoire, but an early refusal to 'draw out
the thread of their verbosity finer than the staple of their argument'.

In his middle and later plays, Shakespeare begins to *use* Latinisms,
copious diction and even compounds as indicators of particular
styles. This will be illustrated more fully in the later chapters of this
book which attempt to characterise those styles. But meanwhile we
can glance at some individual effects which do not seem to reverber-
ate beyond their particular play. *All's Well* is a muted play linguistically. There are no set pieces in the manner of Claudio on death in
the contemporary *Measure for Measure*. The King does not dominate
sufficiently; Bertram is brave but hardly heroic; Parolles is fool and
coward, not villain. It is Parolles who comes closest to possessing a
manner of his own, but even in his case what is notable is what is
said about him rather than what he says himself. Bertram does not
really see through Parolles until the business of the drum, when he is
revealed as 'your devoted friend, sir, the manifold linguist and the
armipotent soldier' (IV.iii.230). Lafew does, and already at II.v.43
recognises that 'The soul of this man is his clothes'. Later he informs
the Countess:

> No, no, no, your son was misled with a snipped-taffeta fellow there,
> whose villainous saffron would have made all the unbaked and doughy
> youth of a nation in his colour. Your daughter-in-law had been alive at
> this hour, and your son here at home, more advanced by the King than
> by that red-tailed humble-bee I speak of.[13]   (IV.v.1–6)

Parolles himself says that the French lords 'wear themselves in the *cap* of the time'. If these metaphors of language and clothes visualise Parolles as something of a later Armado, he is certainly not caricatured to that extent.

For some reason, the prefix *un–* seems to have been a favourite of Shakespeare's and several of his examples are the earliest recorded in *OED*. *Hamlet* is full of instances: *unaneled, unbated, uncharge, uneffectual, unfellowed, unfortified, ungartered, unhand, unhouseled, unimproved, unknowing, unmastered, unnerved, unpeg, unpolluted, unprevailing, unproportioned, unreclaimed, unrighteous, unshaped, unsifted, unsinewed, unsmirched, unwrung* are all unique, whereas *unforced, ungalled, unkennel, unschooled* and *unyoke* occur on one other occasion only. *Un–* was, in any case, increasing in use in the Tudor period, often as a translation of *in* – in French or Italian loan-words. In an interesting recent examination of the use of *un–* in *King Lear*[14], it emerges that Lear uses the prefix quite often up to the end of III.iv. He gives away his kingdom to his daughters 'while we/*Unburdened* crawl toward death' (I.i.41). Cordelia is to him *untender* (I.i.106) and *unfriended* (I.i.203). He threatens Goneril with 'Th'*untented* woundings of a father's curse', i.e. too deep to be probed. Not all *un–* words are Lear's – Gloucester and Kent provide other examples – although some are spoken of him: the Gentleman describes him as running *unbonneted* through the storm (III.i.14) and Kent says that 'His wits begin t'*unsettle*' (III.iv.155). Clearly these unusual epithets are a reflection of Lear's distortion of reality. Later uses of *un–* are both fewer in number and their novelty now represents his increasing perception. *Accommodated* was evidently a new word which Bardolph only half understands and Shallow admires (*2 Hen IV* III.ii.65–80), but to Lear, Poor Tom is *unaccommodated* man (III.iv.103). Cordelia finally refers to his *untuned* and jarring senses (IV,vii,16).

The whole of *Troilus and Cressida* is permeated with Latinate diction and with compounds. In this play of the breakdown of love admidst the posturings of two war-weary armies, it is not surprising that many of the compounds (especially those of Thersites) are pejorative, even insulting. But the amount of obviously Latinate diction and the apparently unusual nature of much of it are strange in a play of this date (? 1600). *Corrivaled, attributive, appertainments, assubjugate, abruption, calumniate, commixtion, deceptious, constringed* (closer to the Latin than the French-derived *constrained*), *insisture, monstruosity, maculation, multipotent, mirable, protractive, primogenity, oppugnancy, propugnation, refractory, unplausive, uncomprehensive, subduements* are unique within the Shakespeare canon, and rare elsewhere according to *OED*. One or two other words, such as *deracinate, medicinable, unrespective, prenominate* and *recordation*, each occur only once more in Shakespeare, although it is fair to point out that in a few instances the existence of other words from the same root – *corrival, monstrous, transport* – might make recognition easier. Ulysses among the Greeks and Hector on the Trojan side seem especially prone to Latinisms, but Agamemnon and Nestor too have been accused of 'verbal flatulence'.[15] Ulysses' famous 'degree' speech in Act I, scene iii, is full of all the marks of the high style: lists at lines 86–8, 96–9, 103–7; the conversion *vizarded* (83); the images of the hive, the untuned instrument, the wolf and the fever. And yet the gist of the speech is easily understood. Ulysses often uses formal metaphorical language to clothe quite simple ideas. Hector, too, is not one to use a straightforward word where a more impressive one will suffice:

> The obligation of our blood forbids
> A gory emulation 'twixt us twain.
> Were thy commixtion Greek and Troyan . . .   (IV.v.121–3)

The play seems full of 'words, words, mere words, no matter from the heart' (V.iii.107) and the idiom of the characters is insufficiently distinctive.[16]

Perhaps part of the explanation of the unusual amount of Latinate diction in *Troilus and Cressida* lies in its curious textual history. Permission was granted to James Roberts to print the play in 1603 (when it had evidently been acted by the Lord Chamberlain's company), but apparently it did not appear in print until the 1609 quarto, the new printers of which claim that it was 'neuer stal'd with the Stage, neuer clapper-clawd with the palmes of the vulgar'. One suggestion is that the play was performed before a sophisticated and cynical audience at one of the Inns of Court. That may have been so – such an audience might certainly respond to the play's Latinate diction – but it is most unlikely that the play was *composed* with such an audience in mind. Perhaps it had not been any too successful on the public stage. The epistle to the 1609 quarto calls the play a comedy, but its title page calls it a history and it appears in the section of the First Folio containing the tragedies. Either the Elizabethan terminology for describing genres was unbelievably lax (Polonius, at least, knew several sub-divisions) or else, then as now, the play presented its problems.

After *Troilus and Cressida*, copious language, where it occurs at all, is hardly ever for mere augmentation but usually for dramatic contrast (as we shall see in *Lear* and *Othello*). It is rare indeed in Shakespeare, to find words like Tourneur's *insculption* ('inscription') and *circumvolved* ('enveloped') occurring for no apparent reason. Even in Tourneur, the Latinate diction is sometimes deliberate, part of the verbose Puritan jargon of Languebeau Snuffe:

> Sir, I want words and protestation to insinuate into your credit, but in plainness and truth, I will qualify her grief with the spirit of consolation.
> (*Atheist's Tragedy* I.ii.143–5)

All's Well, for example, yields only *prejudicates, captious* and *intenable, facinerious* and *consolate* by way of Latinisms, and the *–ate* suffix probably appears more unusual to us than it did to the Elizabethans. When uncommon words appear in the tragedies and after, the play sometimes slows down to let us savour them, perceive their significance in that particular context:

> And what was he?
> Forsooth, a great arithmetician.   (*Oth* I.i.18–19)

where the preceding short line prepares us for *arithmetician* and Iago's contempt for the theorist Cassio, or:

> If it were done when 'tis done, then 'twere well
> It were done quickly. If the assassination
> Could trammel up the consequence, and catch
> With his surcease, success.   (*Mac* I.vii.1–4)

where *it* is revealed in all its enormity, *assassination*. Both *arithmetician* and *assassination* occur only here in Shakespeare.

The progress of *The Winter's Tale* is very like that of *King Lear*, from the hero's refusal to recognise an obsession to the shattering realisation that all his beliefs were mistaken, from complexity of language to simplicity. But the manifestation of these changes is different in the two plays. Whereas Lear demonstrated – at least to himself – his royal demeanour by copiousness of diction, Leontes uses synonyms to savour them, to elaborate, and usually to degrade. The 'friendship' of Hermione with Polixines may be genuine *entertainment* (I.iii.110) but its outward demonstrations make it 'entertainment / My bosom likes not' (118). Occasionally the distinction is achieved by punning:

> Go play, boy, play: thy mother plays, and I
> Play too – but so disgraced a part . . .   (I.ii.187–8)

57

> Why, that's my bawcock. What, hast smutched thy nose?
> They say it is a copy out of mine. Come, captain,
> We must be neat – not neat but cleanly, captain.
> And yet the steer, the heifer, and the calf
> Are all called neat. Still virginalling
> Upon his palm? – How now, you wanton calf!
> Art thou my calf? (I.ii.121–7)

Neat also means 'horned cattle', and a *calf*, whilst young (like Mamillius) may also be *wanton* (like Hermione). Latinate words give way to more blunt compounds:

> More, she's a traitor, and Camillo is
> A *fedary* with her, and one that knows
> What she should shame to know herself
> But with her most vile principal – that she's
> A *bed-swerver* . . . (II.i.89–93)

or less precise words lead to more explicit, coarser terms:

> My wife is *slippery*? If thou wilt confess –
> Or else be impudently negative
> To have nor eyes, nor ears, nor thought – then say
> My wife's a *hobby-horse* . . . (I.ii.273–6)

These compounds are the peasant's view of the aristocracy as no better than they should be, not a ruler's own belief in himself; Leontes here is more like the old shepherd taking up the abandoned child:

> Sure, some scape, Though I am not bookish, yet I can read waiting
> gentlewoman in the scape: this has been some stair-work, some
> trunk-work, some behind-door-work. (III.iii.70–3)

Leontes has a trick of repeating words: 'my heart dances / But not for joy, not joy'; 'It is but weakness / To bear the matter thus, mere weakness'; 'But we have been / Deceived in thy integrity, deceived'; and

> *Camillo* Bohemia stays here longer.
> *Leontes*   Ha?
> *Camillo*   Stays here longer.
> *Leontes* Ay, but why?
> *Camillo* To satisfy your highness, and the entreaties
>   Of our most gracious mistress,
> *Leontes*   Satisfy?

Th'entreaties of your mistress? Satisfy?
Let that suffice.   (I.ii.230–35)

This is, of course, a feature of colloquial speech, but it also serves to call innocent words into suspicion.[17] Not that all the words are innocent: in this quotation *sluiced* and *fished* are deliberately offensive and the repetition of *neighbour* is preceded by the allegorisation *Sir Smile*:

                    Go play, boy, play. There have been,
Or I am much deceived, cuckolds ere now;
And many a man there is, even at this present,
Now, while I speak this, holds his wife by th'arm,
That little thinks she has been sluiced in's absence,
And his pond fished by his next neighbour, by
Sir Smile, his neighbour.   (I.ii.190–6)

It is true, he thinks, not just of Hermione but of several others, and it is immediately true, 'even at this present, / Now, while I speak this' – true, perhaps, for some of the audience.

And so to early in Act III when the messengers return with the oracle's pronouncement that Hermione is innocent and that Leontes's suspicions are groundless. Act IV takes place wholly in Bohemia and Leontes does not appear in it. By Act V, with Mamillius (really) and Hermione (supposedly) long since dead, Leontes, like Lear, uses a more deliberate, straightforward speech. Even in the first three acts, however, there have been occasional stylistic contrasts to the demented style of Leontes. These do not come wholly from Polixines or from Hermione. The rational controlled style of Camillo (I.ii.249 –67), which even verges on euphuism in the opening prose scene, and still more the directness of Paulina, remind us that not everything in the court is awry. Paulina uses synonyms to discriminate, not like Leontes to degredate:

                    I'll not call you tyrant;
But this most cruel usage of your queen –
Not able to produce more accusation
Than your own weak-hinged fancy – something savours
Of tyranny, and will ignoble make you,
Yea, scandalous to the world.   (II.iii.115–20)

In the concluding speech of *The Winter's Tale*, Leontes picks Camillo as a husband for Paulina. Loyalty is rewarded, and these two, upholders of careful, considered diction are brought together. Shakespeare's progress with vocabulary reflects an increasing discrimination: not to use Latinisms, doublets or poetic compounds simply because they were fashionable or expected of an Elizabethan dramatist, but, by letting them stand out from the surrounding words, to allow them to make their own point as determiners of an appropriate style.

NOTES AND REFERENCES

1. Bradbrook (1951), p.83.
2. Marlowe is quoted from *Complete Plays and Poems*, ed. E. D. Pendry, Dent (1976).
3. *Discoveries, Works*, ed. C. H. Herford and P. and E. M. Simpson, Clarendon Press, Oxford (1947), VIII, p.587.
4. Peet (1959).
5. Text in Bullough (1957), I, pp.284–363.
6. Marlowe's *Hero and Leander*, Lodge's *Scylla's Metamorphosis*, Drayton's *Endymion and Phoebe* and Shakespeare's *Venus and Adonis* are in *Elizabethan Verse Romances*, ed. M. M. Reese, Routledge & Kegan Paul (1968). The New Penguin edition is used for *The Rape of Lucrece*. For the lexis and syntax of Shakespeare's poems, see Partridge (1976).
7. Brooke (1968), p.54.
8. For *Poetaster*, see *Works* IV and King (1941). Compare *Discoveries*: 'Wheresoever, manners, and fashions are corrupted, Language is. It imitates the publicke riot. The excesse of Feasts and apparell, are the notes of a sick State, and the wantonness of language, of a sick mind.', *Works*, VIII, p.593.
9. *Directions for Speech and Style*, ed. H. H. Hudson, Princeton University Press, Princeton (1935), pp. 24–5.
10. Carroll (1976), pp. 176–82. For remarks on the concluding lyrics I am indebted to Heniger (1974).
11. Ewbank (1972), p.40.
12. Respectively Calderwood (1965) and Matthews (1964); it is fair to add that this is not the conclusion to Calderwood's article. See also Anderson (1971).
13. 'Saffron was used as a starch at the time, hence the link with the clothes of Parolles; it was also used to colour pastry, hence the unbaked and doughy youth of line 3' (New Penguin note, p.205).
14. Roberts (1978).
15. MacAlindon (1969) and Thomson (1969).
16. Greene (1981).
17. As Othello also does, to the puzzlement of Lodovico:
    Ay, you did wish that I would make her turn.
    Sir, she can turn, and turn, and yet go on.
    And turn again. And she can weep, sir, weep.
    And she's obedient; as you say, obedient,
    Very obedient. (IV.i.254–8).

CHAPTER FOUR
The new syntax

Hitherto I have concentrated on vocabulary which is the most obvious and most easily accessible of linguistic features. I have been especially concerned with the Elizabethan expansion of the lexicon by borrowings, chiefly from Latin; the recognition and use of some of the more recent of these borrowings, both singly and in groups; and the suggestion that excessive borrowing might be limited by the development of alternative lexical strategies such as word-formation and archaisms. It is time now to turn to wider matters of clause and sentence, to the Elizabethan achievement of a variety of syntactic styles in English, and to Shakespeare's selection from these for different artistic purposes. To appreciate this we must first turn aside to examine the function of rhetoric.[1]

In classical times, and up to the Renaissance and even later, the word *rhetoric* did not carry its modern, frequently pejorative sense of 'bombast', 'mere hollow words', but meant the art of persuasion. One of its most influential Roman exponents was Cicero, who was an advocate, a calling in which it is naturally important to persuade an audience of the justice of your case. But the argument should be not only convincing but attractive; formality and elegance invite the listener to accept what he is being told without submitting it to the more rigorous tests of logic and reason. Knowledge of the detail of rhetoric passes to the Middle Ages largely through Cicero and through a book wrongly attributed to him, *De Rhetorica ad Herennium* (c. 80 BC). By medieval times, rhetoric was found not only in courts but also in preaching and literature, two other fields in which eloquence was important, and it formed part of the introductory liberal arts course in medieval universities, the Trivium, which consisted of grammar, logic and rhetoric. Several textbooks (in Latin) illustrated the application of rhetoric to literature by numerous examples which were usually taken from classical writers but occasionally from medieval authors too. One such book, the *Nova Poetria* by Geoffrey de Vinsauf (c. 1200), Chaucer certainly knew of, since he mentions it in *The Nun's Priest's Tale*. And of course numerous examples of the figures of speech (*figurae* or *colores*) which were so important in literature could be found in medieval works also.

The practice of rhetoric, as medieval and renaissance writers conceived it, derived from the concept of *decorum*, that different styles are suitable for different subjects: 'the word must be the cousin to the deed', as Chaucer expresses it. But not only was the kind of subject-matter important, so were the intended audience and the literary kind in which the author chose to write, such as tragedy, pastoral or sermon, since the genre chosen would bring its own expectations of the kind of language employed. This has been argued all over again in books on modern stylistics, although there the terminology is different. The middle ages often spoke of the 'high', 'middle' and 'low' styles; these are the most common terms, but the high style, for instance, may be called 'elevated', 'grand' or 'ornate', and the 'low' style is often spoken of as 'plain'. The full range of figures or colours was reserved for the high style of (say) epic or tragedy. Geoffrey de Vinsauf had already suggested that the three levels of style might be applied to the three classes of society: aristocratic, middle and plebian respectively. Kings must talk like kings and peasants like peasants. Puttenham, in 1589, still defines the three levels partly by the kind of literature involved and partly by the sort of characters it deals with. This will often work: Chaucer's Troilus or Shakespeare's Henry V will use the high style for much of the time. But it is not invariable: Chaucer's Miller does not tell the whole of his tale in the low style which the description of him in the *General Prologue* might lead us to expect.

The rhetorical text-books, however, seldom discuss genres like epic or tragedy, nor do they greatly concern themselves with ideas like character or plot which interest modern critics. Typically they consider their subject under five headings:

1. *Inventio* (conception): finding what to say – material may have to be assembled from different sources – and consideration of the subject under several headings (called 'topics' or 'places').
2. *Dispositio* (arrangement): the general planning and ordering of the material. Beginnings were thought to be especially important, and an idea of the whole plan is often given near the beginning of a medieval story or an Elizabethan sermon.

3. *Elocutio* (phrasing): often the longest section of the text-book. Here the ornaments of style are listed and illustrated (64 of them in the *Rhetorica ad Herennium*). Sometimes these figures or colours are said to be of two kinds. *Tropes* (literally 'turns') involve a change of meaning from that which the word usually has, as in metaphor, hyperbole, pun, irony or allegory (in the latter the word has an additional 'covered' or 'secret' meaning). *Schemes* organise the thought rather than the individual words, e.g. antithesis, or the periodic sentence in Elizabethan writers. The words are employed in their literal sense but are arranged in an unusual or artificial way.
4. *Memoria* (memorising): concerned with tricks to improve the memory.
5. *Pronunciatio* (delivery): such things as modulation of the voice, facial expression, gesture.

Of these, sections 4 and 5 were often brief, although they are important in such periods as the middle ages, where oral delivery was more common than silent reading, and as time went on rhetoric became more and more concerned with section 3, the ornaments of style. These devices are particularly used for elaboration and illustration, for amplification was much more attractive than contraction – another aspect of copiousness in Renaissance literature. Some of these ornaments are common enough today (metaphor, antithesis) or are obvious to us as we read earlier literature (*descriptio*, description of persons or places; *digressio*, deliberately introduced digression), but many need to be explained since they are much less familiar now. In the text books, most of them have Latin or Greek names reflecting their origin, although Puttenham gives alternative English nomenclature, sometimes rather amusing, as when he speaks of hyperbole as 'the Ouer-reacher, otherwise called the loud lyer'. Here is a list of the more common ones in Elizabethan literature which may not be immediately recognisable from their titles; alternative names are given in round brackets:

adnominatio (*traductio, paronomasia*): repetition of the same word in a different form, e.g. similar words formed from the same root or the same word used in different senses.

anaphora (*repetitio*): repetition of the same word(s) at the beginning of successive clauses or of lines of poetry.

apostrophe (*exclamatio*): highly-charged emotional comment, frequently shown in successive lines beginning with 'O' or 'Alas!'

epistrophe: the same word ending successive clauses (the opposite of anaphora).

gradatio (*climax*): the final word(s) of one clause repeated at the beginning of the following clause, thereby advancing the argument since the second use will usually add extra detail or qualification.

isocolon: balance of two clauses of equal length.

parison: balance of two clauses of corresponding syntactic structure (isocolon and parison are often found together).

paromoion: deliberate patterning of sounds within the clause.

ploce: repetition of the same word or phrase, sometimes after the intervention of one or two other words.

stichomythia: a form of dialogue in which single lines are uttered by alternate speakers.

zeugma: using the same verb with two very different objects (as Pope's society lady may 'stain her honour or her new brocade').

I have omitted from this list those figures which we would easily recognise today, such as antithesis or periphrasis, nor have I thought it necessary to distinguish the various types of pun, for example. I have not included either figures such as *occupatio* (mentioning something or somebody under cover of a pretended omission: 'Time would fail to speak of A and B and C'), *effictio* (description of outward appearance as opposed to moral worth), or *litotes* (understatement, frequently by negatives, 'He's no fool'), which seem to be more germane to the appreciation of medieval than Elizabethan literature. What is important is that the rhetorical figures provided writers with a ready-made means of organising material, especially passages of some emotional heightening which needed, as Puttenham said, to be distinguished from our ordinary talk. Jonson takes the same view: '. . . talking and Eloquence are not the same: to speake and to speake well are two things'.[2] Because these figures were widely recognised – had indeed often been learned at school in handbooks which combined definitions with some of the charm of an anthology – the audience was left free to concentrate on their use as a means of characterisation or of deliberate embellishment. Their very familiarity, far from restricting the author, enabled him to emphasise what he felt to be important.

I have already referred to some of the best-known Elizabethan works of rhetoric, such as those by Puttenham and Wilson. Wilson, incidentally, constantly envisages a court with judges who have to be persuaded of the truth of a particular case, and we are reminded of the rise of rhetoric in classical trials. Another and generally a more entertaining book of rhetoric is John Hoskins' *Directions for Speech and Style* (probably 1599).[3] Hoskins, both lawyer and man of letters, was a friend of Jonson (whose *Discoveries* incorporated passages from the *Directions*), Raleigh (for a time a fellow-prisoner in the Tower), Donne, Daniel and probably Sidney whose *Arcadia* he greatly admires and frequently quotes from. The book is addressed to a young man whose father was a friend of Hoskins, and its aim is to improve not only the pupil's writing but also his public speaking and conversation. Anaphora, for instance, 'beats upon one thing to cause the quicker feeling in the audience, and to awake a sleepy or dull person'. Hoskins, like other Elizabethan rhetoricians, lists and illustrates the figures of rhetoric, and, like them, is in no doubt that 'to amplify and illustrate are two the chieftest ornaments of eloquence'. The Preface sees rhetoric as the hallmark not only of the speaker himself but even of what he has to say:

> Careless speech doth not only discredit the personage of the speaker but it doth discredit the opinion of his reason and judgment, it discrediteth the truth, force, and uniformity of the matter and substance.

Each of the three kinds of style, high, middle and low, has its appropriate 'vice' or exaggeration which may produce verbal flatulence or slackness. It was just as possible for the Elizabethans as it is for us to distinguish between artifice and plain words. Cordelia says that she lacks 'that glib and oily art/To speak and purpose not' by means of which Goneril and Regan have falsely professed their love for Lear. The historian Holinshed, seeking the write in the plain (or low) style suitable for conveying information, states that 'My speech is plaine, without any rhetoricall show of eloquence, having rather a regard to simple truth than to decking words'.[4] Herbert uses this same term, *decking*:

> When first my lines of heav'nly joyes made mention,
> Such was their lustre, they did so excell,
> · That I sought out quaint words, and trim invention;
> My thoughts began to burnish, sprout, and swell,
> Curling with metaphors a plain intention,
> Decking the sense, as if it were to sell.   (*Jordan 2*)

He also employs the technical word *invention* and naturally thinks of elaboration ('burnish, sprout, and swell') as the mark of an obviously rhetorical style. *Painted* is another word often used in the Renaissance to describe this false rhetoric. Harrison (1534–93) says that he has tried in his *Description of England* 'truly and plainly to set forth such things as I minded to entreat of, rather than with vain affectation of eloquence to paint out a rotten sepulchre'.[5] Compare Shakespeare's Sonnet 82:

> And do so, love; yet when they have devised
> What strained touches rhetoric can lend,
> Thou, truly fair, wert truly sympathized
> In *true plain words* by thy true-telling friend:
> And their *gross painting* might be better used
> Where cheeks need blood; in thee it is abused.

In an age far less hygenic than our own, women's faces were painted to hide dirt or disease as well as to emphasise beauty, 'Fairing the foul with art's false borrowed face', as Sonnet 127 expresses it. Morally, painting may be equated with sin, as in revenge tragedy or in Harrison's 'rotten sepulchre'. When Bacon, in *The Advancement of Learning* (1605), seems to be advocating less rhetoric, his argument is that the figures of speech have too often submerged the subject-matter: the balance of decorum had been destroyed. Although by the mid-late seventeenth century fewer works are obviously and consistently rhetorical, we still employ rhetoric today ('You could have heard a pin drop.' 'She has hundreds of dresses.').

If rhetoric, even where correctly employed in earlier literature, seems to us to overvalue the synthetic as opposed to the creative talent, to imply that writers can be made rather than be born, and to presuppose a separation of form and content, we should remember that some intellectual pleasure was presumably derived from the mere recognition of the figures and that, when Shakespeare began to write, his audience was accustomed to narrative and dramatic verse which deliberately and ostentatiously employed rhetorical artifice. In his own early plays, Shakespeare can sometime disappoint because he does not seem to us to have achieved the correct balance between style and subject-matter:

> [He] is deliberately at his most artificial where one would expect him, in terms of natural psychology, to aim at spontaneity. Hence one's impression of bad taste in the early word-play, its alienation rather than enlistment of sympathetic response. . . . The limitation of the method is that the surface brilliance tends to obscure by distraction at the same time as it strives to articulate feeling.[6]

But Elizabethan theories of composition were not ours. The plain style was not then considered especially virtuous: it was simply one amongst several possible styles. And, to go further, prose was not thought of as inferior to poetry but simply different. The work of prose-writers like Sidney, Hooker or Raleigh could contain easily as much rhetoric as poetry. A considerable writer, whether in poetry or prose, will learn to use his rhetorical devices for deliberate effect and will not simply show them off. Consequently, more than one of the three styles will appear in the same work. The high style often generalises, with a pronounced tendency towards the abstract and the static: humanity rather than the individual is its main concern. The middle style (which often uses the first person) is more persuasive and analytical, but it is essentially a polite style in which a reader is expected to share the writer's ideas of what is socially or artistically important. The plain (or low) style explains or describes, sometimes denigrates, but with a simplicity of lexis and syntax suitable to its often pragmatic approach.[7] Shakespeare will often write impressive rhetorical passages either because the subject under discussion at that moment demands them (e.g. the heightened language used for affairs of state) or as an indication of how we are to react to a particular character (an obvious instance would be the ridiculously inflated style of Osric which Hamlet parodies). Or there may be a deliberate breach of decorum where the style is clearly inappropriate to the subject, often to make a criticism of social behaviour.

Of those writers before Shakespeare who had been most notable for the balance and refinement of their style, the two most important are probably Lyly and Sidney. Lyly's *Euphues* (1578) is a tale of a student who leaves learning for the more attractive and glittering life of Naples. The hero (whose name means 'gentleman') acquires a close friend whom he betrays when he falls in love with the friend's intended wife; the girl, however, jilts Euphues who repents of his frivolous life and vows to return to study. The plot – if one can call it that – is, though, simply a peg upon which to hang a series of set speeches full of rhetorical embellishment, examples from natural history and knowledge culled from classical writers. There are few obvious Latin loans and the fewer doublets used are unremarkable, but the decoration and balance of the style can be illustrated from almost any page:

> Too much studie doth intoxicate their braynes, for (saye they) althoughe yron, the more it is vsed the brighter it is, yet siluer with much wearing doth wast to nothing, though the Cammocke, the more it is bowed the better it serueth, yet the bow, the more it is bent & occupied the weaker it waxeth, though the Camomill, the more it is trodden and pressed downe, the more it spreadeth, yet the violet the oftner it is handled and touched, the sooner it withereth and decayeth. Besides thys, a fine wytte, a sharp sence, a quicke vnderstanding, is able to atteine to more in a moment or a very little space, then a dull and blockish heade in a month; the sithe cutteth farre better and smoother then the sawe, the waxe yeeldeth better and sooner to the seale, than the steele to the stampe or hammer, the smooth & plaine Beeche is easier to be carued and occupyed then the knotty Boxe. For neyther is ther any thing, but yt hath his

contraries: Such is the Nature of these nouises that thincke to have learning without labour, and treasure without trauayle, eyther not vnderstanding or els not remembring, that the finest edge is made with the blunt whetstone, and the fairest Iewell fashioned with the harde hammer.

For as the Bee that gathereth Honny out of the weede, when she espyeth the faire flower flyeth to the sweetest: or as the kynde spanyell though he hunt after Byrdes, yet forsakes them to retryue the Partridge: or as we commonly feede on beefe hungerly at the first, yet seing the Quayle more dayntie, chaunge our dyet: So I, although I loued *Philautus* for his good properties, yet seing *Euphues* to excell him, I ought by Nature to lyke him better: By so muche the more therefore my change is to be excused, by how much the more my choyce is excellent: and by so much the lesse I am to be condemned, by how much the more *Euphues* is to be commended. Is not the Dyamonde of more valewe than the Rubie, because he is of more vertue? Is not the Emeraulde preferred before the Saphyre for his wonderfull propertie? Is not *Euphues* more prayse worthy than *Philautus* being more wittie?[8]

It must be one of the easiest styles to parody, as Falstaff does in a well – known passage from *1 Henry IV*, adapting an illustration from the first of our two extracts:

> For though the camomile, the more it is trodden on the faster it grows, yet youth, the more it is wasted the sooner it wears. (II.iv.393–5)

Earlier he uses the same style, although he concludes his intricately-balanced sentence with two puns of his own (*countenance*: 'face' and 'protection' and *steal*: 'move silently' and 'rob'):

> Marry then, sweet wag, when thou art King let not us that are squires of the night's body be called thieves of the day's beauty. Let us be Diana's foresters, gentlemen of the shade, minions of the moon. And let men say we be men of good government, being governed as the sea is, by our noble and chaste mistress the moon, under whose countenance we steal. *(1 Hen IV* I.ii.23–9)

Shakespeare's debt to Lyly, however, lay far less in parody than in the realisation that balance and precision (especially in prose) can be made a staple of comic wit and intrigue. For Lyly also wrote plays (in the second quotation Falstaff intends his audience to recall *Endimion*) and whilst his drama still has occasional comparisons from natural history, they are not nearly so numerous or so obvious as in *Euphues*, so that the attention is directed even more towards the construction of the speeches:

> A heate full of coldnesse, a sweet full of bitternesse, a paine full of pleasantnesse; which maketh thoughts haue eyes and harts eares; bred by

desire, nursed by delight, weaned by ielousie, kild by dissembling, buried by ingratitude; and this is loue! Fayre Lady, wil you any?

(*Galathea* I.ii.16–20)

Who would haue thought that *Tellus*, being so fayre by nature, so honourable by byrth, so wise by education, would haue entered into a mischiefe to the Gods so odious, to men so detestable, and to her freend so malicious?

(*Endimion* V.iii.1–3)

Lyly's plays also included a number of clever, prattling boys, not surprisingly since they were chiefly acted by the children's companies. Their speech, too, is pointed and balanced, but it is wit rather than humour. It is influenced by the tradition of the clever servant, frequently a slave, in classical comedy, and it shows itself in the patter of Moth in *Love's Labour's Lost* or the Dromios in *The Comedy of Errors*.

As we might expect, it is in his comedies that Shakespeare most realises the advantages of the kind of mannered rhetoric Lyly had practised. *Love's Labour's Lost* has already been discussed in terms of his perception of the significant features of the expanding vocabulary. Its syntax is almost equally dependent on contemporary fashions. The delight in punning and in elaborately patterned language generally is the hallmark of the opposing quartets, the men from Navarre and the ladies from France. Shakespeare improves on Lyly's elegance, but the subject of comedy is still courtship. Although there is occasional copious lexis:

About surrender up of Aquitaine
To her decrepit, sick, and bed-rid father   (I.i.136–7)

He made her melancholy, sad, and heavy;
And so she died. Had she been light, like you,
Of such a merry, nimble, stirring spirit,
She might ha' been a grandam ere she died.   (V.ii.14–17)

the complexity in this play is as much a matter of syntax, as perhaps seeming more appropriate for aristocrats: every fool can play upon the *word*. Their intricate style is often very like that of contemporary sonnets, and Shakespeare was almost certainly writing his own sonnets at this time:

Why, all his behaviours did make their retire
To the court of his eye, peeping through desire.
His heart, like an agate with your print impressed,
Proud with his form, in his eye pride expressed.

69

> His tongue, all impatient to speak and not see,
> Did stumble with haste in his eyesight to be;
> All senses to that sense did make their repair,
> To feel only looking on fairest of fair.
> Methought all his senses were locked in his eye,
> As jewels in crystal for some prince to buy;
> Who, tend'ring their own worth from where they were glassed,
> Did point you to buy them, along as you passed.
> His face's own margent did quote such amazes
> That all eyes saw his eyes enchanted with gazes.   (II.i.234–47)

The positioning of *behaviours, court of his eye, heart, tongue, All senses, His face*, all near the beginning of the line, assists us to make our way through this elaborate speech by Boyet, the attendant lord on the Princess and her ladies – only a moment before he had spoken of *the heart's still rhetoric* – but the amount of the imagery and the subordination in the syntax make it rather difficult going. In an earlier speech by Berowne, one pun leads to another:

> Why, all delights are vain, but that most vain
> Which, with pain purchased, doth inherit pain:
> As, painfully to pore upon a book,
> To seek the light of truth, while truth the while
> Doth falsely blind the eyesight of his look.
> Light seeking light doth light of light beguile;
> So, ere you find where light in darkness lies,
> Your light grows dark by losing of your eyes.
> Study me how to please the eye indeed
> By fixing it upon a fairer eye,
> Who dazzling so, that eye shall be his heed
> And give him light that it was blinded by.   (I.i.72–83)

Pain is both agony and difficulty; *light* both illumination (truth) and brightness; the verb *blind*, similarly, is literally to deprive of eyesight and metaphorically to conceal the truth. After she has listened to a later exchange of this kind between two of her own ladies, Rosaline and Katharine, the comment of the Princess is

> Well bandied both! A set of wit well played.   (V.ii.29)

Tennis, we recall, was a favourite Elizabethan game, and in *Henry V* the Dauphin sends Henry a set of tennis balls. A similar comment by Silvia (*Two Gentlemen of Verona* II.iv.32): 'A fine volley of words, gentlemen, and quickly shot off', and Portia's reply to Nerissa: 'Good sentences, and well pronounced' (*Merchant of Venice* I.ii.10) indicate by their mocking tone that already Shakespeare was using this elaborately-patterned syntax for deliberate exaggeration.

The style of *As You Like It*, a play with several resemblances to *Love's Labour's Lost*, such as its multiple wooings and a preference for conversation over action, has less of such polished symmetry than one might expect from its source, the euphuistic prose romance, Lodge's *Rosalynde*. But Shakespeare's Arden is more of a real forest than the usual pastoral idyll of euphuism, and anyway at the end the major characters (except Jaques) troop back to the court. Perhaps Orlando comes closest to the euphuistic vogue:

> I beseech you, punish me not with your hard thoughts, wherein I
> confess me much guilty to deny so fair and excellent ladies anything.
> But let your fair eyes and gentle wishes go with me to my trial:
> wherein if I be foiled, there is but one shamed that was never gracious;
> if killed, but one dead that is willing to be so. I shall do my friends no
> wrong, for I have none to lament me; the world no injury, for in it I
> have nothing: only in the world I fill up a place which may be better
> supplied when I have made it empty.   (I.ii.171–80)

Even so, Orlando talks less than the heroes of Shakespeare's other comedies. Brilliance of language is becoming less important for its own sake and more important as an indication of character.[9]

In *Much Ado About Nothing*, on the other hand, as C. A. Owen says, 'Beatrice and Benedick pursue a journey into self-knowledge without the help of supernatural agents, of a Forest of Arden, or of sexual disguise.'[10] Benedick, though, becomes a changed man following his gulling by Don Pedro and the others. In his first soliloquy he is 'full of confidence in his ability to keep the world at a proper distance for witty observation'; one hundred lines later 'love has released him from the tyranny of elaborate syntax', although he salves his conscience with a neat double antithesis ('When I said I would die a bachelor, I did not think I should live till I were married'). By this stage of his career Shakespeare is using euphuism as one possible dramatic style which can be rejected when the plot demands it. This, then, is the early Benedick:

> May I be so converted and see with these eyes? I cannot tell; I think not. I
> will not be sworn but love may transform me to an oyster; but I'll take
> my oath on it, till he have made an oyster of me, he shall never make me
> such a fool. One woman is fair, yet I am well: another is wise, yet I am
> well; another virtuous, yet I am well; but till all graces be in one woman,
> one woman shall not come in my grace. Rich she shall be, that's certain;
> wise, or I'll none; virtuous, or I'll never cheapen her; fair, or I'll never
> look on her; mild, or come not near me; noble, or not I for an angel; of

good discourse, an excellent musician, and her hair shall be of what
colour it please God. (II.iii.21–33)

The balance ('One woman . . . my grace'), the punning (*noble/angel*),
the final throwaway phrase which nevertheless, since it is a little longer than its predecessors, elegantly rounds off the speech – all these
imply a cleverness and self-satisfaction which is asking to be given a
cold douche of reality. Beatrice's early style is less obviously symmetrical than Benedick's, for the lady is usually allowed to be less
dogmatic and inflexible so that she may eventually yield gracefully.
Her advice to Hero is, at first sight, euphuistic:

> For hear me, Hero: wooing, wedding, and repenting, is as a Scotch jig, a
> measure, and a cinquepace: the first suit is hot and hasty, like a Scotch jig,
> and full as fantastical; the wedding, mannerly-modest, as a measure, full
> of state and ancientry; and then comes repentance and, with his bad legs,
> falls into the cinquepace faster and faster, till he sink into his grave.

Yet *the first suit . . . the wedding . . . repentance* do not form the exact parallel (*first . . . second . . . third*) that the schematic rhetoric of true
euphuism might have produced.

Euphuism has been aptly characterised as 'verbal pirouetting'.
Certainly it often has an air of artificiality, if not of superficiality, and
in the later 1580's it lost favour to Sidney's Arcadianism. *Arcadia* was
published in 1590 although composed some time before; a fuller version was printed in 1593. It is a prose romance, and the complexity
of its adventures is matched by an equally complex style: its prose requires time for proper appreciation. In his dedication Sidney calls it
an 'idle work' and 'a trifle, triflingly handled', although clearly he
hoped for the admiration of his audience. Lyly's prose elaborates,
frequently by describing the same subject in different parallel
phrases; Sidney's is much more varied because it almost always contains more subordination. It is still, however, subject to rigorous
control. His model is Cicero, but Elizabethan English simply did not
contain the number of grammatical devices by which Latin signifies
agreement. Sidney therefore needs a good deal of linguistic signpost-
ing, and it is a tribute to him that we (and his contemporaries) can
find our way through a long and complex sentence – in which the
main verb, in true Ciceronian fashion, is often held back to the end –
without losing the thread of his argument. Consider this passage
from *Arcadia*:

> And therefore, *where* most princes, seduced by flattery to build upon false

grounds of government, make themselves, as it were, another thing from the people, and so count it gain what they can get from them and, as if it were two counter-balances, that their estate goes highest when the people goes lowest, by a fallacy of argument thinking themselves most kings when the subject is most basely subjected; *he, contrariwise,* virtuously and wisely acknowledging that he with his people made all but one politic body whereof himself was the head, even so cared for them as he would for his own limbs; never restraining their liberty without it stretched to licentiousness nor pulling from them their goods which they found were not employed to the purchase of a greater good; but, in all his actions showing a delight in their welfare, brought that to pass that, while by force he took nothing, by their love he had all.[11]

It is one long sentence which pivots on the *where* and the *he contrariwise* which I have italicised (*they* did this, but *he,* contrariwise, did that). Within each half of the balance, however, there are degrees of subordination, incorporating rhetorical devices like parison and paromoion ('their estate goes highest when the people goes lowest') or, in a chinese-box manner characteristic of Sidney, containing further pairs of pivoting correlatives (*never . . . nor . . . but*) within the larger structure. There is, in fact, a good deal of conversation in *Arcadia,* as in *Euphues,* but the speeches in both are excessively long and excessively formal, so that they seldom seem natural. A second passage from Sidney shows his achievement of variety within the same long sentence: it is this, above all, which makes him far more readable than Lyly. The extract is from the *Apology for Poetry,* 1595, (i.e. a defence, not of poetry against prose but of fiction against fact, especially against the allegedly superior claims of history and philosophy):

The historian scarcely giveth leisure to the moralist to say so much, but that he, loaden with old mouse-eaten records, authorising himself (for the most part) upon other histories, whose greatest authorities are built upon the notable foundation of hearsay; having much ado to accord differing writers and to pick truth out of partiality; better acquainted with a thousand years ago than with the present age, and yet better knowing how this world goeth than how his own wit runneth; curious for antiquities and inquisitive of novelties; a wonder to young folks and a tyrant in table talk, denieth, in a great chafe, that any man for teaching of virtue, and virtuous actions is comparable to him.[12]

Again, this is most carefully structured. The main clause, *The historian . . . (he) . . . denieth . . . that any man . . . is comparable to him,* spans the sentence and is not complete until its end. Subordination begins by participles (which in Latin would of course agree with their antecedents but in English have to be emphasised by positioning each at the beginning of its clause): *loaden . . . authorising . . . having . . . acquainted . . .*

knowing; but when this pattern has been established it is varied, but not lost, by the use first of an adjective (*curious*) and then of a noun in apposition (*a wonder*) in the same initial position in the subordinate clause. The minor clauses themselves once more contain lower levels of subordination ('histories, whose greatest authorities are built upon the notable foundation of hearsay') and have their own balance (the antithesis of 'curious for antiquities and inquisitive of novelties', with its additional invitation to speculate on the possible difference in tone between *curious* and *inquisitive*).

With Sidney's rhetorical style in romance we might compare Hooker's as he discusses the nature of the heavenly host. We have considered the passage on page 16 from the point of view of lexis: its syntax is equally complex, equally copious. Similarly the Donne passage below it, while not truly Ciceronian in style, for Donne prefers to elaborate the same idea at paragraph length rather than to refine and concentrate, is planned on a large scale. The first of its two long sentences proceeds via the repeated *Let me . . . let me . . .* to pivot on *yet if . . . if . . .* The following sentence, even longer, with its crescendo of seven *when's*, rises to the twice-repeated the *Almighty God himself*, the second occurrence of which introduces the counter-balance, the *pondus gloriae*, without which *we are weighed down* (fortissimo) *irreparably, irrevocably, irrecoverably, irremediably*. And this was, of course, preached, in the majesty of St Paul's. Within this single extract the rhetorical devices of subordination, such as anaphora, antithesis, isocolon and parison, are evident, yet the structure is looser than Sidney's and, being a sermon, contains more redundancy. The complication arises less from Sidney's type of complex subordination than from parallelism and repetition. For Donne, who was painted in his funeral shroud and who preached his last sermon on the subject of 'Death's Duel', is nothing if not dramatic and expansive.

It was easy, therefore, for Shakespeare to find examples of rhetoric in the prose – and verse – of his contemporaries; he would have been hard put to it to avoid them. The benefits of rhetorical structuring are, however, more evident from early comedy than from early tragedy. Too often the set speech of Senecan tragedy is isolated from its surroundings. In static drama like this we miss any interaction of the characters, and the formal parallelism of much of the style in a play like *Gorboduc* serves little purpose beyond repetition of ideas simple enough in the first place. The Epilogue of *Arden of Feversham* (a much better play) speaks of 'this naked tragedy / Wherein no filed points are foisted in', as if rhetoric were a kind of top dressing. Kyd is better than this. Although dialogue is often set out in the formal,

line by line exchange, *stichomythia*, and although rhetorical set
speeches (which stylised, declamatory Elizabethan acting encouraged) are still frequent, there is a greater variation of tempo than
hitherto.[13] Nevertheless, the rhetoric is easy to see:

> His men are slain, a weakening to his realm,
> His colours seiz'd, a blot unto his name,
> His son distress'd, a corsive to his heart.   (I.ii.141–3)

> King   Say, worthy prince, to whether dids't thou yield?
> Balthazar   To him in courtesy, to this perforce:
>   He spake me fair, this other gave me strokes;
>   He promis'd life, this other threaten'd death;
>   He won my love, this other conquer'd me;
>   And, truth to say, I yield myself to both.   (I.ii.160–5)[1]

Both passages, coming close together, are spoken by Balthazar who
also shares with Bel-Imperia an example of *stichomythia* at I.iv.77–
89. Lorenzo begins the exchange reasonably and plainly enough and
concludes it with a plea to cease *these ambages* and use plain terms.
Lorenzo's style is much more direct than Balthazar's rhetoric, and his
sheer delight in villainy and the complexity of its execution are a
foretaste of Iago. Yet too little of Kyd's writing strikes us as natural
speech and the rhetoric obtrudes all too often.

Characters in these early plays, in fact, talk *at* one another; they
seldom listen or respond, nor is there sufficient change of pace or
tone. Too many moments are made into theatrical 'occasions' and
conversation is infrequent. The *Henry VI* trilogy largely conforms to
this pattern, although Shakespeare, by an indirect stage direction
such as 'Observe' or an invitation to the actor to supply his own ges-
tures, does make some attempts to involve other characters who
would otherwise be standing idle on stage. Usually, however, a
character is first *described* and the general category in which he is then
seen to fit is illustrated by almost all of his actions: Talbot's bravery
and patriotism, Buckingham's ambition. This is still the morality
tradition in which characters seldom need to reveal their nature in action. One would like to believe, with Clemen[15], that the mention of
the *silly stately style* (*1 Hen VI* IV.vii.72) is Shakespeare's recognition
of such shortcomings; in fact, Joan of Arc's remark is more likely to
refer to the dead Talbot's list of imposing titles.

There is a straightforward passage of *stichomythia* in *1 Henry VI*
(IV.v.34–47) between Talbot who tries to persuade young John Talbot to leave the battle and his son who is determined to stay and

fight, and another in *3 Henry VI* (III.ii.32–75) as Lady Grey misunderstands Edward's offer of love. In a similar but longer passage, *Richard III* I.ii.68–141, the antiphonal effect of the single-line responses is varied by two, three or four-line passages and the exchanges are occasionally even broken up into half lines. In this scene the formality of the rhetoric accentuates the outrageous nature of Richard's request to Elizabeth for his daughter's hand. *Stichomythia*, however, can occur in comedy as well as in tragedy. In *Love's Labour's Lost* it is more in the nature of banter, as is the repartee between Juliet and Paris (*RJ* IV.i.18–26). The first of two passages in Act I of *A Midsummer Night's Dream*, I.i.136–40, reveals the shared affection of Lysander and Hermia whose responses echo each other's love, despite parental opposition. In the second, 194–201, the figure points the contrast between the speakers, as it generally does: Helena yearns for Demetrius's love which Hermia would willingly repudiate.[16]

Rhetoric works best when it is contained within a clearly-perceived framework such as the paragraph (in prose), the set speech or the short poem. Take Sonnet 73:

> That time of year thou mayst in me behold
> When yellow leaves, or none, or few, do hang .
> Upon those boughs which shake against the cold,
> Bare ruined choirs where late the sweet birds sang.
> In me thou seest the twilight of such day
> As after sunset fadeth in the west,
> Which by and by black night doth take away,
> Death's second self, that seals up all in rest.
> In me thou seest the glowing of such fire
> That on the ashes of his youth doth lie,
> As the deathbed whereon it must expire,
> Consumed with that which it was nourished by.
> > This thou perceiv'st, which makes thy love more strong,
> > To love that well which thou must leave ere long.

The first line of each quatrain and of the concluding couplet has a similar syntactic structure (*thou mayst in me behold; In me thou seest* (twice); *This thou perceiv'st*). *What* is seen achieves a similar grammatical cohesion by the repetition of noun + *of* + noun (*That time of year; the twilight of such day; the glowing of such fire*). Lexical cohesion is managed by grouping words from nature in the first two quatrains (*yellow leaves, boughs, cold, birds sang, twilight, sunset, night*). In the third quatrain the prevailing metaphor of day ending is changed to that of fire consuming, and a different lexical set is therefore necessary: *glowing, fire, ashes, expire, consumed*.[17]

It is most unlikely that the Sonnets, as we have them in the 1609 quarto, are in chronological order or otherwise specially arranged.[18] There is some general evidence of grouping: numbers 1–17 argue that the young man should marry and perpetuate his own virtues in his children. 1–126 seem to be addressed to this young man, 127–154 to a dark-haired woman; sonnets 40, 42, and 144 perhaps suggest an affair between the young man and the woman. But the publication of the sonnets was most probably not authorised by Shakespeare, and hence they may not have been revised for publication. Francis Meres speaks of Shakespeare's 'sugared sonnets among his private friends'. (*Palladis Tamia*, 1598). Many shorter Elizabethan poems are private in the sense that they were coterie poetry, meant to be shared by a small circle of friends. This may explain their frequent compactness and difficulty: their more abstruse poetic effects could be savoured at leisure. In a similar way we have to quote Donne's sonnets, both divine and secular, from the edition of 1633 (he died in 1631). Shakespeare's sonnets, although evidently written at different times, are likely to be early. Sonnet writing was a literary fashion in the 1590's and it had passed its peak by 1600. The sonnets of the 1590's, though, are frequently different in tone from Shakespeare's, 'always sweet, always lachrymose, always unreal' in Patrick Crutwell's words,[19] mellifluous, but, if one reads many at a stretch, monotonous too. Their conventional diction is satirised by Shakespeare in Sonnet 130 ('My mistress' eyes are nothing like the sun').

There are indications that the sonnet form was early seen by Shakespeare as potentially leading to artificiality. The occasional sonnets in *Love's Labour's Lost* have already been mentioned. Lady Capulet describes Paris (a cardboard lover if ever there was one) in terms of a book (I.iii.82–95) and the description takes the form of a sonnet. The book image is also a *conceit*. By the later sixteenth century *conceit*, originally meaning simply 'thought', 'concept', signified a witty thought. The wit lay in the comparison of two objects which appeared to be completely unlike; by bringing together characteristics of each, the conceit uses the one to explain and analyse the other. In Lady Capulet's conceit 'This precious book of love, this unbound lover' conceals his love just as a bound volume conceals its contents. The comparison is made continuous through the number of shared lexical items: *volume, writ, pen, content, margent* (what we would call footnotes were often written in the margin in Elizabethan books), *unbound, cover, clasps, story*. An extended comparison of this sort often involves puns. Here, for instance, *content* is both the content(s) of the book and also satisfaction: Paris is *unbound* (like the book) but also not yet bound by marriage ties. Sonnet 122 makes a somewhat similar comparison:

> Thy gift, thy tables, are within my brain
> Full charactered with lasting memory,
> Which shall above that idle rank remain
> Beyond all date, even to eternity;
> Or, at the least, so long as brain and heart
> Have faculty by nature to subsist,
> Till each to rased oblivion yield his part
> Of thee, thy record never can be missed.
> That poor retention could not so much hold,
> Nor need I tallies thy dear love to score.
> Therefore to give them from me was I bold,
> To trust those tables that receive thee more.
>   To keep an adjunct to remember thee
>   Were to import forgetfulness in me.

Tables are memorandum books (compare Hamlet and his tables), which are naturally *charactered* (written); *rank* could possibly mean 'leaves' (of a book); *rased* is our 'erased'; *record, retention, tallies* prolong the image which closes with a return to the *tables* of the opening line. The concluding couplet reveals the point of the conceit: the poet needs no memento (*adjunct*) since he could never forget his beloved. Sonnet 80 employs the rather conventional conceit of the storm-tossed lover, as does the second quartain of 116. Sonnet 133 achieves lexical cohesion by images of slavery, imprisonment and torture.

Berowne, we may remember, was *conceit's expositor* (*Love's Labour's Lost* II.i.72). Romeo (II.vi.24) invites Juliet to poeticise (*blazon*) their mutual joy, and she replies

> Conceit, more rich in matter than in words,
> Brags of his substance, not of ornament.

A poem's success depends not only on the freshness (even the novelty) of the comparison but on whether the conceit appears merely cerebral or else emotional with the speaker passionately involved with his subject. The flaccid comparisons of Tudor poetry are often contrasted with the more complex and intense conceits of Donne who, as well as the celebrated compasses and absent lovers (*A Valediction: Forbidding Mourning*) sees souls in terms of gold leaf (the same poem), tears in terms of coins, globes and floods (*A Valediction: Of Weeping*), and lovers in terms of angler and fish (*The Bait*). The occasional unpoetical and rather bizarre images should not surprise us either. Many Elizabethan writers were not only men of letters but made a career in politics, diplomacy or the church (as eventually with Donne). Science, philosophy, religion, as well as literature, were all of interest to the cultivated society within London and out-side it (in the country houses that increasingly reflected wealth and status) for which these poems were originally designed. Such poems made demands on the reader and were expected to be read more than once before they yielded up their secrets. It is no accident that the 1920's, with their credo that poetry *must* be difficult if it is to reflect the variety and complexity of modern civilisation, saw a revival of interest in metaphysical poetry.

About the turn of the century there seems to have been a vogue for unusual and witty comparisons. It can be seen in some of the essays of Bacon in the first (1597) edition: 'Men fear death as children fear to go into the dark'; 'Fortune is like the market, where, many times, if you can stay a little, the price will fall'; 'Wives are young men's mistresses, companions for middle age, and old men's nurses'. Several of the character-writers round off their essays by a para-doxical or punning sentence:

> . . . when the time, or term, of his life is going out, for Doomsday he is secure; for he hopes he has a trick to reverse judgement.
>
> (Earle, *An Attorney*)

The rhetorician Hoskins suggests that the comparison of 'things seeming unequal' is especially 'forcible':

> But this is not so forcible an amplification . . . as when things seeming unequal are compared, and that in similitudes as well as examples; as in my speech of a widow compared to a ship, *both ask much tackling and sometimes rigging*. And you shall most of all profit by inventing matter of agreement in things most unlike, as London and a tennis court: for *in both all the gain goes to the hazard*. (p. 18)

Bacon himself, despite his stress on scientific observation as opposed to received authority, can be surprisingly 'conceitful', even in his more philosophical prose. He argued that his illustrations trans-formed 'conceits intellectual to images sensible', and will occasional-ly include several in the same paragraph:

> For men have entered into a desire of learning and knowledge, sometimes upon a natural curiosity and inquisitive appetite; sometimes to entertain their minds with variety and delight; sometimes for ornament and reputation; and sometimes to enable them to victory of wit and contradiction; and most times for lucre and profession; and seldom sincerely to give a true account of their gift of reason, to the benefit and use of men: as if there were sought in knowledge a couch whereupon to

rest a searching and restless spirit; or a terrace for a wandering and variable mind to walk up and down with a fair prospect; or a tower of state for a proud mind to raise itself upon; or a fort or commanding ground for strife and contention; or a shop for profit or sale; and not a rich storehouse for the glory of the Creator and the relief of man's estate.[20]

In passages of this kind, Bacon would have considered that he was using metaphor to illustrate and to demonstrate, and so to comprehend – not in the least as mere decoration or elaboration.

Sometimes poets – or poetically-inclined characters in drama – pretend to be worried at their inability to produce the expected illustrations in sufficient number and unlikeliness for a conceit. George Herbert spoke of his early determined search for witty comparisons:

> When first my lines of heav'nly joyes made mention,
> Such was their lustre, they did so excell,
> That I sought out quaint words, and trim invention;
> My thoughts began to burnish, sprout and swell,
> Curling with metaphors a plain intention,
> Decking the sense as if it were to sell.   (*Jordan 2*)

Richard II passes some of his imprisonment in devising usual poetic correspondences:

> I have been studying how I may compare
> This prison where I live unto the world;
> And for because the world is populous,
> And here is not a creature but myself,
> I cannot do it. *Yet I'll hammer it out.*
> My brain I'll prove the female to my soul,
> My soul the father, and these two beget
> A generation of still-breeding thoughts,
> And these same thoughts people this little world,
> In humours like the people of this world.
> For no thought is contented.   (V.v.1–11)

One of the best-known sonnets (18) begins conventionally 'Shall I compare thee to a summer's day?' But the next line immediately denies the validity of the comparison: 'Thou art more lovely and more temperate', and the poem proceeds to explain why the conceit would be inappropriate. Most interesting of all, Shakespeare's Sonnet 76 seems to express some early dissatisfaction with his own poetry:

> Why is my verse so barren of new pride,
> So far from variation or quick change?
> Why with the time do I not glance aside
> To new-found methods and to compounds strange?

Why write I still all one, ever the same,
And keep invention in a noted weed,
That every word doth almost tell my name,
Showing their birth, and where they did proceed?
O, know, sweet love, I always write of you,
And you and love are still my argument.
So all my best is dressing old words new,
Spending again what is already spent:
    For as the sun is daily new and old,
    So is my love still telling what is told.

Why does he *keep invention in a noted weed* ('go on writing in the same old style') and spend his time *dressing old words new* instead of following contemporary fashion with its *new pride* (decoration), *variation, quick change* or *compounds strange* ('compositions' or 'compound words', or perhaps both)? In terms of the sonnet's argument, the reason is the continually renewed freshness and satisfaction of his love, but in terms of Shakespeare's developing poetic skills it may be that he preferred to explore the 'intense immediacy of individuals caught in a stock situation'.[21] Certainly he is not above a 'metaphysical' conceit when occasion serves, as in Othello's final words:

I kissed thee, ere I killed thee; no way but this,
Killing myself, to die upon a kiss.   (V.ii.354–5)

but one's impression is that occasion did not serve any too often.

What sonnet writing perhaps taught Shakespeare most, was the art of cohesion within a clearly defined (fourteen line) passage. This cohesion is frequently lexical, as has been shown, but may be simply a matter of repetition of a phrase in the same metrical position, just as each quatrain of Sonnet 49 begins 'Against that time . . .' or Sonnet 64 'When I have seen . . .'. Sonnet 4 is rather more complex:

Unthrifty loveliness, why dost thou spend
Upon thyself thy beauty's legacy?
Nature's bequest gives nothing but doth lend,
And being frank she lends to those are free.
Then, beauteous niggard, why dost thou abuse
The bounteous largess given thee to give?
Profitless usurer, why dost thou use
So great a sum of sums yet canst not live?
For having traffic with thyself alone,
Thou of thyself thy sweet self does deceive.
Then how when Nature calls thee to be gone,
What acceptable audit canst thou leave?
    Thy unused beauty must be tombed with thee,
    Which, used, lives th'executor to be.

Unthrifty, spend, legacy, bequest, lend, frank . . . free (both 'generous'), *niggard, largess, usurer, sums, traffic, audit, use* ('invest' or 'use up'), *executor* form a remarkable lexical set, but there are syntactical parallels too: *why dost thou spend, why dost thou abuse, why dost thou use*, and *unthrifty loveliness, beauteous niggard, profitless usurer*, all terms of address, all adjective plus noun, all near-paradoxical. The vocabulary of the sonnets is in itself not very remarkable. There are not very many obvious loans, a few – mostly adjectival – compounds, such as *world-without-end* hour (57) and *proud-pied* April (98). Little reminds us of the idioms of speech: 'My love is as fair/ *As any mother's child*'(21); 'In sleep a king, but waking *no such matter*' (87); And Death once dead, *there's no more dying then*' (146). The 'speaking voice' occurs now and then in the sonnets by Shakespeare's contemporaries, although usually in those of a later date, for example in Drayton, writing in 1619:

> Since, ther's no helpe, come let us kisse and part,
> Nay, I have done: You get no more of me.[22]

The formality of Shakespeare's diction in the sonnets contrasts with the colloquial opening of several Donne poems ('Here, take my picture'; 'For God's sake hold your tongue and let me love') with the aggression of their imperatives ('*Go* and *catch* a falling star . . .', followed by *Get, Tell, Teach, Find*). Donne's is a world where the man, usually the speaker, calls the tune, and it is a young man's world where stability in relationships is at a low premium. The imperatives suggest the challenge. When Donne's ideas or conceits seem to defy the laws of probability, they sometimes do so in a deliberately distorted syntax. The deceptively easy beginning of *Love's Growth* is followed by some much more difficult lines:

> But if this medicine, love, which cures all sorrow
> With more, not only be no quintessence,
> But mix'd of all stuffs, paining soul, or sense,
> And of the Sun his working vigour borrow,
> Love's not so pure, and abstract, as they use
> To say, which have no mistress but their muse,
> But as all else, being elemented too,
> Love sometimes would contemplate, sometimes do.[23]

In Shakespeare's sonnets, line ends and syntactical units usually coincide; in Donne's poems far less often. The ratiocination of this poem (as of several other Donne poems) is preserved by the simple connectives (*Because . . . But if . . . But . . . And yet . . . As . . . If . . . For . . . And though . . .*) all placed at the beginning of the line. But Shakespeare seems to make more use than Donne of deliberate parallelisms of

syntax, and his language in the sonnets is both less intemperate and
less colloquial.

In commenting on *The Shepherd's Calendar*, E. K. had been content to point out the rhetorical figures: 'a pretty Epanorthosis . . . and
withall a Paronomasia', but in these early poems of Shakespeare (not
only the *Sonnets* but also *Venus and Adonis* and *The Rape of Lucrece*)
the more positive benefits of rhetorical structuring are beginning to
emerge. By its need to adopt varying viewpoints in a debate, and to
imagine the situations in which different types of speech or different
emotional states could occur, rhetoric provided a training in characterisation through language. R. A. Lanham notes the changing attitudes of Venus: sexual temptress, energetic virago, anxious mother
to a childlike Adonis, disappointed suitor. Each attitude has its
appropriate style.[24] Tarquin tries to control his desire for Lucrece in
terms of a set debate ('madly tossed between desire and dread'), Lucrece's monologues on Night, Honour, Opportunity and Time (764–
1036) foreshadow later set pieces, not always wholly serious, such as
Fauconbridge on Commodity and Falstaff on Honour. And the picture of the Trojan War would have delighted the rhetoricians, not
merely as embellishment but as a functional device.

Within the plays everyone will have his own remembered selection of set speeches. These are usually very tightly structured. The
second half of Henry V's long speech on 'ceremony' in IV.i. – twen-
ty-four lines from 'No, thou proud dream . . .' to ' . . . vantage of a
king' can scarcely be more than two sentences, the second beginning
only three lines from the end ('And but for ceremony . . .') and is
perhaps best seen as one single sentence. Punctuation is, of course,
that of the modern editor; Elizabethan dramatic punctuation is both
less full and more rhetorical – as a guide to speaking aloud – than is
its present counterpart. Again, in *Coriolanus*, Aufidius reveals his
own feelings about the hero (IV.vii.28–57), a puzzled mixture of
admiration and envy. At the centre of the speech is an eleven-line
sentence punctuated by the correlatives *Whether . . . whether . . . or
whether . . . but one of those*. More surprising, perhaps, is the cohesion
of a speech by Iago:

> Virtue? A fig! 'Tis in ourselves that we are thus, or thus. Our bodies are
> our gardens, to the which our wills are gardeners. So that if we will plant
> nettles or sow lettuce, set hyssop and weed up thyme, supply it with one
> gender of herbs or distract it with many, either to have it sterile with
> idleness or manured with industry, why the power and corrigible
> authority of this lies in our wills. If the beam of our lives had not one
> scale of reason to poise another of sensuality, the blood and baseness of

our natures would conduct us to most preposterous conclusions. But we have reason to cool our raging motions, our carnal stings, our unbitted lusts: wherof I take this, that you call love, to be a sect or scion.

(I.iii.316–29)

This begins with allegory ('Our bodies are our gardens'), continues with parison ('plant nettles or sow lettuce, set hyssop or weed up thyme') and antithesis ('either to have it sterile with idleness or manured with industry', and *reason* versus *sensuality*). Some of the words are Latinate (*corrigible, preposterous*) and the same ideas are repeated in different words but in the same grammatical relationship ('our raging motions, our carnal stings, our unbitted lusts'). The garden imagery runs throughout the passage and binds it together.

Drama, however, does not consist solely of set speeches. Some early Tudor drama, including some plays of Shakespeare, had tried to make too many scenes into theatrical spectacles. The practice of rhetoric contributed a welcome tautness to formal exchanges, of whatever kind, but even in comedy, where devices such as parison, antithesis and punning accentuate the wit of the clever characters, Shakespeare early realised that this was only part of the play. In *Love's Labour's Lost* the rhetorical structures helped to characterise the formal, articulate – but also pompous – behaviour of the aristocrats which was finally shown to need correction. In *As You Like It* and *Much Ado*, the rhetoric is far less schematic. In the histories and the tragedies, especially, men need to talk naturally, even inconsequentially, whilst the more deliberate, formal syntax can take its place, together with the copious lexis, as markers of the special occasion.

NOTES AND REFERENCES

1. A good short introduction is Dixon (1971). Vickers (1971) discusses Shakespeare's use of rhetoric.
2. 'Figuratiue speech is a noueltie of language euidently (and yet not absurdly) estranged from the ordinarie habite and manner of our dayly talke and writing.', *The Arte of English Poesie*, ed. G. D. Willcock and A Walker, Cambridge University Press (1936), p. 159; Jonson, *Discoveries, Works*, ed. C. H. Herford and P. and E. M. Simpson (1947), VIII, p. 620.
3. *Directions for Speech and Style*, ed. H. H. Hudson, Princeton University Press, Princeton (1935).
4. Quoted Bullough (1960), III, p. 15.
5. Dedicatory letter to *The Description of England*, ed. G. Edelen, Cornell University Press, Ithaca (1968), p. 6. The sentence is also found in Holinshed's dedication.

6. Hill (1961), pp. 102, 112.
7. See in detail Gilbert (1979a).
8. Quotations from *The Complete Works of John Lyly*, ed. R. W. Bond, Clarendon Press, Oxford (1902).
9. Hunter (1962) p. 345.
10. Owen (1961) and Barish (1974); Beatrice's speech is analysed by Barish.
11. *Selections from Sidney's Arcadia*, ed. R. Syfret, Hutchinson (1966), p. 116.
12. *An Apology for Poetry*, ed. G. Shepherd, Nelson (1965), p. 105.
13. Barish (1966), Palmer (1966), Clemen (1961).
14. Further examples are (reference Craik): I.iv.14–15, I.v.6–9, II.i.19–28, II.i.113–21 (*gradatio*), III.iv.40–5, IV.iv.90–5. A longer example of *stichomythia* occurs at II.iv.24–49.
15. Clemen (1980). See also Burckhardt (1968), 47–67 and Turner (1964).
16. For rhetorical patterning in *MND* and other plays of the mid–1590s, see Brooks (1979) pp. xlv–liii.
17. Sonnet 73 is discussed in detail by Fowler (1975) pp. 79–122 and by Nowottny (1962) pp. 76–82.
18. I am indebted to Booth (1969) and to Crutwell (1954). A recent general book is Muir (1979). For individual sonnets, see Booth (1977) and for an examination of registerial variation, Gilbert (1979b).
19. Crutwell (1954), p. 16.
20. *The Advancement of Learning*, ed. A. Johnston, Clarendon Press, Oxford (1974), p. 36.
21. Hunter (1953). Shakespeare was a professional dramatist, unlike the other major sonneteers.
22. *Poems of Michael Drayton*, ed. J. Buxton, Routledge & Kegan Paul (1953), I, p. 17.
23. *The Songs and Sonnets of John Donne*, ed. T. Redpath, Methuen (1956), p. 50.
24. Lanham (1976), Ch. 4.

CHAPTER FIVE
Loosening the structures

How do we assimilate information? When we listen to speech (as in a theatre) we are helped by the degree of stress, intonation, gesture. Even so, the important statements need to stand out, and this may be partly achieved by rhetorical parallelism. The opening of Act III of *Measure for Measure* is the challenge to the imprisoned Claudio by the disguised Duke: 'Be absolute for death...' After the opening half-line, all the arguments are in fact concentrated in the second half-lines: 'Reason thus with life... a breath thou art... thou art death's fool... Thou art not noble... Thou'rt by no means valiant... The best of rest is sleep... Thou art not thyself... Happy thou art not... Thou art not certain... If thou art rich, thou'rt poor... Friend hast thou none... Thou hast nor youth nor age.' The majority of these clauses begin *Thou art* or *Thou hast*, but there is just sufficient variation of word-order ('Happy thou art not', 'Friend hast thou none') to avoid monotony. The concluding remark, 'What's yet in this...?' also occupies a second half-line. The justification for the Duke's arguments (all the clauses beginning with *for*) and the illustrative imagery comes in the intervening lines.

This, however, is a set speech. Earlier in the same play Claudio needs to explain to Lucio – and so to us – why what has hitherto passed in Vienna as a misdemeanour only now apparently results in imprisonment. The parallelism of this speech is not nearly so marked (I.ii.155–70), but the repetition, both of subject and predicate, conveys the sense: 'The *new* deputy... *newly* in the seat... this *new* governor...' (does what?) 'lets it *straight* feel the spur... Awakes me all the enrolled penalties... puts the drowsy and neglected act / *Freshly* on me...' (and why?) 'for a *name*... 'Tis surely for a *name*'. Apart from the *new(ly)*, *straight* and *freshly*, which are repeated because it is the arbitrary nature of the decision which infuriates Claudio, and the word *name*, which is used twice because he believes the introduction of the new regime is simply to advance Angelo's reputation, the variation of title (*deputy, governor*) and the different images in the predicate prevent the speech from becoming repetitious. Furthermore, this is a single, fifteen-line sentence where, despite the parentheses, we do not lose the thread.

The same multiplicity of parts within a single whole is characteristic of Marlowe's syntax. His sentences are apt to be quite long, but the main clause can almost always be perceived without difficulty. What Shakespeare may have been taught by Marlowe (although this would reinforce a lesson learnt from writing narrative poetry) was the ability to elaborate by way of relative, participial and adverbial clause:

> *The warlike soldiers and the gentlemen*
> That heretofore have fill'd Persepolis
> With Afric captains taken in the field,
> Whose ramsom made them march in coats of gold,
> With costly jewels hanging at their ears,
> And shining stones upon their lofty crests,
> Now living idle in the walled towns,
> Wanting both pay and martial discipline,
> *Begin in troops to threaten civil war,*
> *And openly exclaim against the king.*   ·   (*1 Tam* I.i.140–9)

> And if we should with common rites of arms
> Offer our safeties to his clemency,
> *I fear the custom proper to his sword,*
> Which he observes as parcel of his fame,
> Intending so to terrify the world,
> By any innovation or remorse,
> *Will never be dispens'd with till our deaths.*   (*1 Tam.* V.i.11–17)

> By Cairo runs to Alexandria bay
> Darote's steam, wherein *at anchor lies*
> *A Turkish galley* of my royal fleet,
> Waiting my coming to the river side,
> Hoping by some means I shall be releas'd;
> Which, when I come aboard, will hoist up sail,
> And soon put forth into the Terrene Sea,
> Where 'twixt the isles of Cyprus and of Crete,
> We quickly may in Turkish seas arrive.   (*2 Tam* I.ii.19–27)

> Then in my coach, like Saturn's royal son
> Mounted his shining chariots gilt with fire,
> And drawn with princely eagles through the path
> Pav'd with bright crystal and enchas'd with stars

> When all the gods stand gazing at his pomp,
> So *will I ride through Samarcanda streets,*
> Until my soul, dissevered from this flesh,
> Shall mount the milk-white way, and meet him there.
>
> (*2 Tam* IV.iii.125–32)[1]

It is the sheer flow of the verse – even though the lines are end-stopped more often than not – which as much as any other single feature contributes to the grandeur of *Tamburlaine*. This is what amplification (beloved of the rhetoricians) really meant for Marlowe. Side by side with these passages from Marlowe, we may place Portia's reply to Bassanio who has just correctly chosen the lead casket. The passage (*Merchant of Venice* III.ii.150–65) is rather too long to quote in its entirety, but it is almost certainly intended to be a single sentence. What is noticeable, however, is the variety of construction which avoids monotony: *Though . . . yet . . .* (correlatives), *a thousand times . . . ten thousand times . . .* (lexically and syntactically parallel), *that* ('so that') *. . . but* (coordination) *. . . which* (subordination) *. . . Happy . . . happier . . . Happiest . . .* (parallel clauses introduced by the same adjective). Not all the examples need come from drama. The opening seventeen-line stanza of Spenser's *Prothalamion* coils around a main clause, 'Calme was the day . . . When I . . . Walkt forth', with a wreath of secondary clauses at various levels of subordination. The syntax reflects the slow, therapeutic stroll along the river bank which helps to relieve the poet's discontent.

Copiousness, then, is not merely a matter of vocabulary. The elaboration may be by relative, infinitive or adverbials, as in *Richard III* I.ii.230–6:

> What? I that killed her husband and his father
> To take her in her heart's extremest hate,
> With curses in her mouth, tears in her eyes,
> The bleeding witness of my hatred by,
> Having God, her conscience, and these bars against me,
> And I no friends to back my suit at all
> But the plain devil and dissembling looks?

where the infinitive in fact acts as the main verb in colloquial usage: 'I'm actually going to take her . . .' Or the noun itself may be extended, not simply by adding further nouns but by noun phrases in apposition:

> Macbeth does murder sleep – the innocent sleep,
> Sleep that knits up the ravelled sleave of care,
> The death of each day's life, sore labour's bath,

Balm of hurt minds, great nature's second course,
Chief nourisher in life's feast. (*Mac* II.ii.36–40)

The simple, additive, colloquial structure allows us to concentrate on
the imagery.

In her book *Shakespeare's Grammatical Style*, Dolores M. Burton
makes a very detailed and technical stylistic comparison of two
plays, *Richard II* and *Antony and Cleopatra*. She finds the style of
Antony and Cleopatra typically periodic: 'sentences with a structure
rather like an onion, whose minor syntactic elements surrounded the
main clause that lies at the centre'.[2] As a variant of this, the main
clause may be interrupted by an elaborating subordinate clause (or
clauses). The object of the resumed main clause can equally well be
modified, but it is important that the main clause itself remains simple, and usually in as normal a word-order as possible, so that it is
easily assimilated in the theatre:

> *Our slippery people,*
> Whose love is never linked to the deserver
> Till his deserts are past, *begin to throw*
> *Pompey the Great and all his dignities*
> *Upon his son*; who, high in name and power,
> Higher than both in blood and life, stands up
> For the main soldier; whose quality, going on,
> The sides o' th' world may danger. (I.ii.186–93)

This is not a particularly remarkable passage, but it has its own balance. It is looser than the Ciceronian style of Sidney or Hooker, and
it is more natural in that the main verb occurs quite early in the sentence instead of being delayed until near the end. It is therefore more
suitable for drama (the term *periodic* has also been applied to Donne's
style). The sense of roundness and smoothness is characteristic of
much of Shakespeare's later syntax.

It is perhaps too much to expect Shakespeare to have achieved
such smoothness all at once. Three early cases of copious style show
him trying – but perhaps not quite achieving – both lexical expansion
and syntactical parallelism. The first example is from *2 Henry VI*:

> See how the blood is settled in his face.
> Oft have I seen a timely-parted ghost
> Of ashy semblance, meagre, pale and bloodless,
> Being all descended to the labouring heart,
> Who, in the conflict that it holds with death,
> Attracts the same for aidance 'gainst the enemy;

> Which with the heart there cools, and ne'er returneth
> To blush and beautify the cheek again.   (III.ii.160–7)

Here the five epithets applied to *ghost* (one pre-modifier and four post-modifiers) run smoothly, but *Being* apparently refers to blood, *Who* to heart and *Which* once again to blood. *3 Henry VI* I.iv.141–2 is better (and shorter):

> Women are soft, mild, pitiful, and flexible;
> Thou stern, obdurate, flinty, rough, remorseless.

but the four adjectives of the first line are not quite matched by the five of the second and the polysyllabic *obdurate* perhaps comes too early in the series. Similarly, *Titus Andronicus* V.iii.43–4

> A reason mighty, strong, and effectual,
> A pattern, precedent, and lively warrant,

leads us to expect three matching adjectives to follow *pattern*; instead we get noun plus adjective plus noun.

Some further examples, from *Richard III*, are more promising. I.ii.21–25 is more grammatically varied, with adjectives, relative clause and pronoun, but the referent (*child*) is clear, as was not the case in the example from *2 Henry VI* above:

> If ever he have child, abortive be it,
> Prodigious, and untimely brought to light,
> Whose ugly and unnatural aspect
> May fright the hopeful mother at the view,
> And that be heir to his unhappiness!

At I.ii.242–5 the expansion is embedded within the opening and closing lines which together constitute the main clause:

> A sweeter and a lovelier gentleman,
> Framed in the prodigality of nature,
> Young, valiant, wise, and, no doubt, right royal,
> The spacious world cannot again afford.

In this, as in much else, *Richard III* shows a more assured writer at work.

Once the norm of a subordinate, easy-flowing syntax has been established, Shakespeare can exaggerate its characteristics (as he does elsewhere with copious lexis) to achieve a special effect. Claudius is a ruler who has learned all about *policy* and *commodity* (in the Elizabethan senses). On stage he must show some presence. He is apparently an efficient ruler of Denmark; Hamlet's quarrel with him is almost wholly personal, and no one else appears to protest. He has obviously impressed Gertrude, shallow and unthinking as she may be. His strength and decisiveness is seen in the firm syntax of his contemptuous dismissal of the idea that Hamlet has been driven mad by love for Ophelia and his *quick determination* to remove from the court of Denmark the cause of potential trouble:

> Love? His affections do not that way tend;
> Nor what he spake, though it lacked form a little,
> Was not like madness. There's something in his soul
> O'er which his melancholy sits on brood,
> And I do doubt the hatch and the disclose
> Will be some danger; which for to prevent,
> I have in quick determination
> Thus set it down: he shall with speed to England
> For the demand of our neglected tribute.   (III.i.163–71)

Nor has he lost his touch towards the close of the play in his masterly handling of Laertes' rebellion. He agrees that Laertes has a strong case against Hamlet, indeed some case against himself, but he persuades him to handle it his (Claudius') way.

Yet, as his opening speech, with the subordination and parentheses of its syntax, reveals, he is a master of circumlocution too:

> Therefore *our sometime sister*, now our Queen,
> Th'imperial jointress to this warlike state,
> *Have we*, as 'twere with a defeated joy,
> With an auspicious and a dropping eye,
> With mirth in funeral and with dirge in marriage,
> In equal scale weighing delight and dole,
> *Taken to wife*.   (I.ii.8–14)[3]

Once that is over, he turns blandly to the next piece of business: 'And now, Laertes, what's the news with you?' His second long speech to Hamlet maintains its suavity by a lavish use of Latinate adjective with Latinate noun:

> But you must know your father lost a father;
> That father lost, lost his; and the survivor bound
> In filial obligation for some term
> To do obsequious sorrow. But to persever
> In obstinate condolement is a course
> Of impious stubbornness.   (I.ii.89–94)

He speaks diplomatically to Rosencrantz and Guildenstern about Hamlet's *transformation* (II.ii.5).

At the other extreme, colloquial syntax is harder to identify and to describe. The usages we can recognise are often not so much Elizabethan as perennial. Pause-fillers, an essential part of the communicative process, are not neglected. 'Why, now', 'faith', 'Sir', or 'I warrant you' give the illusion of colloquial speech, like our own 'I mean', 'actually', 'Well, then' or 'you know'. Another simple trick is to begin a scene – or indeed a whole play – apparently in the middle of a conversation; a character denies what we have never heard uttered in so many words:

> Nay, but this dotage of our general's
> O'erflows the measure . . .   (*AC* I.i.1–2)

> No, holy father, throw away that thought . . .   (*MM* I.iii.1)

> No, faith, I'll not stay a jot longer.   (*TN* III.ii.1)

Repetition may indicate self-pity, as it does with Gloucester's 'O madam, my old heart is cracked; it's cracked' and 'I know not, madam. 'Tis too bad, too bad!' (ii.i.89, 95), or senility and purposelessness, as with Shallow:

> *Falstaff* You must excuse me, Master Robert Shallow.
> *Shallow* I will not excuse you; you shall not be excused; excuses shall not be admitted; there is no excuse shall serve; you shall not be excused.   (*2 Hen IV* V.i.3–6)

> He hath wronged me; indeed, he hath. At a word, he hath, believe me.
> Robert Shallow, Esquire, saith he is wronged.   '' (*MWW* I.i.103–5)

Lawrence Danson[4] suggests that Shylock, at his first meeting with Bassanio and Antonio, deliberately appears as an absent-minded, doddering, but pedantic old man (a kind of Venetian Shallow) who can barely bring his mind back to Bassanio's bequest:

> *Shy*   Three thousand ducats, well.
> *Bass* Ay, sir, for three months.
> *Shy*   For three months, well.
> *Bass* For the which, as I told you, Antonio shall be bound.
> *Shy*   Antonio shall become bound, well.
> *Bass* May you stead me? Will you pleasure me? Shall I know your answer?
> *Shy*   Three thousand ducats for three months, and Antonio bound.
>   (*MV* I.iii.1–10)

> I had forgot – three months, you told me so.   (I.iii.64)

who explains his poor puns ('land rats and water rats, water thieves and land thieves, I mean pirates') and who is apparently unable to work out the current rate of interest in his head:

> Three thousand ducats, 'tis a good round sum.
> Three months from twelve, then let me see, the rate . . . (I.iii.100–1)

That this is a pose, meant to gratify Shylock's desire to see the Christians squirm, is clear when he rounds on Antonio like the *stranger cur* the latter has called him. Shakespeare apparently realised, early in his career, the dramatic possibilities of deliberate, repetitive speech.[5]

The Nurse in *Romeo and Juliet* and Mistress Quickly in *Henry IV* find it above all difficult to say things simply and without an over-abundance of confirmatory evidence. The Nurse's rambling attempt to establish Juliet's age (I.iii) is good, but Quickly's lengthy prose speeches are perhaps better. She vainly attempts before the Lord Chief Justice to tie down Falstaff to his earlier promises of marriage and repayment of debts (*2 Hen IV* II.i.83–101), but the mere mention of Pistol and his *swaggering* – something of a new word[6] – is enough to set her off:

Hostess	If he swagger, let him not come here. No, by my faith! I must live among my neighbours; I'll no swaggerers. I am in good name and fame with the very best. Shut the door. There comes no swaggers here. I have not lived all this while to have swaggering now. Shut the door, I pray you.
Falstaff	Dost thou hear, hostess?
Hostess	Pray ye, pacify yourself, Sir John; there comes no swaggerers here.
Falstaff	Dost thou hear? It is mine ancient.
Hostess	Tilly-fally, Sir John, ne'er tell me; an your ancient swagger, 'a comes not in my doors. I was before Master Tisick the debuty t'other day, and, as he said to me – 'twas no longer ago than Wednesday last, i'good faith – 'Neighbour Quickly,' says he – Master Dumb our minister was by then – 'Neighbour Quickly,' says·he, 'receive those that are civil, for,' said he, 'you are in an ill name' – now 'a said so, I can tell whereupon. 'For,' says he, 'you are an honest woman, and well thought on; therefore take heed what guests you receive; receive,' says he, 'no swaggering companions.' There comes none here. You would bless you to hear what he said. No, I'll no swaggerers. (*2 Hen IV* II.iv.71–93)

The repetition of *swaggerers*; the rhyming slang *name and fame*; the corruption of *deputy*; the colloquial '*a, by my faith, Tilly-fally, well thought on, You would bless you*, but the fine, legal-sounding *where-upon*; and, above all, the parentheses with their circumstantial detail (*Wednesday last; Master Dumb . . . was by*) and the constant interjection of *says he* (because direct speech is somehow more 'real') – all these establish her as a muddled, sentimental but attractive character, addicted to pause-fillers (*by my troth; look you, I warrant you*), indulged by Falstaff and Doll:

> Hostess Cheater, call you him? I will bar no honest man my house,
>   nor no cheater, but I do not love swaggering; by my troth, I
>   am the worse when one says 'swagger'. Feel, masters, how I
>   shake, look you, I warrant you.
> Doll   So you do, hostess.

Another occasional feature of Shakespeare's syntax which can easily be paralleled from present-day English is the use, for emphasis, of both a noun and a pronoun. We pick out one feature for particular attention and put it at the head of the sentence ('*That dress*, where did you get *it*?') or we wish to emphasise a noun or even a noun clause ('*It's* rather good *coffee, this*', '*It* does surprise me, *what he sees in her.*'). Because this distorts normal word-order, we feel the necessity to make doubly sure by the inclusion of a pronoun. Similarly, in *Measure for Measure*, the excitable, interfering Lucio blurts out:

> But yesternight, my lord, *she and that friar*,
> I saw *them* at the prison. A saucy friar,
> A very scurvy fellow.   (V.i.134–6)

A further example of the same construction occurs in *Cymbeline* when Cloton is trying to force his attentions upon Imogen:

> *The contract you pretend with that base wretch*,
> One bred of alms and fostered with cold dishes,
> With scraps o' th' court, *it is no contract, none.*   (II.iii.115–7)

Jonson's comic style is usually less balanced than Shakespeare's and often nearer to the language of ordinary speech, but one kind of balance found quite often in his verse is a parallelism of strongly-stressed verbs within short clauses:

> Here I *wear* your keys,
> *See* all your coffers and your caskets locked,
> *Keep* the poor inventory of your jewels,
> Your plate, and moneys; *am* your steward, sir,
> *Husband* your goods here.   (*Volpone* I.iii.40–4)

I, that have *preached* these things so oft unto you,
Read you the principles, *argued* all the grounds,
Disputed every fitness, every grace,
Called you to counsel of so frequent dressings . . .

(*Volpone* III.iv.23–6)

I *ga'* you count'nance, credit for your coals,
Your stills, your glasses, your materials;
Built you a furnace, *drew* you customers,
Advanced all your black arts; *lent* you, beside,
A house to practise in.   (*Alchemist* I.i.43–7).

This, too, is a feature of some speech styles. The very few purple passages in Jonson stand out against his realistic norm: Mammon's fantasies of using his newly-acquired riches to lead an aristocratic life with Dol (in reality a prostitute); the delights Volpone offers to Celia; or, rather differently imagined, the prose monologues of Justice Overdo. In these his syntax is much more subordinate than usual. Marston's preface 'To the Reader' states that *The Malcontent* is written 'more honestly than eloquently' and in the play verse turns into prose or prose into verse within the same speech (the effect is less troublesome in the theatre than on the printed page).

Recent editors comment on the 'low-keyed formality' and the self-defeating complexity of the syntax of *All's Well That Ends Well*,[7] as if Shakespeare was working towards, but had not yet achieved, the looser style of the final plays. It seems to me that the syntax of this play, like the characters, is a melange of styles which have not been properly integrated. Bertram who has, at best, proved weak and gullible, finally accepts Helena ungraciously. Helena appears to act out of character in herself suggesting the bed-trick (it is put *to* Isabella) and the introduction of the talisman – the ring placed on Bertram's finger in bed – is similarly artificial. Likewise the syntax: several passages are cast as couplets, especially the lengthy exchanges between Helena and the King (II.i.130–210) and the King's attempt to persuade Bertram to accept her (II.iii.124–43; here the switch from blank verse occurs in the middle of the speech). These may be intended to suggest an incantatory, aphoristic style, just as the formal sonnet form of Helena's letter in III.iv. conveys the *opposite* of her true feelings for Bertram. Act I, scene i had promised better. Helena's first verse speech establishes her as a straightforward, likeable girl, with its colloquialisms, one or two metaphors, and her ability to recognise Parolles for what he is (as Bertram cannot). Later oxymoron (168–70) and her witty replies to Parolles (187–202) show

that she is intelligent too, in the manner of earlier comic heroines.
Unfortunately all this does not last.

   Timon of Athens, perhaps to be dated 1607 but not printed until the
First Folio and possibly worked on spasmodically, contains some
passages whose syntax seems unnecessarily difficult. When Apeman-
tus visits Timon in the woods, his speech begins with the rhythm
which we shall see to be characteristic of *Macbeth*: if *this*, then *that; the
one . . . the other*. But by trying to repeat as an aphorism what the earlier lines have stated more forcibly by means of antithesis (*courtier/
beggar, misery/pomp*), the concluding three lines become almost im-
possibly concentrated:

> If thou didst put this sour cold habit on
> To castigate thy pride, 'twere well; but thou
> Dost it enforcedly. Thou'dst courtier be again
> Wert thou not beggar. Willing misery
> Outlives incertain pomp, is crowned before.
> The one is filling still, never complete,
> The other at high wish. Best state, contentless,
> Hath a distracted and most wretched being,
> Worse than the worst, content.   (IV.iii.240–9)

Not much of *Timon* is, however, of this kind. Timon's soliloquy in
IV.i., his prayer to the gods as he looks back on the Athens he has
left and heaps curses on the city, is as carefully balanced as almost
anything in Shakespeare. Lines 1, 4, 6, 8, 10, 12, 13, 15, 21, 23, 25,
28, 30 and 32 all have a heavy caesura, but the second half lines show
different grammatical patterns (sometimes paired nouns – *Slaves and
fools; Piety and fear* – sometimes noun followed by imperative – *Bank-
rupts, hold fast; Bound servants, steal*) and also some variation in
metrical structure (*O thou wall* versus *Plagues incident to men*), so
providing variety. The sentences are of roughly equal length, thus
intensifying the hammer-blows of the curses, except for lines 15–19
where the list of features of an *ordered* society, observing 'degree' (religion, peace, justice, truth and the rest) make clear what it is that is
to be overthrown and replaced by confusion. Line 32 marks the
change of subject from the state of Athens to the feelings of the
exiled Timon by a departure from this careful parallelism, and the
speech concludes in a much looser syntax.

   Other speeches in the play demonstrate a less insistent parallelism:
the imperatives of IV.iii.111, 113, 115, 119, 123 all begin strongly-
marked second half-lines, yet the opening of the speech is scarcely
blank verse at all:

> That by killing of villains
> Thou wast born to conquer my country.
> Put up thy gold. Go on. Here's gold. Go on.   (IV.iii.106–8)

The final plays seem to be characterised by a looser, almost experimental syntax. Perhaps 'experimental' is the wrong word, for it
may be that Shakespeare had become so accustomed to writing blank
verse that he was less conscious than we are of the variations in
rhythm and syntax within the established pattern. But I prefer to
think that the syntax of several of the later speeches marks a development beyond the syntax of the earlier tragic soliloquies (which demands separate treatment), that Shakespeare, while retaining the
overall structure of a speech, was now able to convey the impression
of a character thinking as he spoke, often under pressure. Most of us
do not think in a particularly logical fashion; it is only when we re-
arrange or write up our thoughts that firm order and coherence creep
in. In thinking aloud we make qualifications and objections, go off at
a tangent and partially obscure straightforward communication of
ideas. In Shakespeare's final plays, the increase in parentheses
attempts to indicate something of this turmoil.

Since parentheses may be a matter of modern editorial punctuation, I will try to limit myself to obvious examples, and it may
broaden the discussion a little if I begin with an example outside
Shakespeare, from Beaumont and Fletcher's *Philaster*:

> Then thus I turne
> My language to you Prince, you forraigne man!:
> Ne're stare, nor put on wonder, for you must
> Indure me, and you shall. This earth you tread upon
> (A dowry as you hope with this fair Princesse),
> By my dead father (Oh, I had a father
> Whose memory I bow to) was not left
> To your inheritance, and I up, and living,
> Having my selfe about me, and my sword,
> The soules of all my name, and memories,
> These armes, and some few friends, besides the gods,
> To part so calmely with it, and sit still,
> And say I might have beene. I tell thee *Pharamond*,
> When thou art King, looke I be dead and rotten,
> And my name ashes, as I: For heare me, *Pharamond*:
> This very ground thou goest on, this fat earth,
> My fathers friends made fertile with their faiths,
> Before that day of shame, shall gape and swallow
> Thee and thy nation, like a hungry grave,

Into her hidden bowells: Prince, it shall;
By the just gods it shall.   (I.i.173–93)[8]

The sentence 'This earth...by my dead father...was not left to
your inheritance' has been interrupted by two parentheses, and it is
continued in irregular grammar by 'and I up, and living'. This in
turn produces its own subordination ('Having...the gods') before
concluding 'To part so calmely with it'. Elsewhere the emphasis of
speech is indicated by *and you shall* (176), *as I* (187) and *By the just
gods it shall* (193). The status of *made* (189) is at first uncertain: for a
moment it appears to be a main verb, but *shall gape and swallow* (190)
leads us to think that line 189 may be a relative clause without its
pronoun. Of course all this analysis would not be necessary for an
audience; the general tone is clear and the actor's voice can supply the
necessary emphasis. My point is simply that this is the absolute
opposite of 'literary' drama, for the style indicates to the actor how
he is to play the scene.

Cymbeline, probably written in 1610, about the same time as *Philaster*, is full of parentheses. A very early example shows the parenthesis as part of a conversational style:

He that hath missed the Princess is a thing
Too bad for bad report, and he that hath her –
I mean, that married her, alack good man,
And therefore banished – is a creature such
As, to seek through the regions of the earth
For one his like, there would be something failing
In him that should compare. I do not think
So fair an outward and such stuff within
Endows a man but he.   (I.i.16–24)

Lines 21–22, following the strong pause after *his like*, seem to mean:
'Well, even if you found someone to compare with Posthumus, he
wouldn't be his equal', but they are elliptical in the manner of some
conversation. This play also has its share of difficult syntax:

You do seem to know
Something of me or what concerns me. Pray you,
Since doubting things go ill often hurts more
Than to be sure they do – for certainties
Either are past remedies, or, timely knowing,
The remedy then born – discover to me
What both you spur and stop.   (I.vi.93–9)

Yet the short syntactic units of the Queen's speech at III.v.56 or Imogen's soliloquy in III.vi or Posthumus's in V.iv are at least as characteristic of *Cymbeline* as the more difficult passages.

Pericles, on the other hand, has very few parentheses. The story, however, requires Pericles to be a curiously passive figure. His misfortunes do not result from guilt (as do Leontes') or neglect (like Prospero's).[9] The Epilogue speaks of 'Virtue preserved from fell destruction's blast', and a plot like this is less likely to produce difficulties of syntax. Textually, *Pericles* is a mess, but it might be worth considering why we can be reasonably sure that this passage is by Shakespeare:

> A terrible childbed hast thou had, my dear;
> No light, no fire; th'unfriendly elements
> Forgot thee utterly. Nor have I time
> To give thee hallowed to thy grave, but straight
> Must cast thee, scarcely coffined, in the ooze,
> Where, for a monument upon thy bones,
> And e'er-remaining lamps, the belching whale
> And humming water must o'erwhelm thy corpse,
> Lying with simple shells. O Lychorida,
> Bid Nestor bring me spices, ink and paper,
> My casket and my jewels. And bid Nicander
> Bring me the satin coffer. Lay the babe
> Upon the pillow. Hie thee, whiles I say
> A priestly farewell to her. Suddenly, woman.   (III.i.56–69)

The simplicity and colloquialism of lines 56–8 give way to a more subordinate structure allowing time for a compound, *e'er-remaining*, and the striking adjectives *belching* and *humming*. This is followed in turn by the short, matter-of-fact phrases indicating the actions of 65–9 and incorporating their own stage directions. The air of confidence in the writing, the ability to vary pace and style within a short passage, demonstrate the ability of the experienced dramatist.

As Prospero, in Act I, scene ii of *The Tempest* (1611, and possibly Shakespeare's last play) explains to Miranda (and to us, the audience) how they arrived on the island, he appears torn between a natural desire for revenge on his enemies and the realisation that he can now, if he wishes, finally forgive them. Yet we do not see this indecision in soliloquy, and although he relives the experiences as he recounts them to Miranda, there is not the same sense of pressure as in some of the great tragedies or the slightly earlier *Winter's Tale*. Nor is there tension in the plot, for Prospero holds all the cards. There are several parentheses, but they are not as numerous as in *The Winter's Tale* and almost always much shorter. Although subordinate clauses occasionally occur out of their normal position in the sentence, the style is rarely exceptionally puzzling:

> Some food we had, and some fresh water, that
> A noble Neapolitan, Gonzalo,
> *Out of his charity, who being then appointed*
> *Master of this design*, did give us, with
> Rich garments, linens, stuffs, and necessaries
> Which since have steaded much. So, *of his gentleness,*
> *Knowing I loved my books*, he furnished me
> From mine own library with volumes that
> I prize above my dukedom.   (I.ii.160–8)

A later example of distorted syntax:

> You are three men of sin, whom destiny –
> That hath to instrument this lower world
> And what is in't – the never-surfeited sea
> Hath caused to belch up you, and on this island
> Where man doth not inhabit, you 'mongst men
> Being most unfit to live. I have made you mad;
> And even with such like valour men hang and drown
> Their proper selves.   (III.iii.54–61)

may owe its difficulty to the unnecessary addition of *you* (57) after the preceding *whom*, and the addition of 'and on this island . . .' in a manner characteristic of speech idiom. The concluding lines (76–83) of this same speech by Ariel may be deliberately prophetic and puzzling. The well-known speech in which Prospero finally announces that he will abjure his magic powers seems to change construction in midstream and a new sentence to begin at V.i.44 without a finite verb having occurred in the previous sentence. But these are relatively isolated instances, from which *The Tempest* has sometimes acquired a false reputation as a 'difficult' play.

Leontes, in *The Winter's Tale*, is a great analyst of his own emotions, and the complexity of his thought-processes leads to a correspondingly difficult syntax. Sometimes (as with Macbeth) specifics become abstracts: *Bohemia, traitors, the daughter of a king*, not, I think, because he is afraid to name the reality, as Macbeth is, but because it 'proves' to him that his wife is like all women and his close friend deceitful in the manner of some close friends. Like Hamlet, having established the general truth from the particular instance, he proceeds to deduce the particular from the general. He persuades himself that what he believes to be true really is so, nowhere more than in the speech at I.ii.128, formally addressed to Mamillius but as close to a soliloquy as makes no difference. Women (*that will say anything* – once again the generalisation) say that Mamillius resembles Leontes, but *were they false* (131), *yet were it true* ('it would still be true', 134) to say the boy is like him. Leontes wants it both ways; *Affection* ('sexual desire') makes possible what had hitherto been thought impossible. *How can this be?* (140) leads at once to probability: *Then 'tis very credent / Thou mayst* (142–3), and probability to certainty: *thou dost* (143) and *I find it* (144). Leontes needs no Iago. Starting with a facial resemblance between father and son, he has proved, to his own satisfaction, that Hermione is an adulteress. As Thorne has noticed[10] he is fond of indefinite pronouns, *nothing, something, it,* frequently with antecedents which become ever more imprecise:

> Is whispering nothing?
> Is leaning cheek to cheek? Is meeting noses?
> Kissing with inside lip? Stopping the career
> Of laughter with a sigh? – a note infallible
> Of breaking honesty. Horsing foot on foot?
> Skulking in corners? Wishing clocks more swift?
> Hours minutes? Noon midnight? And all eyes
> Blind with the pin and web but theirs, theirs only,
> That would unseen be wicked – is this nothing?
> Why, then the world and all that's in't is nothing;
> The covering sky is nothing; Bohemia nothing;
> My wife is nothing; nor nothing have these nothings,
> If this be nothing.   (I.ii.284–96)

That quotation also demonstrates the quick and broken style characteristic of Leontes in the first two acts. Once more, these are essentially speech rhythms, but their allusiveness and occasional incoherence illustrate his tortured mind. Parentheses are frequent and last longer than usual:

> Ha'not you seen, Camillo –
> But that's past doubt, you have, or your eye-glass
> Is thicker than a cuckold's horn – or heard –
> For to a vision so apparent rumour
> Cannot be mute – or thought – for cogitation
> Resides not in that man that does not think –
> My wife is slippery? If thou wilt confess –
> Or else be impudently negative
> To have nor eyes nor ears, nor thought – then say
> My wife's a hobby-horse, deserves a name
> As rank as any flax-wench that puts to
> Before her troth-plight: say't and justify't.   (I.ii.267–78)

101

Nor night nor day no rest! It is but weakness
To bear the matter thus, mere weakness. If
The cause were not in being – part o'th'cause,
She, th'adult'ress: for the harlot-king
Is quite beyond mine arm, out of the blank
And level of my brain, plot-proof; but she
I can hook to me – say that she were gone,
Given to the fire, a moiety of my rest
Might come to me again.   (II.iii.1–9)

Other examples are at I.ii.325–33, II.i.173–87, III.ii.83–90 and
III.ii.152–70 (which is in fact a soliloquy):

Apollo, pardon
My great profaneness 'gainst thine oracle!
I'll reconcile me to Polixines;
New woo my queen; recall the good Camillo –
Whom I proclaim a man of truth, of mercy:
For, being transported by my jealousies
To bloody thoughts and to revenge, I chose
Camillo for the minister to poison
My friend Polixines; which had been done,
But that the good mind of Camillo tardied
My swift command, though I with death and with
Reward did threaten and encourage him,
Not doing it and being done. He, most humane,
And filled with honour, to my kingly guest
Unclasped my practice, quit his fortunes here –
Which you knew great – and to the hazard
Of all incertainties himself commended,
No richer than his honour. How he glisters
Through my rust! And how his piety
Does my deeds make the blacker!

This last instance is a prayer to Apollo for pardon when Leontes
finally realises that his accusations against Hermione have been
altogether groundless. He begins with a series of resolutions, ex-
pounded by parallel infinitives: *reconcile, woo, recall*. But the mention
of Camillo leads him to remember, in parenthesis, the plot to use
Camillo to poison Polixines. This in turn gives rise to further subordination (*which had been done / But that . . .*). The first sentence ends
with a compressed conditional clause involving two pairs, each with
three components: 'I threatened him with death if he didn't do it, and
encouraged him with reward if he did'. The second, shorter, sentence, containing two brief parentheses, resumes the verbal parallelism of the opening of the speech: *unclasp'd, quit, commended*.

Act V (Leontes does not appear in Act IV) is free of the earlier abstractions, distorted syntax and confused logic, and it clearly indicates a return to sanity. In Act IV too, we have been introduced to more varied language: the simplicity of Perdita, the firm rhetorical structure of Florizel's marvellous tribute to her ('What you do / Still betters what is done...'), even the canting terms of Autolycus. It is not only the open air of Bohemia in summertime that is less oppressive than the court of Sicilia, but also its language. Hermione, it is true, could be movingly simple (II.i.116–24), as well as demonstrating a natural colloquialism in her piling up of adjunct phrases:

> Both disobedience and ingratitude
> To you and toward your friend, whose love had spoke
> Even since it could speak, *from an infant, freely*
> That it was yours. (III.ii.67–70)

> ... lastly, hurried
> *Here to this place, i'th'open air, before*
> *I have got strength of limit.* (III.ii.103–5)

But perhaps she is linguistically compromised by the deliberately flirtatious double entendres she has used in the second scene of the first act, just as later Polixines is not man enough to countenance his own son's affection for a shepherdess. They are proved innocent, but have their words not been liable to misconstruction? As I have suggested earlier, innocence resides rather in Camillo and even more in Paulina. As this quotation shows, she too has her parentheses, but they are often nearly as important as the main sentence:

> Thy tyranny,
> Together working with thy jealousies –
> Fancies too weak for boys, too green and idle
> For girls of nine – O think what they have done,
> And then run mad indeed, stark mad! (III.ii.177–81)

In *The Winter's Tale* Shakespeare appears to have employed almost the whole of his linguistic armoury: synonyms, compounds, occasional Latinisms, both rhetorical and colloquial syntax, but to have developed and refined these to illuminate the pathological obsession of Leontes, the innocence of Perdita and eventually of Hermione, the sturdy commonsense of Paulina. The basis of both diction and syntax is colloquial usage, but if this is 'natural' in Perdita and Paulina, with Leontes it is flawed, 'artful', rather as the carnations and gillyflowers Perdita would not admit into her country garden. The art has come to seem like nature.

The kind of imagery a writer chooses has clear implications for his syntax. Here, however, Shakespeare's development was from a looser to a more concentrated style. In discussing imagery, I am not concerned with the content of the images or indeed their thematic value in the play: for example, the imagery of light and darkness in *Romeo and Juliet* or that of Macbeth, the man in purloined clothes which are too big for him. Instead I shall consider expanded or concentrated images, since this aspect has clear implications for the form of expression. One would automatically associate the expanded image with the greater leisure for development provided by narrative poetry, and there are several examples in *Venus and Adonis* and *The Rape of Lucrece*. In these two poems there are also stanzas where image is added to image, intensifying the idea but achieving no deeper penetration of the subject:

> Unruly blasts wait on the tender spring;
> Unwholesome weeds take root with precious flowers;
> The adder hisses where the sweet birds sing;
> What virtue breeds iniquity devours.   (*VA* 869–72)

King John (1596) IV.ii.9–16 will serve as an example from the early plays:

> Therefore, to be possessed with double pomp,
> To guard a title that was rich before,
> To gild refined gold, to paint the lily,
> To throw a perfume on the violet,
> To smooth the ice, or add another hue
> Unto the rainbow, or with taper-light
> To seek the beauteous eye of heaven to garnish,
> Is wasteful and ridiculous excess.

All the rhetoricians consider amplification at length; this is copiousness for its own sake, and the result is an additive syntax where the subject or complement comprises a series of short clauses each of which usually occupies a single line. It sometimes occurs in the Sonnets too, for example the beginning of Sonnet 35:

> No more be grieved at that which thou hast done:
> Roses have thorns, and silver fountains mud,
> Clouds and eclipses stain both moon and sun,
> And loathsome canker lives in sweetest bud.

But this is a prelude to the admission that the lover deliberately, if reluctantly, accepts his mistress's faults: the diffuse opening is only the first stage in a developing argument, and some bounds to undue expansion are set by the tight metrical form of a short poem. A series of images on the same subject in *Richard III*:

> When clouds are seen, wise men put on their cloaks;
> When great leaves fall, then winter is at hand;
> When the sun sets, who doth not look for night?
> Untimely storms makes men expect a dearth.   (II.iii.32–5)

is perhaps excusable since it is spoken by one of a group of citizens who take up the whole of this short scene and who clearly have a choric function. In another quotation from the same play the figure is close to a conceit, yet the lexical cohesion (*images, mirrors, cracked, glass*) just saves it from banality, and, more important, simile has given way to the concentration of metaphor:

> I have bewept a worthy husband's death,
> And lived with looking on his images;
> But now two mirrors of his princely semblance
> Are cracked in pieces by malignant death,
> And I for comfort have but one false glass
> That grieves me when I see my shame in him.   (II.ii.49–54)

The characteristic image of the early plays is, however, that which demonstrates its correspondence point by point. In this it has something in common with the metaphysical conceit, but it is seldom consciously witty or especially unusual in its choice of comparison. It has clarity, certainly, but lacks dramatic vigour. *3 Henry VI* seems especially prone to this kind of image:

> This battle fares like to the morning's war,
> When dying clouds contend with growing light,
> What time the shepherd, blowing of his nails,
> Can neither call it perfect day nor night.
> Now sways it this way, like a mighty sea
> Forced by the tide to combat with the wind;
> Now sways it that way, like the self-same sea
> Forced to retire by fury of the wind.
> Sometime the flood prevails, and then the wind;
> Now one the better, then another best;
> Both tugging to be victors, breast to breast,
> Yet neither conqueror nor conquered;
> So is the equal poise of this fell war.   (II.v.1–13)[11]

Lines 1 and 13 largely repeat one another and 9–12 are similarly otiose. The passage might be excused as being a rhetorical opening to the scene, and it is perhaps true that the reflective nature of the soliloquy encouraged the use of formal imagery. But when all is said, the passage is simply diffuse and if it were presented unseen perhaps not many critics would unhesitatingly attribute it to Shakespeare. Less protracted but little better are II.i.11–19 (again the concluding lines make everything doubly clear); III.ii.134–43 ('So do I wish the crown...'): III.ii.174–81 ('And from that torment I will free myself...'); and finally V.iv.1–38 which is a notable extended exercise in nautical imagery.

Richard II is another case in point. One of its best-known images is at IV.i.180 where Richard surrenders the crown to Bolingbroke:

> Richard   Give me the crown.
> Here, cousin – seize the crown. Here, cousin –
> On this side, my hand; and on that side, thine.
> Now is this golden crown like a deep well
> That owes two buckets, filling one another,
> The emptier ever dancing in the air,
> The other down, unseen, and full of water.
> That bucket down and full of tears am I,
> Drinking my griefs whilst you mount up on high.

Again, this is explanatory: *full of water* is paralleled by *full of tears* in the following line.[12] Later, when Bolingbroke's triumphant entry into London in the company of the deposed Richard is narrated by York to his wife, there is no continual contrast: Bolingbroke is described first and then Richard.[13] The comparison of Richard to the actor who has the misfortune to follow the star player on stage is clinched by the final two lines:

> As in a theatre the eyes of men,
> After a well graced actor leaves the stage,
> Are idly bent on him that enters next,
> Thinking his prattle to be tedious:
> Even so, or with much more contempt, men's eyes
> Did scowl on gentle Richard.   (V.ii.23–8)

Later still, Richard, musing on the passing of time, indulges in a metaphysical conceit: 'For now hath time made me his numbering clock.' (V.v.50). But the 'proof' ('So sighs, and tears, and groans / Show minutes, times, and hours') is not usually supplied so directly in metaphysical poems.

Madeline Doran believes that the change from a predominantly explicit imagery, where the points of comparison are explored singly, to a rapid succession of images, often suggested rather than elaborated, takes place between *Richard II* and *Henry IV*.[14] In general terms this is, I think, correct. Yet one cannot be too precise. The imagery of *Richard III* (? 1592–3, but definitely preceding *Richard II*) is certainly more taut than that of most of the early plays:

> Who builds his hope in air of your good looks
> Lives like a drunken sailor on a mast,
> Ready with every nod to tumble down
> Into the fatal bowels of the deep.   (III.iv.98–101)

> Richard yet lives, hell's black intelligencer,
> Only reserved their factor to buy souls
> And send them thither.   (IV.iv.71–3)

> The wretched, bloody, and usurping boar,
> That spoiled your summer fields and fruitful vines,
> Swills your warm blood like wash, and makes his trough
> In your embowelled bosoms – this foul swine
> Is now even in the centre of this isle.   (V.ii.7–11)

The play is a storehouse of rhetorical devices, but the formal and often repetitive expression does not extend to the imagery. This may be because so much of the play is either spoken by or about Richard himself. The sardonic self-awareness (so far beyond Marlowe's villains) would go ill with flaccid expansion and embellishment in the imagery. Equally, *2 Henry IV* contains at least one extended and over-explicit image of the old kind:

> When we mean to build,
> We first survey the plot, then draw the model,
> And when we see the figure of the house,
> Then must we rate the cost of the erection,
> Which if we find outweighs ability,
> What do we then but draw anew the model
> In fewer offices, or at least desist
> To build at all? Much more, in this great work –
> Which is almost to pluck a kingdom down
> And set another up – should we survey
> The plot of situation and the model,
> Consent upon a sure foundation,
> Question surveyors, know our own estate,
> How able such a work to undergo
> To weigh against his opposite; or else
> We fortify in paper and in figures,
> Using the names of men instead of men,
> Like one that draws the model of an house
> Beyond his power to build it, who, half-through,

> Gives o'er and leaves his part-created cost
> A naked subject to the weeping clouds,
> And waste for churlish winter's tyranny.   (I.iii.41–62)

However, Professor Doran is certainly correct in pointing out the much more concentrated images of *Henry IV* where double meanings are frequently left implicit:

> . . . two-and-twenty knights
> Balked in their own blood, did Sir Walter see.   (*1 Hen IV* I.i.68–9)

Balked is, as in Middle English, 'piled up (in ridges)', but equally there is a strong implication of 'thwarted'. It would be easy to multiply examples from the rush of images in the middle and later plays (the pace seems to slacken a little in the final plays). Such images are frequently linked:

> Have you not set mine honour at the *stake*,
> And *baited* it with all th' *unmuzzled* thoughts
> That tyrannous heart can think?   (*TN* III.i.115–7)

> And Pity, like a naked new-born babe
> Striding the blast, or heaven's cherubin, *horsed*
> Upon the sightless curriers of the air,
> Shall blow the horrid deed in every eye,
> That tears shall drown the wind. I have no *spur*
> To *prick* the sides of my intent but only
> *Vaulting* ambition which *o'erleaps* itself
> And *falls* on the other.   (*Mac* I.vii.21–8)

The 'naked new-born babe / Striding the blast' is one of Shakespeare's mixed metaphors, like Lady Macbeth's question shortly afterwards: 'Was the hope drunk / Wherein you dressed yourself?' (I.vii.35) or Macbeth's 'Put rancours in the vessel of my peace' (III.i.66); *Macbeth* seems a play especially prone to such conceits. Antony's 'O thou day o' th' world / Chain mine armed neck' (IV.viii.13) or Hamlet taking arms against a sea of troubles (III.i.59) are similarly unanalysable in sensuous terms. They may be explained – or explained away – as symbolic, but perhaps Dr Johnson came nearer to the truth:

> . . . that fulness of idea, which might sometimes load his words with more sentiment than they could conveniently convey, and that rapidity of imagination which might hurry him to a second thought before he had fully explained the first.[15]

One can, in fact, discover the same image handled much more succinctly later:

> I see thy glory like a shooting star
> Fall to the base earth from the firmament.
> Thy sun sets weeping in the lowly west,
> Witnessing storms to come, woe, and unrest.   (*R II* II.iv.19–22)

> Finish, good lady; the bright day is done,
> And we are for the dark.   (*AC* V.ii.193–4)

In the later image, as Miss Holmes (whose example it is) comments, 'There is no lingering twilight, brightness and dark are tropical.'[16] Simile has become metaphor. Where the image is striking, and perhaps unusual in its context, Shakespeare does sometimes explain, but the explanation is not so protracted or so obvious as in the earlier plays:

> And the ebbed man, ne'er loved till ne'er worth love,
> Comes deared by being lacked. This common body,
> Like to a vagabond flag upon the stream,
> Goes to and back, lackeying the varying tide,
> To rot itself with motion.   (*AC* I.iv.43–7)

The initial difficulty, the *ebbed* man who is finally welcomed to power only when he is no longer available, is made more intelligible by the continuation of the same image in *flag* ('reed') and *stream*. (*Lacked* also perhaps gave rise to the following metaphor, *lackeying*.) Other, more directly explanatory instances are:

> The hearts
> That spanieled me at heels, to whom I gave
> Their wishes, do *discandy, melt their sweets*
> On blossoming Caesar.   (*AC* IV.xii.20–3)

> His delights
> Were *dolphin-like; they showed his back above*
> The element they lived in.   (*AC* V.ii.88–90)

> *Ulysses*   We saw him at the opening of his tent. He is not sick.
> *Ajax*   Yes, *lion-sick, sick of proud heart.*   (*TC* II.iii.86–8)

> neither allied
> To eminent assistants, but *spider-like*

109

> *Out of his self-drawing web,* 'a gives us note,
> The force of his own merit makes his way.   (*Hen VIII* I.i.61–4)

> Let music sound while he doth make his choice,
> Then if he lose, he makes a *swanlike end,*
> *Fading in music.* That the comparison
> May stand more proper, my eye shall be the stream
> And watery deathbed for him.   (*MV* III.ii.43–7)

The initial effect of the last image (as with most of the others, the simile is stressed: *dolphin-like, spider-like, swan-like*) is unfortunately spoiled by its prolongation ('That the comparison / May stand more proper...'). But *The Merchant of Venice* is an early play.

At their best, the later images both work by suggestion and are given support by their context. In considering Shakespeare's development as a dramatist between *2 Henry VI* and *Macbeth*, G. R. Hibbard discusses *Macbeth* III.ii.46–50

> Come, seeling night,
> Scarf up the tender eye of pitiful day,
> And with thy bloody and invisible hand
> Cancel and tear to pieces that great bond
> Which keeps me pale.

and remarks:

> Night as the falconer, and day as the suffering falcon, have taken on the attributes of living things through a kind of verbal shorthand that concentrates on action, as distinct from pictorial description. The nouns 'falcon' and 'falconer' are not used at all, but we see why night's hand is 'bloody and invisible'.[17]

The lexical set is in fact continued in *tear to pieces*, and Hibbard may well be correct in suggesting that the implicit pun *seeling / sealing* led to the new image of *that great bond*. In another example of concentrated metaphor, Cornwall and Regan explain their late visit to Gloucester's house:

> Cornwall   You know not why we came to visit you –
> Regan   Thus out of season, threading dark-eyed night.
> (*KL* II.i.118–19)

The needle is not mentioned directly, but *threading* and *eyed* imply it, and *dark-eyed* (unique in Shakespeare and otherwise not especially meaningful) suggests the difficulty of threading a needle in the dark. *Out of season* may again refer to night, or may mean that it is winter, no good time for a journey.[18] All this Shakespeare achieved in a single line.

Jonson's images are compellingly visual and frequently morally reductive; their realism is often a welcome counterbalance to the artificiality of humour comedy:

> Would you would once close
> Those filthy eyes of yours that flow with slime
> Like two frog-pits, and those same hanging cheeks,
> Covered with hide instead of skin (Nay, help, sir)
> That look like frozen dish-clouts set on end.   (*Volpone* I.v.56–60)

> He vomits crooked pins! His eyes are set
> Like a dead hare's hung in a poulter's shop!   (*Volpone* V.xii.25–6)

> . . . you did walk
> Piteously costive, with your pinched-horn-nose,
> And your complexion of the Roman wash,
> Stuck full of black and melancholic worms,
> Like powder-corns shot at th' artillery-yard.   (*Alchemist*, I.i.27–31)[19]

They are, too, almost all similes where the more leisurely syntax (as opposed to that of the metaphor) allows us to assimilate the unusual comparison. There are fewer such images in Shakespeare before the last plays, although Falstaff ('My skin hangs about me like an old lady's loose gown. I am withered like an old apple-john', *1 Hen IV.* III.iii.2, and 'you shall see him laugh till his face be like a wet cloak ill laid up', *2 Hen IV*, V.i.77) has the same manner but a very different tone.

Webster's style, on the other hand, is complex, nervous, staccato, and his images sometimes seem deliberately far-fetched, unpoetic in a 'metaphysical' manner, although they are usually briefer than Donne's:

> As men to try the precious unicorn's horn
> Make of the powder a preservative circle
> And in it put a spider, so these arms
> Shall charm his poison, force it to obeying
> And keep him chaste from an infected straying,
> (*White Devil* II.i.14–18)

> He and his brother are like plum-trees, that grow crooked over standing pools, they are rich, and o'erladen with fruit, but none but crows, pies, and caterpillars feed on them. Could I be one of their flatt'ring panders, I would hang on their ears like a horse-leech, till I were full, and then drop off.   (*Malfi* I.i.49–54)

111

> Ferdinand   ... This will gain
>   Access to private lodgings, where yourself
>   May, like a politic dormouse –
> Bosola   As I have seen some
>   Feed in a lord's dish, half asleep, not seeming
>   To listen to any talk: and yet these rogues
>   Have cut his throat in a dream.   (*Malfi* I.ii.204–10)

Some of them seem, at first sight, to resemble Jonson's images in their 'realism':

> There was a lady in France, that having had the smallpox, flayed the skin off her face to make it more level; and whereas before she look'd like a nutmeg grater, after she resembled an abortive hedgehog.
>   (*Malfi*, II.i.29–32)

> A politician is the devil's quilted anvil,
> He fashions all sins on him, and the blows
> Are never heard.   (*Malfi* III.ii.321–3)

>   ... How tedious is a guilty conscience!
> When I look into the fishponds in my garden,
> Methinks I see a thing, arm'd with a rake
> That seems to strike at me.   (*Malfi* V.v.4–7)[20]

But not quite – an *abortive* hedgehog, a *quilted* anvil, a rake in a *fishpond*? There is, in each case, one disturbing feature. A few of them are so clotted that the interpretation, and therefore any real assessment of their effectiveness, is difficult, especially in the theatre:

> We see that trees bear no such pleasant fruit
> There where they grew first, as where they are now set.
> Perfumes the more they are chaf'd the more they render
> Their pleasing scents, and so affliction
> Expresseth virtue, fully, whether true,
> Or else adulterate.   (*White Devil* I.i.45–50)

where *perfumes* is a noun, not the verb it might first seem, and we have to decide whether *affliction* or *virtue* can be true or else adulterate. Or this, which simply has too many images all at once:

> Thou art a box of worm seed, at best, but a salvatory of green mummy: what's this flesh? a little crudded milk, fantastical puff-paste: our bodies are weaker than those paper prisons boys use to keep flies in: more contemptible; since ours is to preserve earth-worms: didst thou ever see a lark in a cage? such is the soul in the body: this world is like her little tuft of grass, and the heaven o'er our heads, like her

looking-glass, only gives us a miserable knowledge of the small
compass of our prison. (*Malfi* IV.ii.124–32)

More memorable are the single dramatic images, although once
again the choice of objects for comparison is unusual: 'I am i' th' way
to study a long silence'; 'I have caught / An everlasting cold. I have
lost my voice / Most irrecoverably'; 'We are merely the stars' tennis-
balls'.

Whether the imagery and its syntax are meant to indicate the
turbulence and the bizarre nature of Italian society (it is noticeable
that the Duchess of Malfi herself, uncontaminated by the corruption
all around her, speaks much more simply) or whether they merely
reflect Webster's notebook manner of composition,[21] his is a distinctive style, at the linguistic limits of Jacobean tragedy. Shakespeare's
later images sometimes have the striking realism of Jonson's and
something of the unusual nature of Webster's. Their increasingly
concentrated expression achieved much greater dramatic import than
the expanded images of the early plays, although they hardly ever
became as impenetrable as some of Webster's. In his syntax generally, Shakespeare learned to reserve pronounced rhetorical expression
for set speeches or special effects of characterisation. Most of his
characters appear, for most of the time, to be 'talking naturally',
although, once again, typical features of colloquial language may be
exploited to show comedy on the one hand or extreme perturbation
on the other.

NOTES AND REFERENCES

1. Marlowe is quoted from *Complete Poems and Plays*, ed. E. D. Pendry,
   Dent (1976).
2. Burton (1968), pp. 52–3.
3. Buckingham in *Richard III* has something of the same cloying rhetoric;
   see Berry (1978), pp. 23–4.
4. Danson (1978), pp. 139–57.
5. A later example of pretended muddleheadedness is Pompey's attempt to
   obfuscate the case tried before Angelo and Escalus, *MM* II.i.117–24.
6. Chapman (1598) speaks of *swaggering* as a new word and it seems to
   appear first in the 1590s (OED). Shakespeare would then be amongst its
   earliest recorded users, and this, as well as her garrulity, may account
   for Quickly's repetition of a word she does not understand. Most of
   Shakespeare's uses are by soldiers or else by lower-class characters.
7. Everett, New Penguin, p. 13; Hunter (1959), p. lvii.

8. Philaster, Beaumont and Fletcher, *Dramatic Works*, ed. F. Bowers, Cambridge University Press (1966), I.
9. Wall (1971), pp. 263–4.
10. I am indebted to three articles: Thorne (1971), Smith (1968) and Neely (1975).
11. Cf. *3 Hen VI*, I.iv.40–3, II.I.129–31, II.ii.11–18. For some similar remarks, including a good example from *Titus Andronicus*, see Hibbard (1971). Two examples of the extended image in *The Spanish Tragedy* are II.i.3–7 and II.ii.7–17.
12. Compare *2 Hen VI* II.iv.53–7, III.i.31–3, III.ii.254–69 and *MV* II.vi.14–19 (with the repetition of both *How like the prodigal* and *the strumpet wind*).
13. Burton (1968), p. 206.
14. Doran (1976), pp. 221–33.
15. *The Yale Edition of The Works of Samuel Johnson*, ed. A. Sherbo, Yale University Press, New Haven and London (1968), VIII, p. 54.
16. Holmes (1929), p. 38.
17. Hibbard (1981), p. 29.
18. Watkins (1950), p. 279. Two further examples are *AC* I.v.10–12 (thoughts as seeds carried by the wind) and III.xiii.65 (rats leaving a sinking ship).
19. Jonson's three chief comedies are conveniently available in the Penguin edition by M. Jamieson, Harmondsworth (1966), from which I quote both here and in Ch. 7.
20. Webster is quoted from *John Webster, Three Plays*, ed. D. C. Gunby, Harmondsworth (1972).
21. Brown (1960), p. xlviii; Mulryne (1960); Kernan (1975), p. 395. Further examples are *White Devil* III.ii.5–7, V.i.159–61; *Malfi* III.iii.58–9.

CHAPTER SIX
Some uses of grammar

We can read Shakespeare much more easily than Chaucer. For that obvious reason I need spend comparatively little time on grammatical matters. However, despite the great simplification in morphology (the shapes of words, including inflexions) between Chaucer and Shakespeare, Shakespeare's grammar and syntax are not yet completely our own. Anyone who wishes to investigate the less important differences – of importance, that is, to the philologist but less so to the literary critic – may find them illustrated in three books whose approach is usually very different from mine: G. L. Brook, *The Language of Shakespeare* (1976), C. Barber, *Early Modern English* (1976), and E. A. Adams, *A Shakespearean Grammar* (published in 1870 and still useful). Nor shall I delay over certain differences which I suspect afford little difficulty to the reader and even less to the theatre-goer. We no longer, with the eighteenth century, wish to correct Shakespeare, and so his double comparisons, double superlatives and multiple negatives do not bother us:

Nor that I am *more better*

Than Prospero, master of a full poor cell.   (*Temp* I.ii.19–20)

This was the *most unkindest* cut of all.   (*JC* III.ii.184)

Nor I know *not*

Where I did lodge last night.   (*KL* IV.vii.67–8)

Nor, really, do the occasional strange-looking forms of the past tense or past participle of strong verbs (those verbs which indicate the change from present to past by a change in the stem vowel, e.g.

sing/sang, drive/drove). Present English has one vowel only throughout the past tense of these verbs and usually (though not always)
another vowel for the past participle (*drove/driven, drank/drunk*). Old
English mostly alternated two vowels within the past tense and had a
third for the past participle. Things had begun to settle down in
Middle English, but even in Shakespeare's time the forms were not
always those we have today:

> I *drave* my suitor from his mad humour of love.   (*AYLI* III.ii.399)

> Even now he *sung*.   (*KJ* V.vii.12)

> Thou hast perpendicularly *fell*.   (*KL* IV.vi.54)

It is fair to add that some of these are alternatives to the 'modern'
form. Even as late as the eighteenth century, the original title of
Gray's poem was 'Elegy *Wrote* in a Country Churchyard'.

Two other points of grammar are also unlikely to make us pause
for long. By Shakespeare's time *who, which* and *that* were all in use as
relative pronouns (Chaucer uses *whose* and *whom* as relatives, but not
who). However, all three could still be used with personal antecedents:

> I am married to a wife
> *Which* is as dear to me as life itself.   (*MV* IV.i.279–80)

> Nor do I think the man of safe discretion
> *That* does affect it.   (*MM* I.i.71–2)

Most older and middle-aged people still pray 'Our father *which* art in
heaven' in the form of the 1662 Book of Common Prayer. Barber
(1976: 218–19) suggests that *who* and *which* became more characteristic of a formal style and *that* of colloquial, informal contexts. In Elizabethan English *which* can also have a resumptive function when it
begins a phrase or clause and refers back to all the items of a preceding catalogue:

> For there, they say, he daily doth frequent
> With unrestrained loose companions,
> Even such, they say, as stand in narrow lanes
> And beat our watch, and rob our passengers,
> *Which* he – young wanton, and effeminate boy –
> Takes on the point of honour to support
> So dissolute a crew.   (*R II* V.iii.6–12)

The possessive *its* was a late arrival in English. It is first recorded in 1598, but it does not appear in the quartos of Shakespeare's plays. There are some ten instances in the 1623 First Folio, interestingly – though perhaps coincidentally – usually in the later plays. In Old English *his* was the neuter genitive ('of it') just as much as the masculine genitive, and this can still be found in Shakespeare:

How far that little candle throws *his* beams!   (*MV* V.i.90)

When yond same star that's westward from the pole
Had made *his* course t'illume that part of heaven.   (*Ham* I.i.36–7)

Shakespeare also uses *it* as a genitive form:

It [the Ghost] lifted up *it* head and did address
Itself to motion like as it would speak.   (*Ham* I.ii.216–17)

That nature which contemns *it* origin.   (*KL* IV.ii.32)

But since editors often normalise to *its*, most modern readers never become aware of the variation. There are, incidentally, no examples of *its* in the Authorised Version of 1611 and only three in Milton. The Authorised Version, too, will sometimes use *his* ('If the salt have lost his savour', 'Every creature after his kind') but more often will employ an alternative word ('The earth is the Lord's and the fulness *thereof*', 'four cubits the breadth *thereof* and three cubits the height *of it*'). By the time of Dryden, towards the end of the seventeenth century, *its* had become usual, although until c. 1800 it is frequently found with an apostrophe, *it's*.

But these usages give rise to little difficulty in practice. One or two others, however, are worth considering more carefully, since they may either give a mistaken impression of deliberately old-fashioned language or today's reader may miss a real grammatical distinction in Shakespeare simply because it is not one we have retained. The first might be the case with the Elizabethan use of *do* and the alternative forms – *eth* and –*s*. The second might apply to the difference in usage between *thou* and *you*.

Do has had a chequered history. From early times it has had the possible meaning of 'perform' ('We must *do* something about that.') or could be used as a substitute verb ('We ought to grow vegetables, like the neighbours *do* (grow vegetables).'). Shakespeare has examples of each of these. But the uses of *do* as an auxiliary verb have changed over the centuries. Nowadays we use the auxiliary *do* to ask questions or for emphasis ('*Do* you have a class at ten on Mondays?' 'Yes, I *do* have a Shakespeare class then.') or in negative constructions if no other auxiliary is present (compare 'I *did* not drive' and 'I *could* not drive'). Elizabethan English could use all these three, although they were not inevitable, as will be seen below. It had lost another, earlier, use of *do*, the Middle English causative, corresponding to *have* or *get* in present English ('I had my house painted', 'I got my car repaired').

In Elizabethan English, questions could be asked in two ways: by using *do*, as with most verbs in present English, or, a much older way, by simply inverting subject and verbs:

> Where *sups he? Doth* the old boar *feed* in the old frank?
>
> (*2 Hen IV* II.ii.139)

> Why *look you* so pale?
> Who *sent you* hither? Wherefore *do you come*?   (*R III* I.iv.173–4)

> What *did he* when thou sawest him? What *said he*? How *looked he*?
> Wherein *went he*? What *makes he* here? *Did he ask* for me?
>
> (*AYLI* III.ii.213–15)

Inversion is usual when the sentences begin with an interrogative (Rosalind's *What? How? Wherein?*), and of course this type of question is still used with a few modal verbs ('Why should he go?', 'When can he come?'). The eventual spread of *do* in questions was perhaps helped by its preservation of the usual word-order – subject, verb, object/complement – of English declarative sentences. 'Did he ask for me?' simply precedes this by an auxiliary verb: aux SVO/C. Negatives without *do* are similarly common in Shakespeare:

> Indeed I think the young King loves you not.   (*2 Hen IV* V.ii.9)

but almost half of his negative sentences were already using *do* with a word-order exactly that of present English:

> I know your lady does not love her husband.   (*KL* IV.v.23)

But Shakespeare had one further use for *do* which we have since lost. *Do* (present) and *did* (past) were employed as 'dummy' auxiliaries, semantically empty, merely signalling tense but not altering the meaning of the main verb. 'I do love him' means the same with or without the *do*; 'I did love him' equals 'I loved him', and any extra emphasis is simply because the main verb may be postponed a little. For example:

Which of you shall we say *doth love* us most,
That we our largest bounty may extend
Where nature *doth* with merit *challenge*.   *(KL* I.i.51–3)

                in which our valiant Hamlet –
For so this side of our known world esteemed him –
Did slay this Fortinbras; who, by a sealed compact
Well ratified by law and heraldry,
Did forfeit, with his life, all those his lands.   *(Ham* I.i.84–8)

This usage seems to have arisen in the later Middle English period, and at first it is found especially in poetry (where it has the advantage of providing an extra syllable if needed) although by Shakespeare's time it was fully accepted in prose as well. It seems to have been losing ground by the mid seventeenth century, and at that stage the emphatic *do* begins to appear more often, as does the negative use. There seems to have been a limit on the number of uses of *do* at any one time, and the limit is obviously imposed by ambiguity. The 'dummy' *do*, however, brought occasional extra benefits. It could act as an additional tense marker in long and complex Elizabethan sentences.[1] It could assist the assimilation into English of new Latin borrowings; *illuminateth*, for instance, would sound clumsy. It could remedy ambiguities: *eat* and *ate* sound alike in sixteenth-century pronunciation, so the Authorised Version uses *did eat*, not *ate* (at least in the gospels).

In the years just before Shakespeare, *–eth* and *–s*, as endings for the third person singular of the present indicative, were apparently genuine alternatives. So they often are for Shakespeare himself:

Raz*eth* your cities, and subvert*s* your towns   *(1 Hen VI* II.iii.64)

or the well-known lines from *The Merchant of Venice*:

The quality of mercy is not strained,
It dropp*eth* as the gentle rain from heaven
Upon the place beneath. It is twice blest,
It bless*eth* him that give*s* and him that take*s*.   (IV.i.181–4)

As with the *do*-periphrasis, prosody may have played its part: *subverts* has two syllables, *subverteth* three. In Middle English, *–s* had been a feature of Northern, or at least North Midland, dialect; Chaucer, writing in London, had used – *eth*. But *–s* was spreading south in the later fifteenth century, and by the sixteenth century is part of London

English; at first it may have been regarded as colloquial and informal. –s is more common in prose than in verse, and its eventual pre-
dominance in prose may have had the effect of making *eth* sound formal and even a little old-fashioned. Yet the latter continued as a
possible form, especially when there was nothing to be gained metri-
cally by using –s (*useth, teacheth, judgeth*, but *loves* rather than *loveth*).
It has been calculated that, in Fl, there are almost four times as many
–*eth* as –*es* endings in plays composed before 1600: afterwards –*es*
outnumbers *eth* by about six to one.[2] *Hath* and *doth*, though, are always much more common than *has* and *does*, and in these cases there
may have been very little difference in pronunciation.

In the case of the 'dummy' *do* and the –*eth* inflexion, it would
appear that both were possible forms for Shakespeare but that they
may have suggested a rather dignified, slightly old-fashioned use.[3] It
is difficult to be sure of shifts of tone within the small change of language and over a comparatively short period, but it seems permissi-
ble to use these two forms as corroborative evidence when I later try
to distinguish certain formal styles.

We might well miss subtleties in Shakespeare's use of the second
person unless alerted to the possibilities. If we go right back to the
early Middle English period, there are four unambiguous forms: *thou*
(nominative singular), *thee* (accusative singular), *ye* (nominative plural) and *you* (accusative plural). Nowadays, if we exclude religious
language as a special register, we have only the single form *you*. Two
factors have combined to produce this state of affairs, one grammatical and one social. The social one seems to have become operative
first. From about the mid thirteenth century, and perhaps (like much
else in Middle English) influenced by French practice, *ye* and *you*, as
well as continuing for the plural, began to be used as a mark of re-
spect in the *singular* when addressing a person regarded as one's superior. As this use of the 'polite' singular *ye/you* spread to include
equals as well as superiors, so, by contrast, *thou* and *thee* were increasingly employed to inferiors – a master talking to his apprentice,
say, or an older man to a very much younger one. It could also be
deliberately insulting; Sir Toby teaches Sir Andrew how to pick a
quarrel:

> Taunt him with the licence of ink. If thou 'thou' –est him some thrice it
> shall not be amiss. (*TN* III.ii.42–3)

Thou/thee could also indicate familiarity, from parent to child or between close friends. If it is asked how two almost opposite atti-

tudes – insult and affection – could co-exist, the answer would seem to be that they would never occur within the same context. More and more, *thou* or *thee* was becoming a marked (unexpected) form, used in implied contrast to an unmarked (usual, expected) form, *ye* or *you*.

This, remember, was a social phenomenon. The original grammatical distinction between subject and objective forms continued longer, although increasingly *you* was used 'wrongly' for the subject. The Authorised Version, with its conservative, religious language, continues to distinguish them ('*Ye* have not chosen me but I have chosen *you*.'; '*Ye* in me and I in *you*.') but Shakespeare is not so precise. Take Prospero's 'farewell' speech in *The Tempest* (V.i). It begins gramatically enough: '*Ye* elves of hills . . .', but within four lines we have '*you* demi-puppets . . . and *you* whose pastime is . . .'. In fact, during the seventeenth century, *you* became the regular form for both nominative and accusative and both singular and plural, although *you was* (singular) and *you were* (plural) are sometimes found as late as the eighteenth century.

So, for our study of Shakespeare's style, the social distinction between *thou* and *you* is the more important. An amusing example from Deloney's *Jack of Newbury* (? 1597) shows the same usage in another writer. The hero is married twice; wife A has formerly been his employer and wife B his servant. After marriage he keeps on using *you* to A, but with B he uses both *thou* and *you*. Old habits died hard. It is easy enough to find examples from Shakespeare. In *1 Henry IV* III.ii, King Henry upbraids Hal for his wild life. He speaks more in sorrow than in anger, and so uses *thou* to his son; the Prince calls his father *you*. The same happens in the long conversation between them in *2 Henry IV* IV.v, where the dying king believes Hal cannot wait to get his hands upon the crown. Here Hal's *you* is not only respectful but a sign of remorse at having offended his dying father. When Hotspur is about to ride off to the wars (*1 Hen IV*, II.iii), his wife Kate enters:

> Hotspur How now Kate? I must leave *you* within these two hours.
> Kate   O my good lord, why are *you* thus alone?

But after the opening unmarked *you* (aristocrats, anyway, normally use *you*), Kate switches to *thou* for the rest of the speech:

> Tell me, sweet lord, what is it that takes from *thee*
> *Thy* stomach, pleasure, and *thy* golden sleep?   (42–3)

But when Hotspur seems unappreciative of this wifely concern, and, worse, appears not to be listening, she switches back to *you* (76).

Hotspur responds with an affectionate *thou* or two, but Kate is not convinced:

> Do *you* not love me? Do *you* not indeed? (99)

Hotspur continues to tease her, but when war threatens wives must be kept in their place:

> Come, wilt *thou* see me ride?
> And when I am a-horseback, I will swear
> I love *thee* infinitely. But hark *you*, Kate
> I must not have *you* henceforth question me
> Whither I go, nor reason whereabout. (103–7)[4]

A single switch of pronoun can indicate social class:

> *Falstaff* Dost *thou* hear, hostess?
> *Hostess* Pray *ye*, pacify yourself, Sir John. (*2 Hen IV* II.iv.77–8)

Disreputable he may be, but he is still a knight. Or a change from *you* to *thou* may show affection. Madeleine Doran notes that Antony uses *thou* of Caesar for the first time in his funeral oration.[5] Claudius calls Hamlet *you*, except for the one occasion when he is despatching him to England – he can afford to be expansive then. Hamlet calls Claudius *you* also, not only as subject to monarch but because there is so little love lost between them. He calls Horatio *thou* (his only friend in Denmark?) but Horatio uses *you* to his prince. The Ghost and Hamlet *thou* each other – perhaps to emphasise the affection between father and son as distinct from the cold formality between uncle and nephew – but on the occasion of the Ghost's brief second visit in III.iv, while he continues with *thou*, Hamlet once uses *you*, possibly conscious of his almost blunted purpose. Hamlet and Laertes hurl *thou's* at each other in the insults of the fight in Ophelia's grave ('I'll rant as well as *thou.*'), but in his dying speech Laertes affectionately uses *thou* to Hamlet. Polonius, Laertes and Ophelia *you* each other (a not very united or affectionate family?) except at I.iii. 57–81, Polonius's farewell to Laertes leaving for France.

It may be objected that some of the inferences I have drawn go too far, and I suspect that the *thou/you* dichotomy is not so clear-cut as some critics have argued. Consider the scene between Gertrude and Hamlet in her bedroom. He has always called her *you*, but she has varied between *thou* and *you* according to whether she wants to cajole him or is beginning to lose patience with him. So at III.vi.10:

Hamlet, *thou* hast *thy* father much offended.

Thy father is, to her, Claudius. How nice it would be if they could all settle down and live happily ever after. Hamlet will have none of this. His immediate reply is:

Mother, *you* have my father much offended.

Everyone gets the antithesis: *thy father* (Claudius), *my father* (old Hamlet). But Shakespeare underlines it by the switch from the affection of *thou* to the formality of *you*. I doubt, on the other hand, whether the *thou* and *you* would, by themselves, have been sufficient to signal the change of tone.[6] So while there are several fairly clear indications that the distinction could be useful to Shakespeare, we must remember that one *thou* does not constitute a glorious summer or a single *you* a winter of discontent. Nevertheless, the English language is now the poorer:

You are a secret *thou*.
Fumbling amongst the devalued currency
Of 'dear' and 'darling' and 'my love'
I do not dare to employ it –

Not even in a poem, not even
If I were a Quaker, any more.
Beginning as an honorific, the unaffectionate *you*,
For English speakers, has put *thou* out of business.

So, in our intimate moments,
We are dumb, in a castle of reserve.

And He alone
From Whom no secrets are hid, to Whom
All hearts be open,
Can be a public *Thou*.[7]

One of Shakespeare's most exciting linguistic usages lies on the borderline between vocabulary and grammar. This is the phenomenon called either conversion or functional shift, using one part of speech as if it were another. We still do it, of course: a *key* man (noun as adjective); to *down* tools (adverb as verb); it's a *must* (auxiliary verb as noun). But it is exciting in Shakespeare because of its comparative newness. This plasticity of language would not have been easily possible before. In the heavily-inflected Old English, a noun is a noun because it has a noun-like ending. Even in Middle English, where the inflections have often decayed or even disappeared entirely, there is not much evidence of functional change.[8] But by the Renaissance, parts of speech were often not distinguished at all by grammatical inflection. Here, surely, is Shakespeare exploiting the linguistic situation of his age. It is noteworthy that his contemporaries show fewer and individually less remarkable examples of the process than he does. Conversion seems to work through the listener's shock when he finds the word used in an unfamiliar manner. His attention is thus concentrated on that word for a moment, and this is exactly what Shakespeare wants, for his best examples are not only grammatically novel but metaphorical too. 'I'll *mountebank* their loves', says Coriolanus, as he finally agrees to hide his true feelings and apologise to the plebs (III.ii.132). Fabian (*Twelfth Night* III.ii.18) tells poor Sir Andrew that Olivia is showing favour to Cesario only 'to awake your *dormouse* valour' (which in Sir Andrew's case is very small and anyway asleep). The populace, almost always fickle in Shakespeare, 'Goes to and back, *lackeying* the varying tide' (*Antony and Cleopatra* I.iv.46).[9] The two best examples are, I think, first Lear's description of Goneril and Regan as 'those *pelican* daughters' (III.iv.72). The mother pelican will allow its young to peck its breast when desperate for food, but this sacrifice is the parent's own doing. With Lear, his daughters are deliberately tearing him to death. The other example is of Cleopatra's vivid premonition of defeat followed by something akin to the Roman triumph in which

> Antony
> Shall be brought drunken forth, and I shall see
> Some squeaking Cleopatra *boy* my greatness
> I' th' posture of a whore.   (V.ii.218–21)

One can only marvel that there was a boy actor capable of playing Cleopatra, indeed of speaking these very lines. In fact Shakespeare occasionally goes beyond simple functional shift and the conversion becomes part of a new compound:

> Come you spirits
> That tend on mortal thoughts, *unsex* me here.   (*Mac* I.v.38)

> Wine loved I deeply, dice dearly, and in woman *out-paramoured* the Turk.   (*KL* III.iv.87)

> Though in this city he
> Hath widowed and *unchilded* many a one.   (*Cor* V.vi.152)[10]

> If his occulted guilt
> Do not itself *unkennel* in one speech,
> It is a damned ghost that we have seen.   (*Ham* III.ii.90)

The prefix *un-* was a favourite with Shakespeare. It is pointless to speculate why, unless it was that it helped to break the bonds of convention to show heroes (and villains) hitherto capable of being imagined but hardly satisfactorily created through the dramatist's language. Just as conversion breaks through the fetters of Elizabethan grammar.

NOTES AND REFERENCES

1. Samuels (1965). See also Samuels (1972), pp. 173–6.
2. Taylor (1976).
3. Cusack (1970).
4. Rees (1978), p. 109, contrasts the language of *Julius Caesar* II.i., another scene in which a wife complains that her husband is keeping something important from her.
5. Doran (1976), p.132. For a further example, see McIntosh (1963). Mulholland (1967) is more cautious.
6. The apparent similarity at I.ii.118 ('Let not *thy* mother lose her prayers, Hamlet') is not in fact a parallel. This is a court scene not a private conversation, and Hamlet's reply ('I shall in all my best obey *you*, madam.') keeps courtly etiquette.
7. John Heath-Stubbs, *Selected Poems* (1965), OUP, p.103. I owe this reference to the kindness of Professor S. B. Greenfield.
8. Some remarks on conversion in Chaucer are included in Donner (1978).
9. Other notable examples of conversion are: 'He *childed* as I *fathered*' (*KL* III.vi.108); *womaned* (*Oth* III.iv.191); *maggot* (*LLL* V.ii.410); *candy* (*1 Hen IV*, I.iii.247); *discandy* (*AC* IV.xii.22) and *discandying* (*AC* III.xiii.165); *pageants* (*TC* I.iii.151); *cormorant* (*TC* II.ii.6 and *Cor* I.i.119); *bower* (*RJ* III.ii.81); *sharked up* (*Ham* I.i.98); *prank* (*Cor* III.i.23); *Vinegar* (*MV* I.i.54); *furnaces* (*Cym* I.vi.66). But any moderately careful reader can compile his own list.
10. Wales (1978) notes that the *–ed* suffix may be either adjectival and (usually) stative or participial and dynamic; she compares *KL* III.iv.31 where *windowed* is adjectival with *AC* IV.xiv.72 where it is participial.

CHAPTER SEVEN
Register and style

The reader who has borne with me thus far will realise that the techniques of lexical and syntactical and rhetorical expansion, illustrated in the early chapters, are far from being innovations by Shakespeare. He produced better examples than his contemporaries, usually tailored to his context in a way that theirs were often not. He learnt a good deal about his art from the writing (and reading) of narrative and occasional poetry. What we are evidently concerned with is a number of group styles available to Elizabethan dramatists from the 1590s onwards and eventually developed by Shakespeare to an extent his contemporaries were either incapable of imagining or incapable of expressing. We are far from reality if we imagine Shakespeare scratching his head with the end of a quill pen waiting for the appropriate language to come. For one thing the hunger of the Elizabethan audience for new plays would make this picture unlikely. The second part of this book will attempt to show Shakespeare exploiting some of these accepted styles in his middle and later career. The styles I try to characterise are far from being the only ones, but they are among the most important and their description may help to sharpen the reader's or theatre-goer's awareness of what was increasingly taken for granted by the more experienced and sophisticated members of the Elizabethan audience. *Hieronimo* and *Andronicus* became shorthand terms for the flamboyance and exaggeration of one sort of tragic style and acting. In Beaumont's *Knight of the Burning Pestle* (produced 1607) the Citizen and his wife keep up a running commentary on the action, constantly intervene, and once or twice change the course of the play. Thereby they reveal not only their social pretensions but their almost complete lack of literary sophistication: they simply want a re-run of their favourite scenes from pre-

vious plays. Yet the same play burlesques different types of Elizabethan literature and therefore their appropriate styles. A barber is
described like a giant from romance and is challenged and beaten by
a 'knight' who is a grocer's apprentice; another apprentice disguises
himself as his own ghost.

I have been talking about Elizabethan 'styles', but style is predominantly something we recognise on the page. Where it reflects a
type of language according to use, depending less on the speaker
than on the occasion, a better word might be *register*. This is a comprehensive term for a number of features of both vocabulary and
syntax commonly associated with particular subjects or events, so
easily recognised that we speak confidently of a legal register, say, or
a military register, or a religious register, the kind of language we
expect from people and situations 'like that'. If we turn from life to
literature, certain genres (epic, pastoral) bring an expectation of certain kinds of writing, since literary language has already consciously
selected from normal usage, so that here register and style overlap.
Idiolects reflect the character of the speaker by representing his own
distinctive selection of language features. But there is perhaps rather
less of this individuality in Shakespeare than is sometimes supposed.
In the final chapter of his book *The Language of Shakespeare*, G. L.
Brook discusses the idiolects of Gower (in *Pericles*), the Host of the
Garter (*Merry Wives of Windsor*), Armado, Mistress Quickly, Pistol
and Falstaff.[1] Opinions will naturally differ about what is distinctive,
but while I shall later try to illustrate something of the language of
the Host and of Pistol, I would exclude Gower and Armado from
the list. The choruses spoken by Gower contain several archaisms
from Middle English but nothing especially characteristic of the style
of Gower himself. The intention is presumably to create an atmosphere of far away and long ago thought suitable for romance (Gower
had told this story too), but eventually octosyllabics give way to
blank verse so that a line like 'That even her art sisters the natural
roses' (Chorus V.7) is thoroughly Renaissance in content, metre and
expression. The Quarto of *Love's Labour's Lost* refers sometimes to
Armàdo but sometimes to 'Braggart', suggesting something of a
stock figure whose linguistic usages are largely exaggerations of a
style fairly easily paralleled elsewhere. Quickly and Falstaff are de-
batable cases. The former is an extreme example, in one person, of
the malapropisms, mispronunciations and repetitive syntax characteristic of other lower-class comic characters: possibly the accumulation of all these does indeed constitute an idiolect. Falstaff's *use* of
elaborate syntactical structures to avoid accepting responsibility for

his previous actions and of certain lexical features (such as the outrageous compounds normally used for insults but in his case also as
terms of affection to Hal) again seems to be sufficiently distinctive.

The most subtle exponent of registers in drama is, perhaps, not
Shakespeare but Jonson. What really interested him was the connection between language and manners. His is not the world of *Love's
Labour's Lost* but the language of 'real life' Elizabethan London:
'deeds and language *such as men do use*' or, in the Prologue to *Bartholomew Fair*:

> Your Majesty is welcome to a Fair;
> Such place, such men, *such language* and such ware,
> You must expect.

Plays like *Bartholomew Fair* or *The Alchemist* demand not one but a
number of specialised dictions: alchemy, fencing, the military profession, the canting terms used earlier by Greene's thieves and vagabonds (*doxy, foist, shark, firk* and others occur in *The Alchemist*) – in
fact, several questionable ways of making a living ('the grammar and
logic / And rhetoric of quarrelling', *Alchemist* IV.ii.64 for example). In
Jonson, the jargon is most often spoken by the knaves who are
opportunist enough to use it to persuade and cheat the fools who
seem pathetically eager to imitate these cult languages.[2]

The various Jonsonian registers are not simply employed to create
an air of verisimilitude. The technical terms of alchemy itself ('What
a brave language here is! next to canting', exclaims Surly) is naturally found throughout the play, but Subtle and Face, in the opening
scene, actually quarrel in alchemical terms, while Dol vainly tries to
keep the peace:

> Raised thee from brooms and dust and wat'ring-pots?
> Sublimed thee and exalted thee, and fixed thee
> I' the third region, called our state of grace?
> Wrought thee to spirit, to quintessence, with pains
> Would twice have won me the Philosopher's Work?
>
> (*Alch* I.i.67–71)

Later Subtle and Face engage in a sort of alchemical catechism to deceive Ananias (II.ii). The simple-minded Ananias believes alchemy is
inappropriate to puritanism, that the means are not justified by the
ends, so his superior, Tribulation Wholesome, needs to use the technical puritan vocabulary to persuade him:

> Whenas the work is done, the Stone is made,
> This heat of his may turn into a *zeal*,
> And stand up for the *beauteous discipline*

Against the *menstruous cloth and rag of Rome*.
We must await his *calling*, and the *coming*
Of the good spirit. You did fault, t' upbraid him
With the *Brethren's* blessing of Heidelberg, weighing
What need we have to hasten on *the work*,
For the restoring of the *silenced Saints*,
Which ne'er will be but by the Philosopher's Stone.   (III.i.30–9)

The hypocrisy of the Puritans is revealed in another play when Zeal-of-the-Land Busy 'proves' that the eating of pig may indeed be made acceptable, even in the tents of Bartholomew Fair:

> Surely it may be otherwise, but it is subject to construction – subject, and
> hath a face of offence with the weak, a great face, a foul face, but that face
> may have a veil put over it, and be shadowed, as it were, it may be eaten,
> and in the Fair, I take it, in a booth, the tents of the wicked. The place is
> not much, not very much; we may be religious in midst of the profane,
> so it be eaten with a reformed mouth, with sobriety, and humbleness; not
> gorged in with gluttony or greediness; there's the fear: for, should she go
> there, as taking pride in the place, or delight in the unclean dressing to
> feed the vanity of the eye or the lust of the palate, it were not well, it
> were not fit, it were abominable, and not good.   (I.vi.67–78)

Here the satire is not merely a matter of appropriate diction (*the weak, the tents of the wicked, sobriety, and humbleness, the vanity of the eye or the lust of the palate*); the syntax is deliberately repetitive and the dogmatism is that of the jack-in-office ('He was a baker, sir, but he does dream now, and see visions: he has given over his trade.'). Again, in Busy's opinion, 'it were a sin of obstinacy, great obstinacy, high and horrible obstinacy' not to follow the delicious aroma of roasting pork (III.ii.76). The opposite style, abrupt, often disconnected speech, extreme Senecanism, is fitting for angry characters, such as Kastril or Wasp.

Shakespeare did not examine the seamier side of Elizabethan London, except, to some extent, in the Eastcheap scenes of *Henry IV*. Nor does he write more obviously 'city' comedies, in the manner of Dekker's *Shoemaker's Holiday* (1599 – 'A Pleasant Comedy of the Gentle Craft') or *Eastward Ho!* (1605), a collaborative work by Jonson, Chapman and Marston, with a good deal of obviously colloquial and proverbial language, a firm sense of its London riverside setting, several joking references to previous plays (including some of Pistol's lines) and a sustained alchemical metaphor in the characters Touchstone, Quicksilver and Golding. All this was presumably meant to appeal to the more literate private theatre audience. *The*

The literary language of Shakespeare

Merry Wives of Windsor (? 1600) is not city comedy in this sense; it is set in a country town and much of its imagery is correspondingly domestic and 'natural'. Its interests are, however, wider than this: the discomfiture of Falstaff, Quickly's malapropisms, Evans and Caius who 'make fritters of English', and the sheer normality of Brook and Page and their wives.

The swaggering bully Pistol wanders in and out of *2 Henry IV, Henry V* and *The Merry Wives of Windsor*, his mind crammed with half-remembered or misremembered scraps of old plays, his manner that of the braggart and coward who will turn to any kind of cheating or trickery that seems to promise easy pickings, his language spattered with contractions, inversions and outdated usage. The general impression is clear. But how is it achieved? How much is colloquial, obsolescent or even meant to be easily intelligible? This is a question difficult to answer precisely, since it would involve re-creating the whole linguistic climate of the Elizabethan age to an extent that may be beyond us now. Through the pamphlets of Greene, we can recapture a good deal of the coney-catching background and some of the argot. The Boy in *Henry V* says Pistol *breaks words, and keeps whole weapons* (III.ii.35) and calls him *this roaring devil i' th' old play* (IV.iv.69). His very name is appropriate, for a pistol was still at the experimental stage, erratic and apt not to go off at all, but if it did, to cause a notable explosion and almost as likely to injure its owner as his enemy. A stage direction in *The Atheist's Tragedy* makes Borachio's pistol give *false fire*. Or, as Jorgensen says[3], the name might alternatively derive from Italian *pistolfo* which Florio's dictionary of 1611 defines as 'a rousing beggar, a cantler, an upright man that liveth by cosenage'. But this brings us into the somewhat murky areas of colloquial language and semantic change, for why should an *upright* man live by cosenage? The second chapter of Thomas Harman's *A Caveat for Common Cursitors* enlightens us:

> An upright man, the second in sect of this unseemly sort, must be next placed, of these ranging rabblement of rascals; some be servingmen, artificers, and labouring men traded up in husbandry. These, not minding to get their living with the sweat of their face, but casting off all pain, will wander, after their wicked manner, through the most shires of this realm. These upright men will seldom or never want; for what is gotten by any mort, or doxy, if it please him, he doth command the same . . . Here you see that the upright man is of great authority. For all sorts of beggars are obedient to his hests, and [he] surmounteth all others in pilfering and stealing.[4]

So an upright man is not 'upright' at all, in our sense of the word, but aggressive and domineering.

130

Near the beginning of *The Merry Wives of Windsor*, Slender calls
Bardolph, Nym and Pistol *coney-catching rascals*. Even Falstaff sees
himself coney-catching as a last desperate remedy:

> There is no remedy. I must cony-catch, I must shift.   (I.iii.32)

> I myself sometimes, leaving the fear of God on the left hand and hiding
> mine honour in my necessity, am fain to shuffle, to hedge, and to lurch.
> (II.ii.23–6)

Although *shuffle, hedge* and *lurch* are part of the coney-catchers' vocabulary (all three meaning 'cheat' or 'steal'), Shakespeare does not use
very much of this special register, canting language, as it came to be
called. The audience, however, is obviously familiar with this type
of ragged, cheating scoundrel, for Autolycus in *The Winter's Tale* is
another example. These 'sturdy beggars' seem to have been recruited
from ex-soldiers, such as Pistol himself, who laments at the end of
Henry V:

> Old I do wax, and from my weary limbs
> Honour is cudgelled. Well, bawd I'll turn,
> And something lean to cutpurse of quick hand.
> To England will I steal, and there I'll – steal;
> And patches will I get unto these cudgelled scars,
> And swear I got them in the Gallia wars.   (V.i.80–5)

or discharged serving-men, or tenants evicted as a result of the
change from arable to sheep-farming which required fewer hands.
The elite of the coney-catchers (*coney* meant rabbit, but in this argot
'dupe') formed a fraternity with a strong element of 'professional'
training and a jargon of its own, partly to conceal from any eaves-
dropping worthy citizen the thievery intended, but partly also as a
status symbol. The best and most readable of the literature of coney-
catching is the collection of pamphlets (1591–2) by Robert Greene.
Greene's criminals hardly ever work alone; a con-man set-up involving three or four of them is quite common. The subject-matter is fascinating in itself: *The Second Part of Coney-Catching* covers horse-
stealing, cheating at bowls and at cards, the activities of the nip and
the foist (cutpurse and pickpocket), shoplifting and burglary (including casing the premises first.) Greene clearly enjoys his exposé, and
one imagines that his middle-class audience had the comforting feeling of knowing about the practice while remaining at a comfortable
distance from it (as with modern newspaper 'revelations' of, say, the
drug scene).[5] Stylistically, though, this is the literary exploitation of

one kind of colloquial vocabulary and speech rhythm not used
hitherto. This extract demonstrates not only Greene's journalistic,
coordinate style, full of *and's, but's, then's* and *for's* but also the clear
definition of the function of each of the villains:

> . . . and the whiles he begins to resolve which of them most fitly may be
> lifted, and what garbage (for so he calls the goods stolen) may be most
> easily conveyed, then he calls to the Mercer's man and says, 'Sirrah, reach
> me that piece of velvet or satin, or that jewel, chain or piece of plate', and
> whilst the fellow turns his back, he commits his garbage to the marker:
> for note, the lift is without his cloak, in his doublet and hose, to avoid the
> more suspicion. The marker, which is the receiver of the lift's luggage,
> gives a wink to the santar that walks before the window, and then the
> santar going by in great haste, the marker calls him and says, 'Sir, a word
> with you; I have a message to do unto you from a very friend of yours
> and the errand is of some importance'. 'Truly, sir', says the santar, 'I have
> very urgent business in hand, and as at this time I cannot stay'. 'But one
> word and no more', says the marker, and then he delivers him
> whatsoever the lift hath conveyed unto him, and then the santar goes his
> way, who never came within the shop and is a man unknown to them all.
> Suppose he is smoked and his lifting is looked into, then are they upon
> their pantofles, because there is nothing found about them. They defy the
> world for their honesty, because they be as dishonest as any in the world,
> and swear as God shall judge them they never saw the parcel lost; but
> oaths with them are like wind out of a bellows, which being cool kindleth
> fire. So their vows are without conscience, and so they call for revenge.[6]

Smoked is 'discovered' (smoked out) and *upon their pantofles* means
'on their dignity'; pantofles were exotic, high-heeled slippers (as it
happens Shakespeare does not use the word, preferring *chopines*). All
the rest of the technical language is explained within the passage, and
to punctuate the extract for Modern English, adding inverted com-
mas for example, destroys much of Greene's breathless manner.

Coney-catchers had made their appearance in drama a few years
before Pistol and his cronies. In *Arden of Feversham* (published 1592)[7]
Black Will and Shakebag are coney-catchers but they do not use the
argot. They do begin by speaking prose, but at iii.83, and for no
apparent reason, move into verse. Occasionally they display something of the braggadocio that was to become the fustian style of Pistol and is already suspect:

> And therefore thus: I am the very man,
> Marked in my birth-hour by the destinies,
> To give an end to Arden's life on earth;
> Thou but a member but to whet the knife
> Whose edge must search the closet of his breast.   (iii.153–7)

Black night hath hid the pleasures of the day,
And sheeting darkness overhangs the earth,
And with the black fold of her cloudy robe
Obscures us from the eyesight of the world,
In which sweet silence such as we triumph.
The lazy minutes linger on their time,
As loath to give due audit to the hour,
Till in the watch our purpose be complete,
And Arden sent to everlasting night.   (v.1–9)

But Arden will be safe: no one who spends time talking like that is going to be capable of giving a mortal wound, however dark the night and however sharp the weapon. Pistol, while just as much a coward, is far more flamboyant and far less poetical.

Towards the close of 2 *Henry IV*, he arrives in Gloucestershire with news from court

Pistol	Sweet knight, thou art now one of the greatest men in this realm.
Silence	By'r lady, I think 'a be, but goodman Puff of Barson.
Pistol	Puff?
	Puff i'thy teeth, most recreant coward base!
	Sir John, I am thy Pistol and thy friend,
	And helter-skelter have I rode to thee,
	And tidings do I bring, and lucky joys,
	And golden times, and happy news of price.
Falstaff	I pray thee now, deliver them like a man of this world.
Pistol	A foutre for the world and wordlings base!
	I speak of Africa and golden joys.
Falstaff	O base Assyrian knight, what is thy news?
	Let King Cophetua know the truth thereof.
Silence	And Robin Hood, Scarlet, and John.
Pistol	Shall dunghill curs confront the Helicons?
	And shall good news be baffled?
	Then, Pistol, lay thy head in Furies' lap. (V.iii.87–106)

When Silence cannot understand the significance of Falstaff's elevation, Pistol turns on him in his usual ranting style, composed of four parts aggression to every one of sense. *Recreant*, 'one who has yielded in battle', has the proper military ring which is made to sound even more impressive by the inversion in *coward base*. *Lucky joys/And golden times* is not in his usual vein, but the phrases are probably traditional collocations. A *foutre* is indecent and almost certainly accompanied by the appropriate gesture. Falstaff joins in with a parody of Pistol's style in which there is no real sense in the linking of *Assyrian knight* (the Elizabethans regarded Assyrians as brigands) and the old

133

ballad of King Cophetua and the beggar maid. Helicons and Furies are much more Pistol's stock-in-trade, and *baffled*, which seems odd, even for Pistol, was possibly a new word. Olivia's 'Alas, poor fool, how have they *baffled* thee' and Richard II's 'I am disgraced, impeached and *baffled* here' suggest that Pistol may mean 'confounded' and be wrongly applying the word to *news*.[8] Later news, however, is not so good:

> My knight, I will inflame thy noble liver,
> And make thee rage.
> Thy Doll, and Helen of thy noble thoughts,
> Is in base durance and contagious prison,
> Haled thither
> By most mechanical and dirty hand.
> Rouse up Revenge from ebon den with fell Alecto's snake,
> For Doll is in. Pistol speaks naught but truth.   (V.v. 31–9)

Base durance, contagious prison and *haled* are once again predictable phrases for him. Doll Tearsheet is scarcely a Helen; his later epithet ('the lazar kite of Cressid's kind', *Hen V*, II.i.73) is more appropriate. But Revenge might well come from some kind of *ebon den*; he emerges from the underworld in some contemporary tragedies ('Enter the Ghost of Andrea, and with him Revenge').[9] Alecto is one of the Furies who were indeed represented with snakes in their hair, and the last line is, surprisingly, straight information.

To penetrate the layers of Pistol's mind would need not a psychologist so much as an archaeologist, for phrases and characters from old plays are overlaid with scraps of colloquial Elizabethan English. It is possibly futile to try. Alliteration occasionally appears together with archaisms, not to mention *Couple a gorge*, one of the few French phrases he thinks he knows:

> *Pistol* An oath of mickle might, and fury shall abate.
>   Give me thy fist, thy forefoot to me give;
>   Thy spirits are most tall.
> *Nym*   I will cut thy throat one time or other, in fair terms, that is the
>   humour of it.
> *Pistol* *Couple a gorge!*
>   That is the word. I thee defy again!   (*Hen V* II.i.63–9)

He is inclined to invert not only adjective and noun but also verb and object (*thy forefoot to me give; I thee defy*). *Tall*, 'valiant' was still used of warriors, although less and less often as our sense, 'of great height' (not recorded before 1530) became established. Falstaff is, to Bardolph at least, *a tall gentlamen* (*2 Hen IV* III.ii.60). In the mechanicals' play in *A Midsummer Night's Dream*, Pyramus is *sweet youth and tall* (V.i.143). The Second Murderer of *Richard III* encourages his companion: 'Spoke like a *tall* man that respects thy reputation' (I.iv.154). The Clown in *The Winter's Tale* offers, four times over, to swear that Autolycus is a *tall fellow* (V.ii.160–9). But nobody – except Pistol – seems to speak of *tall spirits*. He cannot even announce himself without a departure from normal word-order: 'My name is Pistol called' (*Hen V* IV.i.62), and this too is probably old-fashioned usage. Elsewhere the grand gesture is what counts:

> Let floods o'erswell, and fiends for food howl on!   (*Hen V* II.i.89)

> Perpend my words, O Signieur Dew, and mark.
> O signieur Dew, thou diest on point of fox.   (*Hen V* IV.iv.8–9)

> Let gallows gape for dog; let man go free,
> And let not hemp his wind-pipe suffocate.   (*Hen V* III.vi.41–2)

Heroic-sounding phrases (whatever they may *mean*) jostle with the language of coney-catchers: *gourd and fullam* and *high and low* both refer to loaded dice:

> Let vultures gripe thy guts! For gourd and fullam holds,
> And high and low beguiles the rich and poor.   (*MWW* I.iii.85–6)

No doubt the audience's delight, if the editor's despair. With Pistol, Shakespeare goes far beyond the register of rogues and vagabonds and creates a genuine dramatic idiolect.

In Shakespeare's own day one of the best and most amusing examples of a deliberate clash of registers and styles is Dekker's *The Gull's Horn Book* (1609). A horn-book was originally a leaf of paper containing the alphabet, some basic spelling, the Lord's prayer, and so forth, protected by a thin plate of translucent horn. It is therefore an elementary book of instruction, a primer. A gull is a credulous person, someone easily imposed upon. Dekker gives directions on how the would-be gentleman setting up in London should behave throughout the day. It is at once a parody of contemporary courtesy books and a moral work showing the worthlessness of such a style of life by his exposé of it. The deliberate contrast between the middle style (with high style phrases) of the gull in his social aspiration of becoming a dandy and the low style reality of his vanity and penury is the source of Dekker's irony. In this passage the gull visits the middle aisle of St Paul's, a favourite meeting-place:

Now for your venturing into the Walk, be circumspect and wary what pillar you come in at and take heed in any case, as you love the reputation of your honour, that you avoid the Servingman's Log, and approach not within five fathom of that pillar but bend your course directly in the middle line, that the whole body of the church may appear to be yours. Where in view of all, you may publish your suit in what manner you affect most, either with the slide of your cloak from the one shoulder (and then you must, as 'twere in anger, suddenly snatch at the middle of the inside if it be taffeta at the least, and so by that means your costly lining is betrayed) or else by the pretty advantage of compliment. But one note by the way do I especially woo you to, the neglect of which makes many of our gallants cheap and ordinary: that by no means you be seen above four turns, but in the fifth make yourself away either in some of the sempsters' shops, the new tobacco office or amongst the booksellers where, if you cannot read, exercise your smoke and enquire who has writ against 'this divine weed', etc. For this withdrawing yourself a little will much benefit your suit, which else by too long walking would be stale to the whole spectators.

But howsoever, if Paul's jacks be once up with their elbows and quarrelling to strike eleven, as soon as ever the clock has parted them and ended the fray with his hammer, let not the Duke's Gallery contain you any longer, but pass away in open view. In which departure if by chance you either encounter or aloof off throw your inquisitive eye upon any knight or squire being your familiar, salute him not by his name of 'Sir Such-a-One' or so but call him 'Ned' or 'Jack', etc. : This will set off your estimation with great men. And if (though there be a dozen companies between you, 'tis the better) he call aloud to you (for that's most genteel) to know where he shall find you at two o'clock, tell him at such an ordinary or such (and be sure to name those that are dearest and whither none but your gallants resort). After dinner you may appear again, having translated yourself out of your English cloth cloak into a light Turkey grogram (if you have that happiness of shifting) and then be seen for a turn or two to correct your teeth with some quill or silver instrument and to cleanse your gums with a wrought handkerchief. It skills not whether you dined or no (that's best known to your stomach) or in what place you dined, though it were with cheese of your own mother's making in your chamber or study.[10]

The firm sense of place is evident: St Paul's Walk, the Servingman's Log (the bench where the servants gossiped), the new tobacco office, the booksellers, the ordinary (eating-house). The high, literary style of *venturing, circumspect, bend your course, pretty advantage of compliment*, the figures having *ended the fray* as the clock strikes, *aloof off throw your inquisitive eye* (with its reversal of normal word-order), *correct your teeth*, shows the gallant. The colloquialisms, such as *'twere, by the way, by no means, etc., or so*, and in particular the parentheses (*as 'twere in anger, for a turn or two, for that's most genteel, of your own mother's making*) which at times approach stage-directions, undercut this fashionable pose by showing that it is all play-acting. The mock-conversational style, with its use of *you* and its several imperatives, creates a close relationship with the reader, and the clothing puns (*publish your suit, your costly lining is betrayed, translated yourself, if you have that happiness of shifting*) reveal that these fine feathers conceal a very close-plucked bird.

The Gull's Horn Book achieves its double approach to the character of the would-be man-about-town by its regular and deliberate juxtaposition of different registers and styles. Shakespeare sometimes achieves the same effect in the Sonnets. Sonnet 46 is a case in point:

> Mine eye and heart are at a mortal war
> How to divide the conquest of thy sight;
> Mine eye my heart thy picture's sight would bar,
> My heart mine eye the freedom of that right.
> My heart doth plead that thou in him dost lie –
> A closet never pierced with crystal eyes;
> But the defendant doth that plea deny,
> And says in him thy fair appearance lies.
> To 'cide this title is impaneled
> A quest of thoughts, all tenants to the heart;
> And by their verdict is determined
> The clear eye's moiety, and the dear heart's part:
>> As thus – mine eye's due is thy outward part,
>> And my heart's right thy inward love of heart.

The lexical set *war, divide the conquest, bar,* is confined to the first quatrain, and is succeeded in the second and third quatrains by a new set of terms: *freedom, plead, defendant, plea, deny, title impaneled, quest, tenants, verdict, determined, moiety, part.* But is not law, too, a kind of warfare, and ought love to be discussed in terms of either? *Eye and heart,* together in line one, have been drifting more and more apart throughout the sonnet, and are contrasted in the concluding couplet. Sonnet 134 also, with its mention of *mortgaged, forfeit, surety-like, bond, statute, sue,* suggests a love which, on the woman's side, is devoid of affection and is characterised by materialistic, business-like relationships.

Drama does not readily lend itself to a continuous use of this technique. What Shakespeare often does is to deflate rather obviously poetic language by a deliberate colloquialism. Hubert of Angers suggests that if King John's niece, Blanche of Spain, will marry Lewis the Dauphin, the city need not be destroyed. The Bastard Fauconbridge is magnificently unimpressed by his rhetoric. Incensed at having been *bethumped with words,* he reasserts reality by his deliberately bathetic and monosyllabic concluding line:

> He speaks plain cannon – fire and smoke and bounce;
> He gives the bastinado with his tongue.
> Our ears are cudgelled; not a word of his
> But buffets better than a fist of France.
> Zounds! I was never so bethumped with words
> Since I first called my brother's father dad!   (*KJ* II.i.462–7)

At the King's final appearance, he prepares for death in a line whose colloquialisms do not detract from the solemn setting:

> Ay, marry, now my soul hath elbow-room.   (V.vii.28)

Unfortunately, he follows this with several sentimental conceits. Shakespeare had not yet learned to allow direct, monosyllabic language to make its own point about the necessary simplicity of dying:

> Finish, good lady; the bright day is done,
> And we are for the dark.   (*AC* V.ii.193–4)

Or a speech in *2 Henry IV*, which, despite lines like 'The beachy girdle of the ocean / Too wide for Neptune's hips', reaches its climax (in the Quarto, the lines are not in F1) simply and monosyllabically:

> O, if this were seen,
> The happiest youth, viewing his progress through,
> What perils past, what crosses to ensue,
> Would shut the book, and sit him down and die.   (III.i.53)

Or Hamlet, planning to make his *quietus* with a bare bodkin. However, the advantages of plainness are beginning to be realised in a play perhaps a year earlier than *King John*:

> Well, Juliet, I will lie with thee tonight.   (V.i.34)

> O true apothecary.
> Thy drugs are quick.   (V.iii.119)

These lines contrast – although the contrast is not yet made fully explicit – with the extravagant language of the early part of the play, and even with the style of Paris in Act V. *Macbeth* regularly makes the contrast between surface appearance and sordid reality by the juxtaposition of two kinds of diction:

> Is't night's *predominance* or the day's *shame*
> That darkness does the face of earth *entomb*
> When living light should *kiss* it?   (II.iv.8–10)

> Good things of day begin to *droop and drowse,*
> Whiles *night's black agents to their preys do rouse.*   (III.ii.52–3)

So does *Antony and Cleopatra*:

> Welcome, dear madam.
> Each heart in Rome does love and pity you.
> Only th'adulterous Antony, most large
> In his abominations, turns you off
> And gives his potent regiment to a trull
> That noises it against us.   (III.vi.91–6)

where *adulterous, large in his abominations, potent regiment* are negatived by the colloquialisms *turns you off, trull* and *noises it.*

Puns (which Dekker employed as one means of irony) are common in Shakespeare. The Hostess addresses Pistol as 'Good Captain Peesel', *2 Hen IV* II.iv.156, and the spelling indicates a pun on *pizzle* ('bull's penis'), a word which Falstaff uses elsewhere (*1 Hen IV* II.iv.241); the same pun occurs when Falstaff says 'She [the hostess] is pistol-proof' (112).[11] A little later still, Doll Tearsheet calls Pistol *you cutpurse rascal, you filthy bung* (124). In one meaning of *bung* (something that stops a hole) the earlier indecent pun is again in evidence, but *cutpurse* suggests the slang use of *bung* as pickpocket, for in thieves' language *bung* meant purse. Indecent puns are not limited to the Falstaff plays, or indeed to lower-class characters, for Mercutio, Leontes and Beatrice all have their share. The curious may consult Eric Partridge's *Shakespeare's Bawdy* or a glossary for entries under *appetite, charge, hit, hole, lap, lie, occupy* ('an excellent good word before it was ill-sorted'), *stand to it, stewed prunes, tail / tale, tailor, top, weapon* and *will.* Perhaps we see too many examples of word-play, just as we are ready to recognise too many recurrent images.[12] But puns are by no means confined to the funny situations. Gaunt in *Richard II* puns on his name as he lies on his deathbed, as does Donne in *A Hymn to God the Father*:

> And having done that, *Thou hast done,*
> I fear no more.

Hamlet's first words are a pun: 'A little more than kin and less than kind'. Lady Macbeth, trying to recall her husband to practicalities as he begins to realise the enormity of his murder of Duncan, makes what to us would be an unacceptable pun:

> I'll gild the faces of the grooms withal,
> For it must seem their guilt.   (*Mac* II.ii.56–7)

In the best general treatment of the subject, *Shakespeare's Word-play*, M. M. Mahood argues further: that Shakespeare's imagination sometimes worked through puns, and that the puns frequently have not only a local significance but a wider dramatic function such as characterisation or emphasising a dominant idea in the play. The first point is really incapable of proof, but Professor Mahood may well be correct when she argues that, in the following quotation, *knave, queen, heart* produced the metaphor *packed cards* (characteristic in its use of colloquialism to express the always slightly suspect nature of Cleopatra's behaviour) and that this in turn led to *false-played* and *triumph* (the latter itself a pun meaning both 'victory' and 'trump card'):

> Here I am Antony,
> Yet cannot hold this visible shape, my knave.
> I made these wars for Egypt; and the Queen –
> Whose heart I thought I had, for she had mine,
> Which, whilst it was mine, had annexed unto't
> A million more, now lost – she, Eros, has
> Packed cards with Caesar, and false-played my glory
> Unto an enemy's triumph. (*AC* IV.xiv.13–20)

On the wider implications of the puns, it is easy to agree with many of the examples Miss Mahood cites from the comedies. Not only do the lovers seek to out-pun one another, but the heroines sometimes bandy puns with the clown, as in the extended passage of wit which begins Act III of *Twelfth Night*:

> *Viola* Save thee, friend, and thy music. Dost thou live by thy tabor?
> *Feste* No sir, I live by the church.
> *Viola* Art thou a Churchman?

At the other extreme, Hamlet's puns in the play scene certainly provide a momentary relief from tension, both for him and for us. But what about Polonius's advice to Ophelia?

> Do not believe his vows. For they are brokers,
> Not of that dye which their investments show,
> But mere implorators of unholy suits,
> Breathing like sanctified and pious bawds,
> The better to beguile. (*Ham* I.iii.127–31)

Would the audience follow the fourfold pun:

| *brokers* | (i) go–betweens | (ii) second–hand clothes dealers |
| *dye* | (i) appearance | (ii) colour |

Investments	(i) finances	(ii) garments
suits	(i) requests	(ii) clothing

and grasp the secondary meanings of shabby, worthless reality below the attractive surface appearance? Would it need to? Probably all four puns are intentional, although their recognition is not essential to appreciate the drift of Polonius's advice and the way in which his puns seek to ridicule Ophelia's love for Hamlet.

Lower-class life and colloquial language often go together. But not invariably. As Fluellen drives the cowards Nym, Pistol and Bardolph forwards 'into the breach', Pistol cries 'Good *bawcock*, bate thy rage! Use lenity, sweet *chuck*' (*Hen V* III.ii.25). Sir Toby uses the same two words to Malvolio (III.iv.112) and Leontes uses *bawcock* and *captain* as terms of endearment to his son (I.ii.121). Antony calls Cleopatra *chuck* (IV.iv.2) and Virgilia her son *crack*, a lively youngster (I.iii.69). It is probably impossible for us now to recreate the spoken English of lower-class life in Shakespeare's time, especially its grammar and syntax – vocabulary is easier.[13] We get hints of it in the speech at the inn in *1 Henry IV* II.i: *out of all cess, stung like a tench, your chamber-lye breeds fleas like a loach, Troyans, you muddy knave* and 'no foot-landrakers, no long-staff sixpenny strikers, none of these mad mustachio purple-hued maltworms'. Prince Hal believes himself to be an honorary member of the fraternity of East-cheap barmen:

> They take it already upon their salvation that though I be but
> Prince of Wales yet I am the king of courtesy, and tell me flatly
> I am no proud Jack like Falstaff, but a Corinthian, a lad of
> mettle, a good boy – by the Lord, so they call me! – and when I am
> King of England I shall command all the good lads in Eastcheap.
> They call drinking deep 'dyeing scarlet', and when you breathe in
> your watering they cry 'Hem!' and bid you 'Play it off!'
>
> (*I Hen IV* II.iv.8–16)

The fashion for classical names (*Corinthian*) is one shared by the Host of the Garter (*Merry Wives*) and Simon Eyre (Dekker's *Shoemaker's Holiday*). The Fishermen in *Pericles* are more concerned with social comment than with appropriate language; only an occasional phrase, such as *with a wanion, bots on't*, suggests real idiom. The brothel scene in the same play relies on a different register, one closer to similar settings in *Henry IV* or *Measure for Measure*. *Pooped, piece, stir you up, crowns of the sun, fitment, plucked, paced, work her to your manage, doorkeeper, ploughed, Tib*, are suggestive enough, often metaphorical or punning, as is common in such language. William and Audrey might have taken the opportunity to show us what real life – with the real dialect – in Arden was like, but instead they simply give Touchstone a chance to show off his wit.

As was the case with change of meaning, the context will usually give us a clue to the interpretation of colloquial phrases. A few of these have survived to our own times; we experience no difficulty with 'I cannot tell *what the dickens* his name is', 'a man of my kidney' (*MWW* III.ii.16 and III.v.113) or Maria's 'at my fingers' ends' and 'a horse of that colour' (*TN* I.iii.75 and II.iii.160). Other usages which have not survived still give us little trouble. When Goneril says to Regan *let us hit together* (*KL* I.i.302), she most probably means 'fit in together', and when they resolve to do something *i' th' heat* the phrase is clearly analogous to 'strike while the iron is hot'. Occasionally the origin of the phrase is clear too. Menenius says to the Volscian sentries 'it is lots to blanks / My name hath touched your ears' (*Coriolanus* V.ii.10). In Elizabethan lotteries, lots won prizes and blanks didn't. Shylock wants to catch Antonio *upon the hip* (*MV* I.iii.43), the phrase is a wrestling term ('at a disadvantage') with a possible additional reference to the dislocation of Jacob's hip in *Genesis 32*. *Godfathers* was a slang term for jury; hence Gratiano's jibe at Shylock:

> In christ'ning shalt thou have two godfathers.
> Had I been judge, thou shouldst have had ten more,
> To bring thee to the gallows, not to the font.   (*MV* IV.i.395–7)

When the unpleasant Bertram refers to Helena as *my clog* (*All's Well*, II.v.53), this seems to be a metaphorical use of *clog* as a block of wood tied to an animal's leg to prevent it from straying. Don John in *Much Ado* (I.iii.30) complains that he is 'trusted with a muzzle and enfranchised with a *clog*'. Autolycus, who regularly uses colloquialisms, speaks of Florizel 'stealing away from his father with his *clog* [Perdita] at his heels' (*WT* IV.iv.674). *Slubber* clearly means 'scamp' in *The Merchant of Venice*: '*Slubber* not business for my sake, Bassanio' (II.viii.39), but when the Duke tells Othello that, in Cyprus, he must '*Slubber* the gloss of your new fortunes with this more stubborn and boisterous expedition' (I.iii.224), 'smear' is a better equivalent. These are the only two uses of the word in Shakespeare, but a shared metaphorical sense of a hurried covering over to conceal the more worthwhile texture beneath seems evident. Metaphor is also behind 'This Doll Tearsheet should be some *road*' ('whore'), Falstaff's direction to Bardolph to push Pistol downstairs, '*Quoit* him down' (*2 Hen IV*, II.ii.160 and II.iv. 187 respectively), and the Nurse's switch of support to Paris: 'O, he's a lovely gentleman! / Romeo's a *dishclout* to him.' (*RJ* III.v.219). Even when we cannot be sure of the explanation, the idea is clear enough. Parolles (*AW* II.iii.278) laughs at the man who, instead of going to the wars, 'hugs his *kicky-wicky* here at home'; this bawdy compound is unique in Shakespeare. Aufidius' 'I'll *potch* at him some way' uses an apparently slang word (Onions thought a Warwickshire dialect word)[14] and one which suggests the unheroic, underhand manner in which he does finally accomplish Coriolanus' death. When the Hostess, assessing Fenton's chances of winning Anne Page, is sure "tis *in his buttons* he will carry't', we may not be able to suggest the origin of the phrase but it presumably means 'it's obvious'. In the same play, *fap* (*MWW* I.i.172), a word often unnecessarily emended, probably means 'drunk' and may be an example from West Midland dialect.[15]

In some cases, colloquial language seems to be used as one means of characterisation. There is a good deal of it in *Twelfth Night*, almost all in the Toby-Andrew-Maria-Fabian scenes. Maria says that Sir Andrew 'hath the gift of a coward to *allay the gust* (offset the delight?) he hath in quarrelling' (I.iii.28). Toby himself uses *coystril* (rogue); *I am a dog at* (very good at) *a catch; sneck up* (push off); *a beagle, true bred* (a marvellous girl); *call me cut* (a fool); *at a cold scent* (from hunting); *play at cherry pit* (be on friendly terms) *with Satan*. Maria has the delightful *Go shake your ears* (oh, shut up!) and *gull him into a nayword* (make a fool of him). Fabian speaks of *the windy side of the law* (the safe side). The racy style aptly matches their high spirits. In *Antony and Cleopatra* the purpose is rather different. Antony tells Octavia *I have not kept my square* (I have wandered from the straight and narrow) and her brother tells Antony we could not *stall* together. But the epithets applied to Cleopatra are far more interesting. To Enobarbus she is a *wonderful piece of work*, an *Egyptian dish*, and he notices that even the priests bless her when she is *riggish*. To Agrippa she is *royal wench*, to Scarus *yon ribaudred nag of Egypt*, and finally to Charmian a lass *unparalleled*. When Antony suspects her of betraying him to Caesar, he calls her a *boggler ever*, and, in an arresting metaphor, one who has *packed cards* with Caesar. She sees herself as *a morsel for a monarch*. These do not merely contribute to the sense of abundant vitality which everyone notices in the play. They also imply that there is something about Cleopatra both unpredictable and unreliable, part of the infinite variety of the queen whom Enobarbus saw not only sailing majestically down the Cydnus but hopping forty paces through the public street.

Slang is ephemeral and, initially, sub-standard too. It aims at a colourful effect, but its very proliferation inevitably destroys much of the novelty, and the word disappears, or, in a few cases, is adopted into the standard vocabulary. Intensifiers, for instance, move in and out of fashion in different ages. How long will *right* ('a right fool', 'a right idler') last? It was certainly very common in Shakespeare's day, as a glance at the *Concordance* will show, although usually with adjective or adverb and only occasionally with noun: *right valiant, right apt, right sorry, right deadly, a right gypsy.* How long a life for *dead* ('dead easy'), not to mention *plumb* easy? *Out-and-out* ('an out-and-out liar'), *desperately* ('desperately tired') and sheer ('sheer force of habit') seem to have been around for some time. Shakespearean drama has its own favourites; not surprisingly they are most common in lower-class dialogue or the colloquial language of upper-class characters. *Whoreson* is used with its literal meaning, 'bastard', by Gloucester at the beginning of *Lear*: 'there was good sport at his making, and the whoreson must be acknowledged', but the instances in *Romeo and Juliet*, 'a merry whoreson' (IV.iv.20) and *Henry VIII*, 'The sly whoresons / Have got a speeding trick to lay down ladies' (I.iii.39), are obviously colloquial. From there it is a short step to 'Thou *whoreson* mad compound of majesty' and 'Thou *whoreson* little tidy Bartholomew boar-pig' (*2 Hen IV*, II.iv.289 and 226) where the word has become an affectionate intensifier. Indeed, it is something of an Eastcheap mannerism in *2 Henry IV*, for the majority of the Shakespearean uses come from that play. Even more of a catch-phrase is *bully*. The Host in *The Merry Wives of Windsor* is especially addicted to the word (*bully* rook, *bully* stale, *bully* knight, or simply *bully* on its own). Sixteen of the twenty recorded instances in Shakespeare are his: two more are used about Bottom, a third by Pistol and the fourth by Stephano to Caliban. *Old*, another intensifier from these plays, is less frequent. Francis the Drawer looks forward to *old utis*, 'a high old time' (*2 Hen IV* II.iv.19). Once Doctor Caius appears, Mistress Quickly – who should know – fears 'old abusing of God's patience and the King's English' (*MWW* I.iv.5). Moving up the social scale, Portia says 'We shall have old swearing / That they did give the rings away '(*MV* IV.ii.15) and Ursula calls back Beatrice because 'Yonder's old coil at home' (*MA* V.ii.86). The Porter's 'If a man were porter of hell gate he should have *old* turning the key' (*Mac* II.iii.2) has a rather similar meaning, although here *old* does not quite look like an intensifier.

    Passing is used as an intensifier on many occasions, in some seventeen different plays and poems. In *Titus Andronicus* poor Lavina, ignorant of her fate or that of Bassanius, has discovered the affair between Tamora and Aaron and says 'This valley fits the purpose passing well' (III.ii.84). Richard III (as yet still Duke of Gloucester) suggests it is no treason to admit that Edward IV's mistress, Shore's wife, 'hath a pretty foot, / A cherry lip, a bonny eye, a passing pleasing tongue' (I.i.93). Desdemona considered Othello's adventures *passing strange* (I.iii.159) and Autolycus offers one from his stock of ballads, 'a passing merry one' (*WT* IV.iv.286). These, and others like *passing fair* are acceptable enough, but *passing cowardly* (*Cor* I.i.201), *passing scornfully* (*Hen V* IV.ii.40) and *passing short* (*AYLI* III.v.138) strike us as odd. For some reason, *The Taming of the Shrew* is especially fond of the word, with seven examples. *Wondrous* is, if anything, even more frequent than *passing*, but most of the collocations: *wondrous fair / strange / heavy / cold / hot / kind / rare*, are clear enough. One at least, Othello's "'twas pitiful, 'twas wondrous pitiful' is one of the best remembered lines of the play. *Monstrous, shrewdly, vengeance* and (one which we have kept) *thoroughly* are far less common. Of the two uses of *monstrous* as intensifier, one is comic, Bottom's 'monstrous little voice' (*MND* I.ii.48) but the other more truly poetic: 'Skill infinite, or monstrous desperate' (*AW* II.i184). *All's Well* also contributes *shrewdly vexed* (III.v.88); the other similar use of the word is *Winter's Tale* V.i.102, where *shrewdly ebbed* continues the metaphor of *flowed* earlier in the line. *Vengeance proud* (*Cor* II.ii.5; compare Menenius's 'What the vengeance.' III.i.261 and present day English 'with a vengeance') is emphatic and arresting, but 'This fellow has a *vengeance* trick o' th' hip' (*Two Noble Kinsmen* II.ii.71) is more puzzling, since the word intensifies a noun rather than the usual adjective or adverb. Shakespeare usually spells 'thoroughly' *throughly*; it occurs four times as an intensifier. *Throughly healed* (*TGV* I.ii.115), *throughly moved* (*MWW* I.iv.89), *throughly weary* (*Cym* III.vi.36) are intelligible enough. Kent's 'My point and period will be *throughly* wrought' is part of a couplet which closes a scene (*KL* IV.vii.96); he seems to mean 'things will come to a head'.

Shakespeare, then, made considerable use of features of contemporary colloquial English, many of which correspond to those of our own day. But he was also sensitive to the vocabulary and syntax of special registers. With characters like the Host of the Garter, on a small scale, and Pistol, on a much larger scale (although we have not quite finished with Pistol yet), he fused these to achieve a literary idiolect of considerable complexity but immensely attractive personality.

NOTES AND REFERENCES

1. Hibbard (1981), pp. 125–8, 174–81 would add the Nurse in *RJ* and Hotspur.
2. Barish (1960).
3. Jorgensen (1962), pp. 70–4.
4. *Coney-Catchers and Bawdy Baskets: An Anthology of Elizabethan Low Life*, ed. G. Salgado, Harmondsworth (1972), pp. 91, 94.
5. They are so natural follies, but so shown
   That even the doers may see, and yet not own
   (*Alchemist*, Prologue, 23–4).
6. *Life and Complete Works of Robert Greene*, ed. A. B. Grosart (edn. of 1964) Russell and Russell, New York, X, pp. 118–20.
7. Included in *Minor Elizabethan Tragedies*, ed. T. W. Craik, Dent (1974).
8. Among the earlier meanings in the *OED* are 'disgrace' (1548) and 'hoodwink' (1590).
9. Opening to *The Spanish Tragedy*.
10. *Thomas Dekker*, ed. E. D. Pendry, Arnold (1967), pp. 88–9.
11. Compare 'With a pistol in his great cod-piece', *Duchess of Malfi*, II.ii.39.
12. As Colman, p. 21 says, ribald punning is often assumed without proof in 'the sex-conscious and irony-loving atmosphere of the later twentieth century'. We see what we want to see.
13. Salmon (1967).
14. C. T. Onions *A Shakespeare Glossary*, Clarendon Press, Oxford (1911); see also Brook (1976), p.180.
15. Oliver (1971), p.13 (note).

CHAPTER EIGHT

Some Shakespearean styles

On the face of it, the primary distinguishing feature of a passage from Shakespeare might seem to be whether it is written in prose or in verse. But it is not quite so simple. There is no prose at all in *Richard II* or in *King John*. *The Merry Wives of Windsor* contains the most prose (and its language may well be the nearest to Elizabethan colloquial English), followed by *Much Ado*, *Twelfth Night* and *As You Like It*. Other plays with marked comic elements – *1 and 2 Henry IV*, for example, in which Falstaff speaks only about a dozen lines of verse – also contain a good deal of prose.[1] Prose, therefore, is most prominent in the middle comedies and some of the histories of about the same date. The earlier comedies, as we have seen, sometimes use patterned euphuistic prose in the manner of Lyly who wrote six prose comedies and only one verse play, and we have to wait for *The Merchant of Venice* (1596) before a major character, Shylock, speaks serious prose. Only in the earliest comedy, and once or twice later (for example where Hal uses prose to Falstaff and his cronies but verse to the nobles) will we find such a clear division as in *The Taming of the Shrew* where the high life is in verse and the low life in prose. Henry V, on the night before Agincourt, speaks prose to his soldiers as he moves among his army in disguise. He later woos Katherine in prose; the soldier has become the lover. Yet in neither of these scenes does the prose seem natural: brief exchanges, characteristic of conversation, are interspersed with longer, more balanced, rhetorical passages:

> Some, peradventure, have on them the guilt of premeditated and contrived murder; some, of beguiling virgins with the broken seals of perjury; some, making the wars their bulwark, that have before gored the gentle bosom of peace with pillage and robbery.   (IV.i.157–61)

> A good leg will fall; a straight back will stoop; a black beard will turn
> white; a curled pate will grow bald; a fair face will wither; a full eye will
> wax hollow; but a good heart, Kate, is the sun and the moon – or rather,
> the sun, and not the moon; for it shines bright and never changes, but
> keeps his course truly. (V.ii.158–63)

The low-life prose of Eastcheap has been abandoned by Henry in the
face of the more serious concerns of *Henry V*.

Not all lower-class characters confine themselves to prose. Mistress
Quickly and Pompey in *Measure for Measure* do, but the Nurse in
Romeo and Juliet speaks verse of a kind, as well as her usual prose, just
as the citizens in *Julius Caesar* use prose in I.i. but verse in III.ii. The
norm of the plays is obviously blank verse, and Shakespeare's au-
thoritative characters – kings, dukes and leaders generally – for the
most part use a verse whose diction includes rather more than the
average number of polysyllables and whose smooth flow conceals a
deliberate control of syntax. But these characters also sometimes use
prose. Prose, then, appears to be used for special reasons of dramatic
contrast.

One of the most obvious uses of prose to reflect something other
than the norm, is to indicate madness, real or assumed. Ophelia in
her madness is a wreck of her former self, and her derangement is
signalled not only by the doggerel verse but also by a change to prose.
Lady Macbeth's monosyllabic prose in the sleep-walking scene is
another case in point. Lear, however, when mad speaks both verse
and prose; perhaps the verse indicates his growing perception of reality. Edgar as Poor Tom usually speaks prose (apart from snatches of
doggerel verse) but blank verse for the soliloquies at the close of
II.vi. and the beginning of IV.i. In the scene where he pretends to
lead the blind Gloucester to the edge of Dover cliffs, both characters
speak blank verse, and Gloucester is consequently puzzled not only
by his preservation but by 'two' characters:

> Methinks thy voice is altered, and thou speak'st
> In better phrase and matter than thou didst. (IV.vi.7–8)

Edgar resumes his disguise of a *bold peasant*, and consequently his
stage Zummerset prose, for the brief altercation with Oswald, but in
Act V, once again Edgar and eventually restored to his rightful position, he uses verse. After he decides to feign madness, Hamlet speaks
prose to everyone except to Horatio (his one confidant), to Gertrude
and the Ghost in the closet scene, and of course in his soliloquies.

But when he returns from the voyage no further pretence of madness is necessary, and the final scene is in blank verse.

Prose, in fact, is not inferior to blank verse. Mercutio, who had earlier been responsible for the poeticism of the Queen Mab speech, dies in prose. It is, of course, capable of balance and wit, and its range can be seen in a character like Falstaff, whose prose increases in complexity as he tries (and usually succeeds) to struggle out of his responsibilities. But, as Vickers says,[2] prose-speaking characters are not heroes, visionaries or romantics, but are sometimes beastly (Thersites), blunt (Enobarbus, Casca) or buffoons (Parolles, Menenius).

THE RATIONAL MAN

To this I would add a further category, the efficient, 'rational' man whose air of common sense may be either real or assumed. Once again, most of these characters alternate prose and verse, so the prose is likely to be contrastive in intention. The Duke in *Measure for Measure* begins Act III with the magnificent verse speech to Claudio, 'Be absolute for death...'. Yet to Isabella later in the same scene, and to Escalus in the next, he employs prose. Perhaps this is partly to emphasise his disguise as a friar, but the balance and spareness of this prose suggests above all a man subject to plan and to command:

> The hand that hath made you fair hath made you good. The goodness
> that is cheap in beauty makes beauty brief in goodness, but grace,
> being the soul of your complexion, shall keep the body of it ever fair.
> The assault that Angelo hath made to you, fortune hath conveyed to
> my understanding, and, but that frailty hath examples for his falling, I
> should wonder at Angelo. How will you do to content this substitute,
> and to save your brother? (III.i.182–90)

Escalus   What news abroad i' th' world?
Duke   None, but that there is so great a fever on goodness that the
          dissolution of it must cure it. Novelty is only in request, and
          it is as dangerous to be aged in any kind of course as it is
          virtuous to be constant in any undertaking. There is scarce
          truth enough alive to make societies secure, but security
          enough to make fellowships accursed. Much upon this riddle
          runs the wisdom of the world. This news is old enough, yet
          it is every day's news. I pray you sir, of what disposition was
          the Duke? (III.ii.211–21)

If we were ever tempted to regard the Duke's temporary abdication as irresponsible, these passages surely remove our doubts. By the close of IV.iii. the plans are completed. Henceforth (and in verse):

> By cold gradation and well-balanced form,
> We shall proceed with Angelo. (98–9)

Brutus, too, is efficient – or believes he is. Both before and after the funeral speech he uses verse, but the oration itself is in prose. Its rhetoric is obvious: the answers to hypothetical questions, the antitheses, the repetitions, the isocolon and parison:

> As Caesar loved me, I weep for him; as he was fortunate, I rejoice at it; as he was valiant, I honour him; but, as he was ambitious, I slew him. (III.ii.24–6)

It is above all reasonable; Brutus had assured the sceptical Cassius that he would show 'the *reasons* of our Caesar's death'. It is also brief. Antony's much longer verse rejoinder is rhetorical too: antithesis in *The evil... The good...*; the repetition of *ambitious, honourable* and *wrong*; the pretence that he is overcome by emotion; the withholding of the will; the affectation of modesty ('I am no orator, as Brutus is'), but these are not so much the figures of speech as that part of rhetoric concerned with the delivery of the speech (*pronunciatio*). At the close, Antony is well-satisfied, and his simple aside, 'Now let it work' indicates his scheming. Brutus, sincere and full of integrity, had appealed in cool prose to the reason, the quality which, in Shakespeare, the populace above all lacks. His idealism comes to seem naive, remote from reality. Intellectual prose is vanquished by passionate blank verse. Coriolanus, too, briefly begs for the citizens' support in prose with an irony they totally fail to perceive. But he regards the whole process as dishonourable and insulting to himself, and so here prose is the mark of an assumed style. Immediately the first group of citizens has gone, Coriolanus returns to blank verse which he continues for a perfunctory appeal to two or three stragglers who must also be placated. The 'plainess' of Coriolanus, however, is best seen in his usual style which I intend to discuss later as an aspect of a deliberately created 'Roman' or 'soldierly' language.

The spare, controlled prose of Brutus is a world away from the prose we have considered hitherto: the euphuism of Lyly, the Ciceronianism of Sidney and Hooker, the looser but still expansive style of Donne. Around 1600, Ciceronianism, with its elaboration of the constituent parts of the sentence, began to lose ground in favour of

the much more terse, epigrammatic, but still balanced style of Seneca
and Tacitus where the ideal became 'the most matter with best con-
ceyt in fewest words'.[3] (Seneca, of course, was not exactly a new author to the Elizabethans.) The distaste for over-refined Ciceronianism, with its deviousness and disproportionate attention to manner at
the expense of matter, is expressed most forcibly in a well-known
passage from Bacon's *Advancement of Learning* (1605):

> There be therefore chiefly three vanities in studies, whereby learning hath
> been most traduced. For those things we do esteem vain, which are either
> false or frivolous, those which either have no truth or no use: and those
> persons we esteem vain, which are either credulous or curious; and
> curiosity is either in matter or words: so that in reason as well as in
> experience, there fall out to be these three distempers (as I may term
> them) of learning: the first, fantastical learning; the second, contentious
> learning; and the last, delicate learning; vain imaginations, vain
> altercations, and vain affectations; and with the last I will begin . . . so that
> these four causes concurring, the admiration of ancient authors, the hate
> of the schoolmen, the exact study of languages, and the efficacy of
> preaching, did bring in an affectionate study of eloquence and copie of
> speech, which then began to flourish. This grew speedily to an excess; for
> men began to hunt more after words than matter; more after the
> choiceness of the phrase, and the round and clean composition of the
> sentence, and the sweet falling of the clauses, and the varying and
> illustration of their works with tropes and figures, than after the weight
> of matter, worth of subject, soundness of argument, life of invention, or
> depth of judgement.[4]

Bacon parodies the excess of eloquence and *copie* ('copiousness')
which he rejects, for the passage 'the choiceness of the phrase, and
the round and clean composition of the sentence, and the sweet falling of the clauses, and the varying and illustration of their works
with tropes and figures' is indeed artfully and elegantly expressed
and contrasts with the hammer-blows of 'weight of matter, worth
of subject, soundness of argument, life of invention, or depth of
judgement'. But Bacon's own prose in *The Advancement of Learning* is
still far from the impersonal prose of later scientists. We are not yet
at the level of absolute plainness advocated in Sprat's *History of the
Royal Society* (1667) or of Hobbes's rejection of metaphor (*Leviathan*,
1651). The essay and the 'character', and in drama the comedies of
Jonson, begin to supply the greater observation and experiment
which Bacon the scientist desired. If brevity was in, copiousness was
not altogether out. But in Jacobean English, it is more likely to be
reserved for a special purpose (the insincerity of Osric or of Timon's
friends) than indulged in for its own sake. One Latin model has
simply been exchanged for two others, and the balance of Bacon's

final phrases (abstract noun + *of* + noun) reminds us that symmetry is still appreciated even if the top-dressing of Ciceronianism is less in vogue.

The eloquent, associative, frequently redundant, sermon style of John Donne (see p. 17) may be contrasted with the pointed, staccato, economic style of Lancelot Andrewes. Andrewes's method is explication; indeed he has been called 'not so much a religious thinker as a religious philologist',[5] and T. S. Eliot's metaphor of squeezing the last drop of meaning from the text is an apt one. Andrewes's style may be conveniently illustrated by an excerpt from his Christmas Day sermon, 1622, well-known for its influence on Eliot's *Journey of the Magi*:

> It is not commended, to stand *gazing up into heaven* too long, on Christ himself ascending: much less on His star. For, they sat not still gazing on the star. Their *Vidimus* begat *Venimus*; their seeing made them come; come a long journey. Venimus is soon said; but a short word: But, many a wide and weary step they made, before they could come to say *Venimus*, Lo, *here we are come; Come* and at our journey's end. To look a little on it. In this their coming, we consider, First, the distance of the place they came from. It was not hard by, as the shepherds' (but a step to Bethlehem, over the fields:) This was riding many a hundred miles, and cost them many a day's journey. Secondly, we consider the way that they came: If it be pleasant, or plain and easy: For if it be, it is so much the better. This was nothing pleasant: for through deserts, all the way waste and desolate. Nor (secondly) easy either: For over the rocks and crags of both Arabies (specially Petrea) their journey lay. Thirdly, yet if safe: but it was not; but exceeding dangerous, a lying through the middest of the black tents of Kedar, a nation of thieves and cut-throats; to pass over the hills of robbers; infamous then, and infamous to this day. No passing, without great troop or convoy. Last we consider the time of their coming, the season of the year. It was no summer progress. A cold coming they had of it, at this time of the year; just the worst time of the year to take a journey, and specially a long journey in. The ways deep, the weather sharp, the days short, the sun furthest off in *solstitio brumali*, the very dead of Winter. *Venimus*, we are come, if that be the one; *Venimus*, we are (now) come, come at this time, that (sure) is another.
> And these difficulties they overcame, of a wearisome, irksome, troublesome, dangerous, unseasonable journey; And for all this, they came. And came it cheerfully and quickly; As appeareth by the speed they made. It was but *Vidimus, Venimus*, with them; They saw and they came: No sooner saw, but they set out presently.[6]

While this, with its several colloquialisms (*much less, hard by, but a step, so much the better, No passing, A cold coming they had of it, sure, No sooner*) and its short sentences (some of them without a main verb) may appear unstudied, it is really no more spontaneous than the expansiveness of Donne. His progress is a logical one (*First . . . Second-*

ly . . . Thirdly . . . Last). He will state a hypothesis, almost immediately to deny it: 'If it be pleasant . . . This was nothing pleasant'; 'yet if safe: but it was not'. The balance of 'The ways deep, the weather sharp, the days short, the sun furthest off' is obvious. The rhetorical figure of *gradatio* is a favourite: 'made them *come*; *come* a long journey', 'the time of their *coming* . . . A cold *coming*'. Andrewes's method is, in his own words here, 'to look a little on it', to probe what the words may mean. And the only occasion he uses copiousness is in the deliberate contrast of 'a wearisome, irksome, troublesome, dangerous, unseasonable journey'.

If the style of Andrewes seems too disconnected, the coordinate but symmetrical syntax of the opening of Bacon's essay *Of Studies* is an example of Senecanism of a less extreme kind. The clauses are mostly of equal length and within them noun matches noun and infinitive answers to infinitive; antithesis is a frequent device:

> Studies serve for delight, for ornament, and for ability. Their chief use for delight is in privateness and retiring; for ornament, is in discourse; and for ability, is in the judgement and disposition of business. For expert men can execute, and perhaps judge of particulars, one by one; but the general counsels, and the plots and marshalling of affairs, come best from those that are learned. To spend too much time in studies is sloth; to use them too much for ornament is affectation; to make judgement wholly by their rules is the humour of a scholar. They perfect nature, and are perfected by experience; for natural abilities are like natural plants, that need proyning by study; and studies themselves do give forth directions too much at large, except they be bounded in by experience. Crafty men contemn studies; simple men admire them; and wise men use them: for they teach not their own use; but that is a wisdom without them and above them, won by observation. Read not to contradict and confute; nor to believe and take for granted; nor to find talk and discourse; but to weigh and consider.[7]

The efficient, rational prose of such characters as Brutus, or the Duke in *Measure for Measure*, is therefore one of several clearly-defined prose styles around the turn of the century. But the surface pragmatism may cloak villainy beneath, as Iago well knew:

> The Moor is of a free and open nature
> That thinks men honest that but seem to be so.   (I.iii.393–4)

Almost everyone in the play calls him *honest* Iago, not only Othello who does it frequently, but also Cassio (III.i.39) and Desdemona (III.iii.5). It is because he was a man 'of honesty and trust' that Othello asked Iago to conduct Desdemona to Cyprus, and he goes on protesting Iago's honesty almost to the very end:

> Ay, 'twas he that told me on her first:
> An honest man he is, and hates the slime
> That sticks on filthy deeds.   (V.ii.146–8)

Iago is careful to use the word about himself (II.i.195, II.iii.259 and 318, III.iii.409, IV.i.279), and from III.iii, by which time the term has become completely attached to him, he begins to stress the disadvantages of being too honest. He does this by deliberate choice of syntactical construction,[8] the difference in English between 'I know X is honest'; 'X is honest, so far as I know'; and 'I don't know that X isn't honest' – the variation from complete certainty, via probability, to some uncertainty:

Othello	Is he [Cassio] not honest?
Iago	Honest, my lord?
Othello	Honest? Ay, honest.
Iago	My lord, for aught I know. (102–3)

Iago	For Michael Cassio,
	I dare be sworn I think that he is honest.
Othello	I think so too.
Iago	Men should be what they seem;
	Or those that be not, would they might seem none!
Othello	Certain, men should be what they seem.
Iago	Why, then, I think Cassio's an honest man, (123–8)

Othello	I do not think but Desdemona's honest.
Iago	Long live she so! And long live you to think so! (223–4)

In this syntactical climate, if Desdemona speaks in support of Cassio, it implies that Desdemona is false to Othello. Iago is even able to portray himself as his own worst enemy:

> O wretched fool,
> That lov'st to make thine honesty a vice!
> O monstrous world! Take note, take note, O world!
> To be direct and honest is not safe.   (IV.i.278–80)

> Alas, alas!
> It is not honesty in me to speak
> What I have seen and known.   (III.iii.372–5)

He constantly *says* he has no proof: 'scattering and unsure observance.' (III.iii.150); I speak not yet of proof' (194); 'not to strain my speech... to larger reach / Than to suspicion' (216); 'yet we see nothing done' (429). As Malcolm Coulthard says, he deliberately creates suspicion by pretending not to understand Othello's questions, so often that Othello comes to believe that Iago is keeping something from him.[9]

How did Iago acquire his reputation for honesty? Again, the answer lies, partly at least, in the kind of language he uses. For much of the time he speaks in prose, although the soliloquies, in which he takes the audience into his confidence, are in verse. Iago gives the impression of balancing his own (admittedly biased) imagination against Othello's natural wisdom and candour. Of course, other remarks by Iago are scurrilous, lecherous, or simply knowingly colloquial in an 'all men together' manner. But there is enough balance to convey the superficial appearance of a careful and rational man. And rational men are often honest men. Often, but not always. They sometimes seem to overturn accepted values and standards simply by virtue of their rational 'modern' thinking. The reductive tone of '[Love] is merely a lust of the blood and a permission of the will' (I.iii.331) is typical of Iago. He is a Machiavellian villain, a political realist, a man who knows, through practical experience, that men do not always by any means act in the way they purport to act and that the world often favours the shrewd operator rather than the man of principle. But if Iago is to persuade Othello that seeing is believing (a typically Machiavellian viewpoint), he starts with the advantage of appearing a rational man. So does another villain, Edmund, who likewise links credulity and honesty:

A credulous father and a brother noble,
Whose nature is so far from doing harms
That he suspects none; on whose *foolish honesty*
My practices ride easy.   (I.ii.175–8)

Edmund is, like other Shakespearean villains, a manipulator of language. He uses both prose and verse, but the balance of his prose to Gloucester is speciously logical:

I do not well know, my lord. If it shall please you to suspend your indignation against my brother till you can derive from him better testimony of his intent, you should run a certain course; where, if you violently proceed against him, mistaking his purpose, it would make a great gap in your own honour and shake in pieces the heart of his obedience. I dare pawn down my life for him that he hath writ this to feel my affection to your honour and to no other pretence of danger.
                                                         (I.ii.80–8)

His contempt, in the same scene, for Gloucester's astrological explanations of his *goatish disposition* is also that of the 'new' Machiavellian man ('Fut! I should have been that I am had the maidenliest star in the firmament twinkled on my bastardizing.'). When he speaks verse his style is equally pared-down and business-like (e.g. II.i.48–55, V.i.55–69), as is that of Goneril and Regan who, interestingly enough, both assume the masculine role in marriage and to whom Edmund becomes attached. Lear's poetic eloquence in the opening scene is brought to earth by the unemotional and calculating prose of Goneril and Regan in the final lines ('Tis the infirmity of his age. Yet he hath ever but slenderly known himself.').

An earlier essay in the balanced language of deceit is Don John in *Much Ado*. He is an uncomplicated villain, but his prose, too, is symmetrical, even rigid:

> I had rather be a canker in a hedge than a rose in his grace, and it better fits my blood to be disdained of all than to fashion a carriage to rob love from any. In this, though I cannot be said to be a flattering honest man, it must not be denied but I am a plain-dealing villain. I am trusted with a muzzle and enfranchised with a clog; therefore I have decreed not to sing in my cage. If I had my mouth, I would bite; if I had my liberty, I would do my liking. In the meantime, let me be that I am, and seek not to alter me.   (I.iii.25–34)

and, as with Iago, seeing is believing:

> If you dare not trust that you see, confess not that you know. If you will follow me, I will show you enough; and when you have seen more and heard more, proceed accordingly.   (III.ii.107–10)

A later Don John would have incorporated within himself the plotting of Borachio, but Borachio is stylistically his own man (II.ii.30–45) and some way ahead of Conrade, as III.iii. makes clear.

THE LANGUAGE OF INSULTS

These various illustrations will not explain all the uses of prose by Shakespeare, for instance the curious scene in prose (where verse might normally be expected) between Autolycus and the three 'Gentlemen' (*Winter's Tale*, V.ii). Probably the prose here is meant simply to convey information in a play whose verse syntax is notoriously difficult. It may be useful, however, to conclude this discussion of prose with an examination of the kind of prose used for insults and scurrilous comment, not least because it shows Shakespeare developing a different kind of compound. If we were inclined to think that all Shakespeare's compounds are 'poetical', several of the examples in the *Henry IV* plays and in *Troilus and Cressida* will soon disillusion us. Falstaff roars into action in the Gadshill robbery:

> Strike, down with them, cut the villains' throats! Ah, whoreson
> caterpillars, bacon-fed knaves! (*1 Hen IV* II.ii.82–3)

His creditors are, to him, equally unreasonable:

> A whoreson Achitophel! A rascally yea-forsooth knave, to bear a
> gentleman in hand, and then stand upon security! The whoreson
> smoothy-pates do now wear nothing hut high shoes and bunches of keys
> at their girdles. (*2 Hen IV* I.ii.34–6)

His pressed soldiers are no better than 'toasts-and-butter, with hearts in their bellies no bigger than pins' heads' (*1 Hen IV* IV.ii.20), but Falstaff himself is to Prince Hal 'this bed-presser, this horse-back-breaker' (*1 Hen IV* II.iv.238) or 'You whoreson candle-mine you' (*2 Hen IV* II.iv.295). Bardolph is 'that arrant malmsy-nose knave' (*2 Hen IV* II.i.37) and Pistol 'you bottle-ale rascal, you basket-hilt stale juggler, you!' (*2 Hen IV* II.iv.127). To the beadle, carrying her off to be whipped, Doll Tearsheet screams:

> Nut-hook, nut-hook, you lie! Come on, I'll tell thee what, thou damned
> tripe-visaged rascal, an the child I go with do miscarry, thou wert better
> thou hadst struck thy mother, thou paper-faced villain.
> (*2 Hen IV* V.iv.7–10)

Thersites ('Who's there? Good Thersites, come in and *rail.*') speaks of his own *spiteful execrations*, and *Troilus and Cressida* provides an impressive list: *thou mongrel, beef-witted lord; thou sodden-witted lord; thou scurvy-valiant ass* (all to Ajax); *short-armed ignorance; idol of idiot-worshippers; clapper-clawing; that stale old mouse-eaten dry cheese, Nestor, and that same dog-fox Ulysses*, and his pièce-de-résistance:

> Now, the rotten diseases of the south, the guts-griping ruptures, catarrhs,
> loads o' gravel in the back, lethargies, cold palsies, raw eyes, dirt-rotten
> livers, wheezing lungs, bladders full of imposthume, sciaticas, lime-kilns
> i' the palm, incurable bone-ache, and the riveled fee-simple of the tetter,
> and the like, take and take again such preposterous discoveries!
> (V.i.17–24)

Elsewhere in the same play, *bed-work, cob-loaf, overproud and under-honest, enlard his fat-already pride, boy-queller, great-sized coward, the*

The literary language of Shakespeare

hold-door trade keep up the level of insults which so often seem a substitute for action. But it is easy to find lists in other plays: Berowne in *Love's Labour's Lost* (V.ii.464–5), Aaron in *Titus Andronicus* (IV.ii.97–8), Capulet to a Juliet who refuses to marry Paris (*RJ* IIII.v.156–7), Kent insulting Oswald (*KL* II.ii.13–22) and, most interestingly, Macbeth's outburst to the unfortunate servant, which expresses his rising panic:

> The devil damn thee black, thou cream-faced loon!
> Where got'st thou that goose look? . . .
> Go prick thy face and over-red thy fear,
> Thou lily-livered boy. What soldiers, patch?
> Death of thy soul! Those linen cheeks of thine
> Are counsellors to fear. What soldiers, whey-face?   (V.iii.11–17)

Not quite all of these are in prose, although most are. What they have in common is their outrageous nature. They are coined for this particular occasion, neologisms, unlikely perhaps to be used again. Here Shakespeare's mentor – if he needed one – was probably Nashe. Nashe was one of the new university-trained men who needed to make a living by his pen. He was twenty-seven when he wrote *The Unfortunate Traveller* which has been called the first picaresque novel in English, but most of his work was in the form of pamphlets, usually controversial, always eye-catching, essentially ephemeral. Nashe, in short, was a journalist before his time, and his extravagant, deliberately shocking, exhibitionist style, which often seems to challenge the reader to do better if he can, is part of his stock-in-trade. Almost any page of Nashe will provide illustrations, but here is a random list: *scholastical squitter-books* (scribblers); *the shop-dust of the sights I saw in Rome; old excellent he was at a bone-ache* (a torturer); *this supereminent principal metropolis of the red fish* (Yarmouth); *shame-swollen toad to have the spit-proofed face* (of one of his opponents in the pamphlet war); *such gargantuan boisterous galliguts* (the Spanish Armada). To those who complained of the harshness of his diction, Nashe retorted:

> To the second rancke of reprehenders, that complain of my boystrous
> compound wordes, and ending my Italionate coyned verbes all in *Ize*,
> thus I replie: That no winde that blowes strong but is boystrous, no speech
> or wordes, of any power or force to confute or perswade, but must bee
> swelling and boystrous. For the compounding of my wordes, therein I
> imitate rich men, who, hauing gathered store of white single money
> together, conuert a number of those small little scutes into great peeces of
> gold, such as double Pistols and Portugues. Our English tongue, of all
> languages, most swarmeth with the single money of monasillables, which

158

are the onely scandal of it. Bookes written in them, and no other, seeme like Shop-keepers boxes, that containe nothing else saue halfe-pence, three farthings and two-pences. Therefore, what did me I, but hauing a huge heape of those worthelesse shreds of small English in my *Pia mater's* purse, to make the royaller shew with them to mens eyes, had them to the compounders immediately, and exchanged them foure into one, and others into more, according to the Greek, French, Spanish, and Italian.[10]

This is another variety of the prose of the 1580s and 1590s to place beside Euphuism, Ciceronianism, or the more realistic style of Dekker. Add the Senecan style of the turn of the century, and it is clear that, in his prose, no less than in his dramatic verse, Shakespeare could select any of several well-established styles.

THE PLAY WITHIN THE PLAY

Pistol was surely a playgoer. Some of his heroic-sounding phrases derive from the more melodramatic speeches in earlier drama, from Marlowe or from Peele (*2 Hen IV* II.iv.158,174). Noun phrases like *lungs military* or *hand terrestial* (both from the Host of the Garter, not Pistol) raise the question whether this portentous style was deliberately used to satirise older-style dramatic verse. If we were asked to identify *tristful visage*, we might well guess Kyd or Marlowe rather than Hamlet in the closet scene:

> Yea, this solidity and compound mass
> With tristful [heated, Q2] visage, as against the Doom,
> Is thought-sick at the act.   (III.iv.50–52)

It is a curious conceit: Hamlet seems to be saying that the earth would be as appalled as the heavens at an act like this. Perhaps the pathetic fallacy spawned the old-fashioned phrase. There are, however, a few distinct 'inset devices', as they have sometimes been called, in Shakespeare. Two, the pageant of the worthies in *Love's Labour's Lost* and the mechanicals' play in *A Midsummer Night's Dream*, are expected to be ludicrous because of their performers. The first is given an unkind reception by the wits of Navarre. What the Athens artisans themselves call 'A tedious brief scene of young Pyramus' and Theseus (having seen it) 'This palpable-gross play', is less subject to aristocratic interruption, and so we get more of its individual flavour. *Dreadful dole* and *Come blade, my breast imbrue* and some of Bottom's frequent apostrophes:

> O grim-looked night, O night with hue so black,
> O night which ever art when day is not! (V.i.167–8)

would not have disgraced Pistol. Elsewhere alliteration, one or two archaisms (*hight, an,* 'if'), an excessive use of *do* as tense-marker, an inversion or two (*lion vile, lion rough*) more often give the impression of well-meaning rustic performers than deliberate parody of earlier drama, but the best in this kind are but shadows.

The extreme reaction to Juliet's supposed death (IV.v.) is almost a 'play within a play' of quite another kind. The exaggerated exclamations of the Nurse ('O lamentable day!'), Lady Capulet ('Accursed, unhappy, wretched, hateful day!'), Capulet ('Death is my son-in-law. Death is my heir.') and Paris ('Beguiled, divorced, wronged, spited, slain!') represent the ritualised grief of uncomprehending Verona. The Friar's motives are good and his theology impeccable, but his conceits on *promotion* and *married* seem too mannered. Only the musicians ('Faith, we may put up our pipes and be gone') show the correct and dignified response. The masque of Herne the Hunter in *The Merry Wives* is in verse – in a play predominantly in prose – as is proper to fairies. The more elevated style of the wedding masque in *The Tempest*, with its many adjectives and compounds, is proper to goddesses. It is narrative rather than dramatic poetry, but 'a most majestic vision, and / Harmonious charmingly' is in any event unlikely to be satirical. There is a great deal of pageantry in *Henry VIII*, but neither Henry's masque nor Katherine's dying vision ever really gets under way.

Which leaves *Hamlet*, both *Aeneas' Tale to Dido* and *The Murder of Gonzago. Aeneas' Tale to Dido* certainly seems a part for the First Player to tear a cat in. Yet Hamlet, and 'others whose judgement in such matters cried in the top of mine' think it an excellent play. How *could* he countenance such phrases as *total gules* (II.ii.455). *baked and impasted* (457), *o'er-sized with coagulate gore* (460), *whiff and wind of his fell sword* (471), *declining on the milky head / Of reverend Priam* (476), *Mars's armour, forged for proof eterne* (488), *threatening the flames/With bisson rheum* (503)? Are not these little better than some of the phrases Pistol uses? Well, not quite. They are, at least, coherent, part of a set speech, even if they are turgid and over-elaborate. Pistol's are disjointed scraps which together make little sense and, however comic, are presumably his comments on a real-life situation. *Aeneas' Tale to Dido* is regarded as fiction. This is the whole tenor of Hamlet's following soliloquy: 'What would he do / Had he the motive and the cue for passion / That I have?' Hamlet considers it a good *play*, and

Elizabethans saw rhetoric as appropriate language: you didn't come across a rugged Pyrrhus every day.

Before *The Murder of Gonzago* comes Hamlet's advice to the players. If *the speech* (III.ii.1) is the one Hamlet has composed specially, he may mean only that he does not want it disproportionately stressed. He evidently accepts 'the very torrent, tempest, and, as I may say, whirlwind of your passion' if the material justifies it; he does not accept ham acting just to please the groundlings or to draw unnecessary attention to the actor. *The Murder of Gonzago*, when it arrives, is if anything more unreal than *Aeneas' Tale to Dido*. It is preceded by a dumb show. There were dumb-shows on the Elizabethan stage, but not, so far as we know, followed by a repetition of the same action within the play proper. (Why did not Claudius react to the dumb show? He later asks Hamlet 'Have you heard the argument? Is there no offence in it?') *The Murder* is distinguished from the style of *Hamlet* proper by its rhymed couplets, its *sententiae*, its long-winded repetition, a few unusual words (*commutual, operant, enactures, confederate season*), some inversions (*Thoughts black, hands apt*), but the language of most of this inset is not very difficult. The opening speech of the Player King and the short speech of Lucianus which finally alarms Claudius (each of them only six lines long) are the only two passages obviously ritualistic and rhetorically strained. As Claire Replogle points out[11], the audience (both at Elsinore and at the Globe) must not be unnecessarily distracted from the events of the play: the point of the performance is, after all, to spring Claudius's guilt. Hamlet constantly criticises exaggerated acting ('pox, leave thy damnable faces, and begin') but not the style. What we have here is archaism maybe, exaggerated rhetoric maybe, theatricality maybe – but certainly not nonsense and hardly burlesque.

Nevertheless, as A. B. Kernan has recently remarked, Shakespeare seems oddly patronising in his portrayal of his own profession:

> He was, after all, a professional writer for what was by all accounts a
> skillful professional company playing in an excellent London theater,
> while the players he portrays in his plays are either members of a touring
> road company or amateurs performing old-fashioned entertainments and
> dramatisations of 'moldy tales' in a pavilion in an open park, the dining
> hall of a great house, and the presence chamber of a court.[12]

Was he contemptuous of the kind of drama which had preceded him, of things he could by now do so much better, biting the hand that had fed him? More likely, I think, he realised, once again, that a demonstrable clash of styles is one of the best ways of achieving dramatic contrast.

AFFAIRS OF STATE

Of the different Shakespearean styles which might be distinguished with some confidence, perhaps the most obvious is the heightened language of affairs of state. Important events concerning important persons require important-sounding language, a kind of linguistic flourish of trumpets. A few of Shakespeare's plays begin with a formal Chorus or Induction: *Romeo and Juliet, 2 Henry IV, Henry V, Troilus and Cressida.* In the short introductory chorus to *Romeo and Juliet,* the compounds (*star-crossed* lovers, *death-marked* love), the empty tense-marker (*doth . . . bury*), the elevated diction (*civil blood, fatal loins, misadventured piteous overthrows*) and the distorted syntax ('Which, but their children's end, naught could remove'; 'What here shall miss, our toil shall strive to mend.') – all these combine to suggest that this is not just a love story, for Romeo and Juliet are members of the two leading families in Verona whose quarrels will determine their tragic love and tragic death. But a better example is the Prologue to *Troilus and Cressida*:

> In Troy there lies the scene. From isles of Greece
> The princes orgulous, their high blood chafed,
> Have to the port of Athens sent their ships,
> Fraught with the ministers and instruments
> Of cruel war. Sixty and nine, that wore
> Their crownets regal, from th' Athenian bay
> Put forth toward Phrygia; and their vow is made
> To ransack Troy, within whose strong immures
> The ravished Helen, Menelaus' queen,
> With wanton Paris sleeps – and that's the quarrel.
> To Tenedos they come,
> And the deep-drawing barks do there disgorge
> Their warlike fraughtage. Now on Dardan plains
> The fresh and yet unbruised Greeks do pitch
> Their brave pavilions. Priam's six-gated city,
> Dardan, and Timbria, Helias, Chetas, Troien,
> And Antenonidus, with massy staples
> And corresp.onsive and fulfilling bolts,
> Sperr up the sons of Troy.

Immures, not walls; *fraughtage*, not freight; *correspsonsive and fulfilling bolts / Sperr up*, rather than 'tightly fitting bolts shut in'. *Ministers and instruments* and *fresh and unbruised* form doublets. *Deep-drawing* barks jostle beneath the *six-gated* city. Grammatically the periphrasic *do . . . disgorge* and *do pitch* achieve a suitable air of formality, as do the phrases *princes orgulous* and *crownets regal* with their un–English word-order of noun plus adjective. Occasional alliteration and sonorous proper names in the manner of Marlowe before, and Milton afterwards, simply increase the air of impressiveness and importance appropriate to the description of perhaps the greatest event of the classical world.

Not surprisingly, this style occurs most frequently in the history plays and the Roman plays. In *1 Henry IV* the opening speech is given by King Henry himself. It is less usual for the monarch to adopt this role, but Henry's language here is characteristic of the 'prologue' style. In addition to the features of diction and syntax mentioned above, he introduces the image of the clashing meteors (a *troubled heaven* reflects a troubled state) and the matter of his postponed pilgrimage to the Holy Land (once the rebellious English are settled he can transfer his attention to God's enemies). *2 Henry IV*, however, opens with an Induction: *Enter Rumour, painted full of tongues*. Rumour is a symbolic figure, not a particularised one, and both his name and his appearance recall *Aeneid IV* and Chaucer's *House of Fame*. In 1553, the Revels Office actually bought a coat and cap painted with eyes, tongues and ears. The *fearful musters* of line 12 might well recall those recently made in the late 1590s to oppose an expected Spanish invasion.[13] A few lines from the middle of the speech will illustrate its copiousness, partly of diction, partly of imagery:

> And who but Rumour, who but only I,
> Make fearful musters, and prepared defence,
> Whiles the big year, swollen with some other grief,
> Is thought with child by the stern tyrant War,
> And no such matter? Rumour is a pipe
> Blown by surmises, jealousies, conjectures,
> And of so easy and so plain a stop
> That the blunt monster with uncounted heads,
> The still-discordant wavering multitude,
> Can play upon it.

But the less admirable aspect of Rumour, its fickleness and coarseness, is indicated by the occasional plain style intrusion ('And no such matter; *Stuffing* the ears of men with false reports').

In this, and other plays, a similar high style is characteristic of those who speak of public affairs. They are frequently minor characters: Gentlemen, Messengers and old men without a name; the Bloody Sergeant in *Macbeth* and the Gardeners in *Richard II* (with their allegory of England as an overgrown garden) with a profession only. Who they are is not significant; what they say and the way in which they say it is. An extension of this 'prologue' style is used in some obvious set pieces, such as Gertrude's account of Ophelia's death or Enobarbus describing Cleopatra in her barge on the river Cydnus. It does not seem important that it is Gertrude who brings the news of Ophelia's suicide: her function here is simply that of messenger. Her initial statement is completely straightforward: 'Your sister's drowned, Laertes'; only then does she begin to speak of *pendent boughs, crownet weeds* and the *envious sliver*. Nor is it significant that it is John of Gaunt who makes the great patriotic speech about *This England*. From 'This royal throne of kings' (*Richard II* II.i.40) to 'this dear dear land / Dear for her reputation through the world' (line 58) is one huge subject, containing within itself lower levels of subordination but kept afloat by the repeated *This*. The predicate 'Is now leased out' does not occur until line 59. How many people who can recite the long high-style opening sequence also know the contrastive plain-style conclusion 'leased out... like to a tenement or pelting farm'? The remainder of the opening scene of 2 Henry IV, following Rumour's Induction, is still concerned with affairs of state, and Morton adopts an appropriately heightened style to describe the death of Hotspur at the hands of Prince Hal with the resultant rout of the rebels. But he concludes in the plain style of places, facts and figures:

> The sum of all
> Is that the king hath won, and hath sent out
> A speedy power to encounter you, my lord,
> Under the conduct of young Lancaster
> And Westmorland. This is the news at full. (I.i.131–5)

I.ii. in deliberate contrast with I.i., opens in a much lower style, with Falstaff and his page. Another example of deliberate style-switching – this time from outside the history plays – occurs early in *Hamlet*. Marcellus asks for an explanation of the military preparations going forward in Denmark and of the general air of anxiety and foreboding: 'Who is't that can inform me?' Horatio replies in the low style:

> That can I.
> At least the whisper goes so. (I.i.79–80)

but immediately changes to a much higher style to explain the national emergency (*emulate pride, sealed compact, seised, moiety competent, gaged, Sharked up, terms compulsory; Did slay, Did forfeit, doth... appear*; the Latinate *which* in lines 91 and 100). He concludes, however, in the same colloquial style as he had begun:

<pre>
                  And this, I take it,
      Is the main motive of our preparations,
      The source of this our watch, and the chief head
      Of this posthaste and romage in the land.   (I.i.104–7)
</pre>

so that the 'public' material is sandwiched between two short conversational passages.

I should like now to consider a rather more extended use of this
style for affairs of state, the opening scene of *King Lear*. Lear does
not merely divide his kingdom, he does it in the grand manner:

<pre>
                  Tell me, my daughters,
      Since now we will divest us both of *rule*,
      Interest of territory, cares of state,
      Which of you shall we say *doth love* us most,
      That we our largest bounty may extend
      Where nature *doth* with merit *challenge*.   (I.i.48–53)
</pre>

(Even before this, the doublet *cares and business*, the reference to
France and Burgundy's *amorous sojurn* and the Latinism *we unburdened*
set the tone.) Goneril is given her ample third of the territory:

<pre>
      Of all these bounds, even from this line to this,
      With shadowy forests and with champains riched,
      With plenteous rivers and wide-skirted meads,
      We make thee lady. To thine and Albany's issues
      Be this perpetual.   (I.i.63–7)
</pre>

Here the syntax achieves most of the desired effect: the inversion of
adjective and noun (a loan-word, anyway) in *champains riched*; the
construction *Of all these bounds . . . We make thee lady*; the grandeur of
Be this perpetual, with the heavy mid-line pause.

And so throughout the first half of the play, especially Act I. Consider, for example, the 'placing' of the Latin borrowings *felicitate*
(I.i.75), *Propinquity* (I.i.114), *derogate* (I.iv.277) and *cadent* (I.iv.282).
This is Lear's conception of his own role: *every inch a king, the name
and all th'addition to a king*. He keeps it up for some time, even in the
early part of the storm scene (e.g. III.ii.49–60) where the imperatives
are now directed to the elements instead of to his subjects.[14] But at
III.ii.67 'My wits begin to turn', and the appearance of Edgar as Poor
Tom in III.iv. seems finally to make Lear lose hold of his sanity. So
far as we know, Lear's madness and the figure of Poor Tom are
Shakespeare's own contribution to the story. At one point language
almost disintegrates, certainly as a tool for communication. Tom's

language reflects simply the concerns of his private world and Lear in his turn can understand it only with reference to *his* world: 'What, has his daughters brought him to this pass?'[15] When Lear finally achieves true knowledge of himself and of events, the exaggerated simplicity of his diction – too simple, surely, for any 'real' speech – with its predominantly monosyllabic cast, and of his syntax, with its short, coordinate clauses, incorporates the change:

> Lear   Pray do not mock me.
>   I am a very foolish fond old man,
>   Four score and upward, not an hour more nor less,
>   And, to deal plainly,
>   I fear I am not in my perfect mind.
>   Methinks I should know you, and know this man;
>   Yet I am doubtful; for I am mainly ignorant
>   What place this is; and all the skill I have
>   Remembers not these garments; nor I know not
>   Where I did lodge last night. Do not laugh at me,
>   For, as I am a man, I think this lady
>   To be my child Cordelia.
> Cordelia   And so I am, I am.
> Lear   Be your tears wet? Yes, faith: I pray, weep not.
>   If you have poison for me I will drink it.
>   I know you do not love me, for your sisters
>   Have, as I do remember, done me wrong.
>   You have some cause; they have not.   (IV.vii.59–75)

The course of the plot is therefore reflected in the changing style. In this last extract even the blank verse is instinctive, not regular. It is no accident that, at the very end of the play, Edgar's recipe for the new regime is to 'Speak what we feel, not what we ought to say'.

The elevated style is not, of course, peculiar to Shakespeare. There are isolated instances in Kyd and Marlowe before him and several more in Jacobean drama. Jonson's tragedies, a little surprisingly, perhaps, do not contain too many distinctive Latinisms. *Sejanus* (1603), a long play on a political subject, has plenty of copious lexis, but individual examples are not very remarkable: *intergatories, iterating, degenerous, importunacies, adscribe* are the most unusual. The later *Catiline* (1611) includes choruses at the end of each of the first four acts, but their style is fairly simple and their metre is different from the usual blank verse of the play. The syntax of some of the longer speeches (Cicero's especially)[16] flows much more smoothly than that of *Sejanus*, and several characters jibe at Cicero's elevated language: 'Now the vein swells', 'a boasting, insolent tongue-man', 'that fine rhetorical pipe of yours', and, most notably, Catiline's:

If an oration or high language, Fathers,
Could make me guilty, here is one hath done it;
He has strove to emulate this morning's thunder
With his prodigious rhetoric.   (IV.ii.403–6)

The diction of *Catiline*, however, is less noticeable for its unusual
Latin loans than for its use of words with their etymological (i.e.
Latin) meanings: *publication* (confiscation), *prosecute* (strive after),
insolent (unusual), *expect* (wait), *frequent* (well-attended), *vindicate* (pun-
ish), *immature* (premature). Compounds are few, although 'the *far-
triumphed* world' would not be out of place in *Antony and Cleopatra*. It
was Jonson who mocked not only the staging but the vocabulary of
the *Henry VI* plays:

> with three rusty swords,
> And help of some few *foot and half-foot words*
> Fight over York and Lancaster's long jars.
> (Prologue to *Every Man in his Humour*, 1616)

In his comedies, at least, Jonson professed (in the same Prologue)
'deeds and language such as men do use'.

We might expect to come across a good deal of the rhetoric of
public affairs in *Henry V*, but this is only partially the case. The only
lengthy example is the long speech of Burgundy (V.ii.) on the de-
vastation in France after the English invasions, with its extended
garden image. The choruses which introduce each act have their
impressive phrases (*ciphers to this great account*, I.17, *High upreared and
abutting fronts*, 21, *imaginary puissance*, 25; *the threaden sails / Borne with
th'invisible and creeping wind*, III.10; *pith and puissance*, 21; *entertain con-
jecture*, IV,1, *chide the cripple tardy-gaited night*, 20; *brook abridgement*,
V.44) but the final impression is not, I think, one of copiousness.
The same is true of Henry's great speeches – 'Once more unto the
breach...', before the walls of Harfleur, on Ceremony, on St Cris-
pin's Day – except, perhaps, for the images in the first three of these:

> Then lend the eye a terrible aspect;
> Let it pry through the portage of the head
> Like the brass cannon; let the brow o'erwhelm it
> As fearfully as doth a galled rock
> O'erhang and jutty his confounded base,
> Swilled with the wild and wasteful ocean.   (III.i.9–14)

> What is it then to me, if impious war,
> Arrayed in flames, like to the prince of fiends,

> Do, with his smirched complexion, all fell feats
> Enlinked to waste and desolation?   (III.iii.15–18)

>   . . . next day after dawn,
> Doth rise and help Hyperion to his horse.   (IV.i.267–8)

with which might be compared a rare conceit:

> And those that leave their valiant bones in France,
> Dying like men, though buried in your dunghills,
> They shall be famed; for there the sun shall greet them,
> And draw their honours reeking up to heaven,
> Leaving their earthly parts to choke your clime,
> The smell whereof shall breed a plague in France.
> Mark then abounding valour in our English,
> That being dead, like to the bullet's crasing,
> Break out into a second course of mischief,
> Killing in relapse of mortality.   (IV.iii.98–107)

Here, surely, is the clue to the function of much of the language of this play. The words themselves must show what the confines of the stage cannot. Jonson's gibe against *Henry VI* is answered directly in *Henry V*, and, as the play itself proves, triumphantly:

> Where – O for pity! – we shall much disgrace,
> With four or five most vile and ragged foils,
> Right ill-disposed in brawl ridiculous,
> The name of Agincourt.   (IV. Chorus 49–52)

The problem is faced squarely from the opening Chorus:

> Suppose within the girdle of these walls
> Are now confined two mighty monarchies,
> Whose high upreared and abutting fronts
> The perilous narrow ocean parts asunder.

and put most succinctly in the final Chorus, the Epilogue:

> In little room confining mighty men.

If *Henry V* is finally an experiment in staging, the imagery assumes a double importance and the diction should not claim undue attention as a result of unusual Latinisms or compounds. The best of the latter are primarily visual: the *worm-holes* of long-vanished days (II.iv.86), that *nook-shotten* isle of Albion (III.v.14), Investing *lank-lean* cheeks and *war-worn* coats (IV Chorus 26), The gum *down-roping* from their *pale-dead* eyes (IV.ii.46). There may be yet another reason.

It has often been observed that in the course of the two *Henry IV* plays, politics increasingly become *policy* (in the Elizabethan sense of scheming) and pragmatism replaces idealism: 'The England which is made by killing Richard, Hotspur and Falstaff is a more efficient but a less vital and less honest realm.'[17] The Hal who views honour as a matter of book-keeping:

> Percy is but my factor, good my lord,
> To engross up glorious deeds on my behalf.
>
> (*1 Hen IV* III.ii.147−8)

for whom the succession is a direct and practical matter, with few of his father's doubts:

> You won it, wore it, kept it, gave it me;
> Then plain and right must my possession be.
>
> (*2 Hen IV* IV.v.220−1)

comes to see his destiny as the efficient ruler England so obviously needs. Ralph Berry notices[18] how Canterbury and Ely, his advisers at the beginning of *Henry V*, open their discussion in I.i. colloquially ('My lord, I'll tell you') but soon pass to public oratory with public rhetoric ('heady currance scouring faults', 'Unseen, yet crescive in his faculty'), arguing by analogy (60−7), but return − especially Ely − to everyday speech for the real bargaining of money and titles ('But, my good lord...', 'How did this offer seem received?'). In its switching of styles this comes close to Horatio's early speech about military preparations in Denmark, but the manner in *Henry V* is opportunist and cynical; these churchmen-politicians expound the Salic Law and invoke the Book of Numbers to bolster a doubtful claim to the throne of France. Berry remarks on the number of *therefore's*, *for's* and *so's* in the play, several of them non-sequiturs. Rhetoric is above all imagery, for example the lengthy simile of the honey-bees (I.ii.187−204) in which the emperor, Henry, replaces the more usual queen. It is often good, stirring stuff, but Henry uses it to smother the deeper questions about the nature and responsibilities of kingship which he cannot − or will not − answer.[19] In a play which dabbles in stage dialect (Fluellen, Macmorris and Jamy − although set against the sobriety of English Gower) and the *franglais* of Henry and Katherine, the surface is glittering, but it remains surface only.

A ROMAN STYLE?

It is sometimes suggested that Shakespeare developed a distinctively 'Roman' style for characters like Brutus, Coriolanus or Octavius and that Antony contrasts with this. I should prefer to speak of a 'soldier-ly' style where, by convention, a plain manner of speech comes to be equated with integrity of character. This extension would allow us to incorporate characters from the English history plays, and others like Claudius and Kent. Such a style – if we can establish it – might show occasional affinities with that used for affairs of state, for these soldiers are frequently involved with matters of great moment, and, since they often use prose, a rather greater correspondence with the balanced prose style previously described. Brutus is the most obvious exponent of balance in his speech, although the clarity and austerity of the style of *Julius Caesar* as a whole owes something to its source in North's Plutarch. Brutus' verse is usually as balanced as his prose (I.ii.161–9 is a good example). An exception is the soliloquy at II.i. 10, 'It must be by his death...'. Cassius is more imaginative than Brutus, more impulsive and histrionic – in his prompt acceptance of Caesar's challenge at swimming or in his offer (IV.ii) to let Brutus stab him to death. He consequently uses more figurative language, although this never obtrudes. Caesar's own style is rather colourless, and it has often been remarked that we really see him only through the opinions of others. Although he sometimes shows evidence of real political judgement, he is perhaps beginning to live the Caesar legend, to listen to flatterers and to speak of himself in the third person. The short syntactical units he prefers emphasise his authority and efficiency.

Cassius pretends to be contemptuous of his opponents, Octavius and Antony:

> A peevish schoolboy, worthless of such honour,
> Joined with a masquer and a reveller.   (V.i.61–2)

Antony makes little impression until after the murder and Octavius does not appear until Act V. What one critic calls Antony's 'easy rhetoric'[20] is evident in the funeral oration, although, as with Goneril and Regan at the end of the first scene of *King Lear*, the exaggerated and hypocritical nature of much of what has just happened is empha-sised by the flat business-like exchange between Antony and his ser-vant immediately afterwards. The true expansiveness of Antony's style becomes evident in *Antony and Cleopatra*, and the very fact that he so seldom shares in the 'Roman' style is no small part of his attractiveness. In this play Egypt stands for indulgence and Rome for the hard work of running the Empire. In the East Antony's pleasure lies, but *business* (his own word) calls him away. On another occasion:

> He was disposed to mirth; but on the sudden
> A Roman thought hath struck him. (I.ii.83–4)

To Pompey he is 'this amorous surfeiter' (II.i.33) and, according to Enobarbus, 'He is already [III.vii.12] / Traduced for levity' in Rome. The death of Fulvia is only one of several reasons why he feels he must return to Rome. Her death is a matter for laconic regret, but is still more a reminder of the contrast between Rome and Egypt:

> She's good, being gone:
> The hand could pluck her back that shoved her on.
> I must from this enchanting queen break off. (I.ii.127–9)

Rome seems to recall the younger, more military-minded Antony and the syntax becomes correspondingly more taut:

> You do mistake your business. My brother never
> Did urge me in his act. I did inquire it,
> And have my learning from some true reports
> That drew their swords with you. Did he not rather
> Discredit my authority with yours,
> And make the wars alike against my stomach,
> Having alike your cause? Of this, my letters
> Before did satisfy you. If you'll patch a quarrel,
> As matter whole you have to make it with,
> It must not be with this. (II.ii.49–58)[21]

It is no accident that this is part of an exchange with Octavius.

Octavius is developed more fully than in *Julius Caesar*. His austere and rather joyless style remains; D. M. Burton notices[22] the marked word order sustained over several sentences, each beginning with an adjunct phrase:

> Octavius   *I' th' market-place on a tribunal silvered,*
> Cleopatra and himself in chairs of gold
> Were publicly enthroned; *at the feet* sat
> Caesarion, whom they call my father's son,
> And all the unlawful issue that their lust
> Since then hath made between them. *Unto her*
> He gave the stablishment of Egypt; made her

171

> Of lower Syria, Cyprus, Lydia,
> Absolute queen.
> Maecenas   This in the public eye?
> Octavius   *I' th' common showplace*, where they exercise.   (III.vi.3–12)

But Octavius uses a surprising number of polysyllabic words too, so that his disciplined style is likely to be an instrument of deliberate policy, to be used as occasion serves. Cleopatra, at least, comes to recognise this:

> He words me, girls, he words me, that I should not
> Be noble to myself.   (V.ii.191–2)

Enobarbus, less puritanical than some of the Roman soldiers, recognises both the discipline of Rome and the attraction of Egypt. His early air of disillusionment makes him the ideal character to describe the magnificence of Cleopatra on her barge (just as the blunt Casca is chosen to relate the marvels seen on the streets of Rome on the night before Caesar's murder). He does, it, furthermore, in blank verse, whereas hitherto he has used more prose than verse. It is a measure of how much Cleopatra inspires him, even though to her face he is unsparing of her faults. But as self-interest gradually overcomes his loyalty to Antony, Enobarbus, in Burckhardt's phrase 'the man who leaves before the play is over'[23], increasingly uses a verse marked by both aphorism and colloquialism:

> Yes, like enough, high-battled Caesar will
> Unstate his happiness and be staged to th' show
> Against a sworder! I see men's judgements are
> A parcel of their fortunes, and things outward
> Do draw the inward quality after them,
> To suffer all alike. That he should dream,
> Knowing all measures, the full Caesar will
> Answer his emptiness! Caesar, thou hast subdued
> His judgement too.   (III.xiii.29–37)

Finally, overcome by Antony's generosity in sending him his treasure, he dies, in a ditch, 'a master-leaver and a fugitive', in a Roman manner but in a most un–Roman style.

In many ways *Coriolanus*[24] maintains the quintessence of Romanness. Almost one-quarter of the text is in prose, an unusually high proportion for a comparatively late play. The hero – like Caesar – is apt to speak of himself in the third person. There is little Latinate diction, however. When Coriolanus speaks of *acclamations hyperbolic-*

al, he is being sarcastic to the plebians. Of Menenius's two coinages,
one, *bisson conspectuities* (II.i.60), is addressed to the tribunes and the
other, *empiricutic* (II.i.112), is a mark of high spirits at receiving a
letter from Coriolanus. The only phrase of this kind that jars is
Th'apprehension of his present portance, used by Sicinius to the citizens
who seem much more literate than their counterparts in *Julius Caesar*.
The tribunes, too, are more adroit politicians than plain men.
Coriolanus has only three soliloquies, none very long and the third –
as he watches his family approach to sue for peace – may more properly be termed an aside. Characteristically, they are all three concerned with the present or the immediate future.[25] His syntax sometimes shows the balance that in the Roman plays suggests strength
and reserves of power. Early in the play he seeks support for yet
another battle:

> If any such be here –
> As it were sin to doubt – that love this painting
> Wherein you see me smeared; if any fear
> Lesser his person than an ill report;
> If any think brave death outweighs bad life,
> And that his country's dearer than himself;
> Let him alone, or so many so minded,
> Wave thus to express his disposition,
> And follow Martius.   (I.vi.67–75)

The repeated *if*, in initial position, emphasises the rhetorical construction. Madeline Doran notes the antitheses and paradox in a later
speech:

> If he [Sicinius] have power,
> Then vail your ignorance; if none, awake
> Your dangerous lenity. If you are learned,
> Be not as common fools; if you are not,
> Let them [the tribunes] have cushions by you. You are plebians,
> If they be senators; and they are no less,
> When, both your voices blended, the great'st taste
> Most palates theirs.   (III.i.97–104)[26]

Once again this is the language of command and of argument between equals which (despite its metaphors) has been pared down to
essentials. A similar syntax characterises Titus Lartius (I.vii.1–5),
the brief, coordinate clauses of Comenius's eulogy of Coriolanus
before the Senate (II.ii.80–120), and the parallel verbs in Aufidius'
speech at V.vi.29–41 (*took . . . made . . . gave . . . let . . . served . . . holp . . .*

took . . . seemed . . . waged . . .). These are all soldiers, all men whom
Coriolanus admires.

Of course Coriolanus' ruin is brought about by his failure to flatter the plebians in the appropriately fulsome language:

> I would not buy
> Their mercy at the price of one fair word.   (III.iii.90–1)

He is no Bolingbroke *wooing poor craftsmen*. Certainly he is, as Menenius points out, *ill-schooled in bolted* [refined] *language*. He himself
admits that he *fled from words*. He calls Virgilia *my gracious silence*. But
it would be wrong to see him as taciturn. He is eloquent as well as
scathing about the attitudes of the plebs in the opening scene and
again in III.i. when they change their minds about supporting him
for the consulship. In this latter scene, people want to *stop* him talking: *No more words*, says a senator; *Come, enough*, from Menenius; *he
has said enough*, from Brutus. What he detests is cowardice, hypocrisy, and undue flattery which he interprets as hypocrisy. It is this
which produces brusqueness and occasionally downright rudeness: 'I
will go wash.' (I.ix.67), 'Will the time serve to tell? I do not think. /
Where is the enemy?' (I.vi.46–7). When his obduracy is finally overcome by Volumnia's double appeal to his patriotism and his regard
for his mother, the change is marked by a new style:

> Hail Lords! I am returned your soldier,
> No more infected with my country's love
> Than when I parted hence, but still subsisting
> Under your great command. You are to know
> That prosperously I have attempted and
> With bloody passage led your wars even to
> The gates of Rome. Our spoils we have brought home
> Doth more than counterpoise a full third part
> The charges of the action. We have made peace
> With no less honour to the Antiates
> Than shame to th' Romans. And we here deliver,
> Subscribed by th' consuls and patricians,
> Together with the seal o' th' Senate, what
> We have compounded on.   (V.vi.71–84)

When previously did Coriolanus speak in such generalities, with
subordinate clauses, with *we* and not *I*? He has finally learned to talk
like a politician, to present a defeat as a victory, but in so doing he
debases himself. For all his previous inflexibility, we admired him
more when he spoke like a Roman. Plutarch's Coriolanus had been

'thought no less eloquent in tongue than warlike in show', but if you trim your hero's style too drastically, you stop the play. There is a limit even to the reticence of an extreme Roman style, and intransigence eventually gives way to maternal pressure and to necessity.

With some qualifications, then, it seems possible to distinguish a basic Roman style, although it is hard to find major characters (except perhaps Brutus) who can be characterised adequately in this manner. Others adapt or temporarily relinquish the style according to situation or audience. The Roman plays do not form a series like the English history plays, however much Rome may have been viewed as the civic model for the Elizabethans. But their central theme does seem to be the relationship between the individual and the state and usually (although not with Antony) the state wins. Public good is placed above private good, and public good demands control, austerity, decisiveness. The comparative restriction of stylistic range – although it does not appear quite in this light when we read the Roman plays – means that the hero, not needing to universalise his situation, makes little use of devices like soliloquy, and when soliloquies occur they are simpler in diction and syntax than in the great tragedies. Traces of the plain, impersonal, sometimes clipped manner of the 'Roman' style can be seen in the English histories and, adapted to rather different purposes, in one or two other plays.

In a negative way it appears in Hotspur's rejection of 'poetic' language as manifested in Glendower's Celtic charm:

> I had rather be a kitten and cry 'mew'
> Than one of these same metre ballad-mongers.
> I had rather hear a brazen canstick turned,
> Or a dry wheel grate on an axle-tree,
> And that would set my teeth nothing on edge,
> Nothing so much as mincing poetry.
> 'Tis like the forced gait of a shuffling nag.   (*1 Hen IV* III.i.123–9)

although Worcester had shrewdly noticed that honour is apt to make Hotspur wax lyrical:

> He apprehends a world of figures here,
> But not the form of what he should attend.   (*1 Hen IV* I.iii.207–8)

The Bastard Fauconbridge in *King John* shows some of the same irreverence, although his contempt is for power politics, but later he is driven, despite himself, to become more involved in the political struggle. As yet (1596?) his mental attitude does not seem to produce an individual style. Horatio's integrity, too, is more a passive than an active virtue: he is the reverse of Hamlet in apparently having no problems at all. Bolingbroke, however, is an altogether different case. He is said by Gaunt to *hoard words*, and we are surely meant to watch the gravitation of power from a king who attitudinises and poeticises, to a man who has no time to waste on unnecessary refinements of language. It has recently been argued, however, that this contrast can be overstated. On occasion Bolingbroke can be as polished as Richard, both in diction and in syntax, while Richard is capable of using a plain style (e.g. at III.iii.200–8 and V.i.59–68). Moreover, Richard's conceits are most numerous in the second part of the play, whereas he had earlier shown some signs of an ability to control events.[27] Stephen Booth argues that the excessive subordination in Richard's early speeches mirrors his ineffectual behaviour, for example the long periphrasis between 'Draw near / And list what with our council we have done' and 'Therefore we banish you our territories' (I.iii.123–39). He might also have cited the heavy modification of noun phrases in this speech, often by 'poetic' compounds. After Richard returns from Ireland in III.ii., Booth notices that, however extravagant his images, his *syntax* is more easily intelligible.[28] Surely the overriding difference between Richard and Bolingbroke is that the latter is an accomplished politician. As spectators we remain uncertain and uncommitted about him: he is a usurper, yet he is also acting to defend his inheritance. (Something of the same deviousness of character continues after he becomes Henry IV.). He does not make the same single, unconvincing shift as Mortimer in Marlowe's *Edward II*, from plain-speaking rough baron and upholder of justice to the Machiavellian protector and lover of Isabella who can quote Latin and philosophise about Fortune. As Edward II is not Richard, so Mortimer is not yet Henry Bolingbroke: hoarding words was far from being Marlowe's genius. Bolingbroke's variations in style seem always motivated by expediency. As do Octavius's and Claudius's in later plays. All three go about getting their own way by a kind of linguistic stealth.

ABSOLUTE INTEGRITY

In *King Lear*, Shakespeare faced (but perhaps did not completely solve) the task of creating a style to suggest absolute goodness. Other characters praise Cordelia generously; she herself appears in only four scenes of the play. The Gentleman's description of her sorrow (IV.iii) is over-metaphorical, artificial and distant, the formal language of public events rather than the tone of deep concern. Cordelia sometimes states what she *cannot* do: heave her heart into her mouth; show a glib and oily art / To speak and purpose not; counterfeit a still-soliciting eye or blown ambition. Occasionally, as with the doublets *aidant and remediate* (IV.iv.17) and *untuned and jarring senses* (IV.vii.16) or the coinage *out-frown false Fortune's frown* (V.iii. 6 – a compound and a personification more characteristic of her father), her language seems too premeditated and contrived. But by this time she is to be seen as Queen of France, a role which does not quite complement that of Lear's daughter. Twice in IV.vii. repetition ('And so I am, I am', 'No cause, no cause') is used to suggest sincerity, but only once, in her first speech of any length in the play, do the simple lexis and straightforward syntax convey her utter integrity:

> Good my lord,
> You have begot me, bred me, loved me.
> I return those duties back as are right fit,
> Obey you, love you, and most honour you.
> Why have my sisters husbands, if they say
> They love you all? Haply when I shall wed,
> That lord whose hand must take my plight shall carry
> Half my love with him, half my care and duty.
> Sure I shall never marry like my sisters,
> To love my father all. (I.i.95–104)

Lear knows that plainness may conceal pride – 'Let pride, which she calls plainness, marry her' – but with Cordelia, no more than with Kent, is he able to recognise true worth when he sees it.[29] Yet, in a strange way, Lear *is* right: nothing will come of nothing. Edgar acts out his suffering and in it assumes different identities: poor Tom, the peasant who witnesses Gloucester's 'fall', a knightly champion, but Cordelia, as John Reibetanz says,[30] simply *is*.

It may well be that there is no special rhetoric to express a feeling as deep as Cordelia's. Elsewhere in Shakespeare this is stated; it cannot be easily demonstrated:

> For truth hath better deeds than words to grace it. (*TGV* II.ii.18)

> Honest plain words best pierce the ear of grief. (*LLL* V.ii.754)

> The silence often of pure innocence
> Persuades where speaking fails. (*WT* II.ii.41–2)

Octavia, of a 'holy, cold and still conversation' and Virginia, too much under the domination of Volumnia, scarcely come alive as Cordelia does, despite her few appearances. The father-daughter relationship seems increasingly to have occupied Shakespeare in his later plays. Both Perdita and Marina do not appear until Act IV, although their earlier adventures have been narrated. Miranda appears much earlier, although her function in I.ii. is simply to act as a willing listener as Prospero recounts the circumstances of his exile from Milan. She is reminded of the hardships she endured as a child; she is not called upon to suffer, as Marina does, within the play itself. The simple style of her speech demonstrates her compassion for those in the shipwreck or later for Ferdinand as he toils to collect logs. Once only is *plain and holy innocence* really challenged to express itself in appropriate language:

> I am your wife, if you will marry me.
> If not, I'll die your maid. To be your fellow
> You may deny me, but I'll be your servant
> Whether you will or no. (III.i.83–6)

Perdita's inability to match Florizel's public avowal of their love:

> I cannot speak
> So well, nothing so well; no, nor mean better.
> By th'pattern of mine own thoughts I cut out
> The purity of his. (IV.iv.377–80)

achieves, by its hesitant syntax and double negatives, something of her goodness and diffidence; she is not surprised when Polixines rejects her as a daughter-in-law (IV.iv.438–47). Florizel *describes* her, but the problem at the sheep-shearing is to show her as 'something greater than herself / Too noble for this place'.

Marina's speech in the brothel, as well as her behaviour, surprises Lysimachus, and her blistering accusations deflate even Boult. Twice in the play, I think, Marina comes closest of all these heroines to achieving by her style both directness and utter candour:

> Why would she have me killed?
> Now, as I can remember, by my troth,
> I never did her hurt in all my life.
> I never spake bad word nor did ill turn
> To any living creature. Believe me, law,
> I never killed a mouse, nor hurt a fly,
> I trod upon a worm against my will,
> But I wept for't. How have I offended,

Wherein my death might yield her any profit,
Or my life imply her any danger?   (IV.i.73–82)

But, good sir,
Whither will you have me? Why do you weep? It may be
You think me an impostor. No, good faith!
I am the daughter to King Pericles,
If good King Pericles be.   (V.i.177–81)

Yet the first of these speeches almost slips into sentimentality. The linguistic problem is acute, perhaps even beyond the range of the mature Shakespeare. In *All's Well*, Helena, concealing her true identity, belies herself:

> . . . all her deserving
> Is a reserved honesty, *and that*
> *I have not heard examined.*   (III.v.60–2)

Perhaps we have here reached the limits of stylistic variation.

NOTES AND REFERENCES

1. Salmon (1967).
2. Vickers (1968). See also Barish (1964).
3. Antony Bacon's introduction to the first English translation of Tacitus (by Sir Henry Savile, 1591); quoted Williamson (1936) p. 327.
4. *The Advancement of Learning*, ed. A. Johnston, Clarendon Press, Oxford (1974), p. 25.
5. Carey (1970), p.399.
6. Quoted from Harris (1968), p.133. See also Eliot (1953), pp. 341–53.
7. *Francis Bacon's Essays*, ed. O. Smeaton, Dent. (1906). *Of Studies* was one of the original ten essays published in 1597.
8. Illustrated in detail, Doran (1976), pp. 63–91.
9. Coulthard (1977), pp. 174–7.
10. 'To the Reader', *Christ's Tears Over Jerusalem* (1954), *The Works of Thomas Nashe*, ed. R. B. McKerrow, Blackwell, Oxford (1958), II, p.184.
11. Replogle (1969). Hibbard (1981), p. 15, points out that, in *The Spanish Tragedy*, 'Soliman and Persida' (unlike the insets in *Hamlet*) is not distinguished in style from the play proper.
12. Kernan (1979), p.80; the plays are *Hamlet, TS, LLL* and *MND* respectively.
13. See the notes, pp. 164–7, in the New Penguin edition by P. H. Davison.
14. De Grazia (1978), p.386.

The literary language of Shakespeare

15. Danson (1974), p.176.
16. E.g. IV.ii.54–73, 403–6. *Cataline* and *Every Man in His Humour* are quoted from *Works*, ed. C. H. Herford and P. and E. M. Simpson, Clarendon Press, Oxford.
17. Kernan (1975), p.288.
18. Berry (1978), pp. 49–59.
19. Kernan (1975), p.295; Danby (1949), p.89; Jump (1975), p.241; Calderwood (1979). The portrait in the National Portrait Gallery suggests something of the same coldness.
20. N. Sanders, New Penguin edition, p.24.
21. Hume (1973); Lloyd (1959); Ingledew (1971), Introduction.
22. Burton (1968), p.141.
23. Burckhardt (1968), p.282.
24. Hill (1964); Calderwood (1966); Sicherman (1972); Vickers (1976); van Dyke (1977). The Introduction to Ingledew (1973) is also useful.
25. McElroy (1973), p.239.
26. Doran (1976), p.190.
27. Baxter (1980), pp. 116–7; Hockey (1964); Potter (1974).
28. Booth (1977).
29. Champion (1976), p.47. See also Leider (1970).
30. Reibetanz (1977), p.65.

CHAPTER NINE
The development of the soliloquy

We must beware of applying to English drama a Darwinian theory of evolution which gives a neat development of mystery plays, moralities, interludes, the 'University Wits' and (finally) Shakespeare. No one of these completely drives out its predecessors and the young Shakespeare could well have seen morality plays acted. But obviously there is some sense of progress, and, in considering how the Elizabethan dramatists developed a syntax for exploring and describing motivation, we may properly begin with the morality plays. Moralities avoid ambiguities and dramatise clear-cut choices, good versus evil:

> When the debate is between some form of good and evil, obviously the right choice can only be of the good; if it is of the evil, tragedy must follow, as in *Faustus* or *Macbeth*. The morality play itself and romantic comedy or tragi-comedy mitigate the harshness of a wrong choice by allowing an escape if a change of heart and a reversal of choice come in time, as in *Mankind* or in *Measure for Measure* or in *The Winter's Tale*. But tragedy keeps its inexorability and its irony by making its reversals of choice, as in *Coriolanus*, always too late. In any case, the impasse created by the presentation of opposing points of view may be broken only by genuine choice.[1]

At its simplest, the choice which the hero has to make is externalised; Faustus's good and bad angels, the seven deadly sins and the old man are all morality figures. With the development of the Senecan villain and the revenge motive, the Machiavel and the Malcontent, the picture becomes more complicated. The Machiavel (Iago, Bosola, Vindice) is completely and remorselessly dedicated to the winning of power for his own ends. The Malcontent (Jaques, Bussy and, in part, Hamlet) would wish to proceed peaceably, but, because of the irrationality of worldly behaviour, he is led to choose more active means of achieving his wishes.² His very isolation from society leads to introspection. The discrepancy between what these characters may say publicly and what they really feel has to be made clear to the audience. In addition, revenge itself gradually became a less straightforward process in which a good clean killing was felt to be too simple. The methods of exacting the revenge – covert stabbing in the midst of festive celebrations, the kissing of a poisoned book, a rigged fencing match – become more various. Circumstances, or his own habit of thinking too precisely on the event, might delay, if not actually prevent, the hero taking revenge. The whole business might, while eliminating the villain, in some way taint the hero himself. The answer to these complexities was, more often than not, the soliloquy (and, less important, the aside), a stage convention to be sure, but in the circumstances a necessary one, and one which, since it needed to show the character resolving conflicting impulses, demanded a deliberate choice of syntax. By convention, too, what the character says in a soliloquy is to be taken as sincere, at least within the limits of his own self-knowledge.

The full possibilities of the soliloquy seem to have dawned on Shakespeare comparatively slowly. Aaron's soliloquy at the opening of the second act of *Titus Andronicus* is simply expository; he decides to use his affair with Tamora to advance himself, but there is no self-analysis. Later he simply makes certain that the audience knows him for what he really is:

> I go, Andronicus, and for thy hand
> Look by and by to have thy sons with thee.
> [*Aside*] Their heads, I mean. O, how this villainy
> Doth fat me with the very thoughts of it!
> Let fools do good, and fair men call for grace,
> Aaron will have his soul black like his face.   (III.i.200–5)

This is no better than the later villain of melodrama who twirls his black moustachios. It demands no special syntax and the concluding couplet simply marks a neat exit. His exaggerated self-confessions in V.i. and V.iii. cannot take the form of soliloquies since his evil must be publicly recognised and punished. He shows no consciousness of any conflicting impulses within himself, and his sole mitigating feature – his desire to keep his illegitimate child – is really an assertion of his own individuality, and characteristically results in yet another killing, that of the nurse.

There are several soliloquies in *Henry VI*, but they either merely keep us abreast of events in those three confusing plays or else flatly

provide information about the character's intentions.[3] Their usual
position is at the end of a scene or, less often, at its beginning.
Perhaps the most moving is that by Henry himself as he sits on the
molehill at Towton, no part of the battle which is to decide his future (*3 Henry VI*, II.v). The soliloquy, however, does not show Henry deciding to abdicate and to embrace the simple life he so much de-
sires. He merely laments, like some of his kingly successors, the
troubles which beset a monarch; he does nothing about them. The
whole soliloquy is too 'poetic' and too rhetorical, and the air of
theatricality is continued by the entry of the son who has unwittingly
killed his father and the father who has killed his son; they are not individuals, merely representative morality figures. Henry can identify
with them but can scarcely help them:

> Sad-hearted men, much overgone with care,
> Here sits a king more woeful than you are.   (*3 Hen VI* II.v.123–4)

Richard III, however, produces the right character for soliloquis-
ing, even if it does not yet achieve a demonstration of decision making – the decisions have already been made – or of moral perturbation.
Useless to protest that contemporary portraits give no hint of de-
formity or that Richard probably had no long-term ambitions for
the crown. These are historians' quibbles; the play emphasises
Richard's larger-than-life character and his personal magnetism. He
is, in Peter Saccio's phrase, both 'demonic jester and archetypal
wicked uncle'.[4] He first really comes alive in a long soliloquy in *3
Henry VI*, III.ii.124–95, where the middle-style platitudes, *golden
time, premeditation, corrupt frail nature, envious mountain, disproportion,
impaled*, together with the similes of the man grazing towards the distant shore and blundering about in the thorny wood, are brought to
earth by the plain-style colloquialisms: *Ay, and all, I look for, And so
I say, some bribe, And yet I know not, between me and home*, concluding
with his determination to achieve the crown, the sole reality, '*Tut,
were it farther off, I'll pluck it down*'. The long soliloquy which
opens *Richard III* indicates his domination of the play and continues
the same technique. Even metaphors can be sardonically trans-
formed: *grim-visaged war . . . capers nimbly in a lady's chamber*. The rhetoric consists of the elaboration of the first-person pronouns at the
beginning of lines 14, 16, 18 and 24 by a series of relative, participial
and noun clauses to show him as so comprehensively out of tune
with the times that machiavellianism becomes the logical alternative:
But I . . . I . . . I . . . Why I . . .

> *And therefore*, since I cannot prove a lover
> To entertain these fair well-spoken days,
> I am determined to prove a villain
> And hate the idle pleasures of these days.
> Plots have I laid . . .   (I.i.28–32)

Certainly his intrigues are so many and so involved that the audience needs to be put in the know, but the soliloquies merely reveal his aims and his relish in furthering them:

> And thus I clothe my naked villainy
> With odd old ends stolen forth of holy writ,
> And seem a saint, when most I play the devil.   (I.iii.335–7)

The *odd old ends* can serve to colour a feigned reluctance to accept the crown ('Aloft, between two bishops') or, supplemented by a Petrarchan conceit or two, help to win over Anne or Elizabeth.

After the opening three scenes there is a long gap before the next soliloquy, by which time Richard is almost king. The plotting has brought tangible rewards, but also further problems:

> But I am in
> So far in blood that sin will pluck on sin.
> Tear-falling pity dwells not in this eye.   (IV.ii.62–3)

So far in blood: the very words are to become Macbeth's ('I am in blood / Stepped in so far . . .') but, unlike Macbeth's, Richard's is no tortured confession. He does not see his diabolical scheming as corrupting his own nature. Only his final soliloquy, where he starts out of the dream in which the ghosts of his victims (pure morality figures employed to externalise internal debate)[5], have appeared to him in turn, shows him faltering, and the hitherto controlled syntax correspondingly changing:

> What do I fear? Myself? There's none else by.
> Richard loves Richard: that is, I am I.
> Is there a murderer here? No. Yes, I am.
> Then fly. What, from myself? Great reason why –
> Lest I revenge. Myself upon myself?
> Alack, I love myself. Wherefore? For any good
> That I myself have done unto myself?   (V.iii.183–9)

The technique of rapid question and answer was one Shakespeare was to employ in later soliloquies, but here the attempt to show

Richard's panic results in a syntax so broken that the audience is hard put to it to follow the quick reversals of thought and the speech is in danger of becoming ridiculous. Towards its end, the soliloquy repeats the same arguments but in less feverish syntax. If we compare a soliloquy by Angelo in *Measure for Measure* (II.ii.161–87), there is the same method of question and answer, but the introduction of imagery (the carrion and the violet, the razing of the sanctuary, the corrupt judges) both allows the audience to get its breath and gives Angelo's dilemma a wider significance.

This is, however, to anticipate. *The Spanish Tragedy* has an early brief soliloquy concluding a scene and telling us no more than we already know:

> Thus have I with an envious, forged tale
> Deceiv'd the king, betray'd mine enemy,
> And hope for guerdon of my villainy. (I.iii.93–5)[6]

but it also uses the soliloquy to show Hieronimo's discovery of the corpse of his son (II.iv). He hears a cry from the garden, someone needing help, perhaps; instead he finds a body, and only as he cuts it down does he see that it is his son who has been hanged; who can have done such a deed, and why? The emphasis is on the gradualness of the discovery and the horror of the scene: he is alone and it is dead of night. The situation is completely right, but there is no real explanation of how all this affects him; instead rhetoric is used to suggest emotion. Nor are subsequent soliloquies, in which Hieronimo first decides to revenge his son's death himself and later discovers the difficulties of achieving a just revenge, very much better. He simply *exclaims*, and although he rejects the idea of suicide and comes to realise the pointlessness of complaint ('But wherefore waste I mine unfruitful words?'), we get nothing of Hamlet's self-disgust and self-condemnation. Only by the device of the play does he obtain his desired revenge. None of his soliloquies calls for a special syntax, since none does anything to question his motives. Only the soliloquy of Isabella, at the close of which she stabs herself (IV.ii), begins to achieve the necessary change of pace. The frenzied cutting of the branches in the arbour ('Down with these branches... Down with them...') gives way to the slower 'Ay, here he died, and here I him embrace', with its succession of monosyllables, quickens again to 'Hieronomo, make haste... Make haste, Hieronimo...', and then the flow of words suddenly breaks as she misinterprets his delay and realises the futility of her own action:

> Ah, nay, thou dost delay their deaths,
> Forgives the murderers of thy noble son,
> And none but I bestir me' – to no end.   (IV.ii.32–4)

Clemen[7] believes that in *Dr Faustus* the soliloquy is, for the first time, used to show the character thinking as he speaks. Certainly this is true of the great final soliloquy. The comparatively smooth syntax of the opening lines, with their *enjambement*, shows Faustus still in some kind of desperate control: a miracle may even yet happen. But his increasing panic is indicated by the broken lines, and other lines which are not full lines at all but only a couple of syllables, the pause allowing the terrible reality of retribution to sink in. Unlike Richard III's final soliloquy, the broken lines are interspersed with others whose greater normality (and even some subordination) suggest possibilities other than a speedy descent to hell. These are developed for a little, only to be interrupted by the striking of the clock and the resumption of a more irregular syntax:

> No, no!
> Then will I headlong run into the earth.
> Earth, gape. O no, it will not harbour me.
> You stars that reign'd at my nativity,
> Whose influence hath allotted death and hell,
> Now draw up Faustus like a foggy mist
> Into the entrails of yon labouring cloud,
> That when you vomit forth into the air
> My limbs may issue from your smoky mouths,
> So that my soul may but ascend to heaven . . .   *The watch strikes.*
>
> My God, my God, look not so fierce on me.
> Adders and serpents, let me breathe awhile.
> Ugly hell, gape not; come not, Lucifer.
> I'll burn my books. Ah, Mephistophilis!   *Exeunt with him.*
>   (V.ii.155–64, 188–91)

Earlier examples of this technique occur at the beginning of II.i. ('Now, Faustus, must thou needs be damn'd . . .') and briefly at II.i.65–70 ('What might the staying of my blood portend?'). Although the Prologue of *The Jew of Malta* is spoken by Machiavelli himself, the soliloquies are almost wholly descriptive. We see Barabas affecting to despise the wealth he so much relishes, his fanatical judaism, his hypocrisy in blaming the Christians for his very own vices, 'malice, falsehood, and excessive pride', and the love for his daughter – all information we need to know to keep abreast of his intrigue and which we cannot easily acquire except by soliloquy. Only at the opening of the penultimate soliloquy (V.ii.28–46) do the short syntactical units show Barabas beginning to worry:

> I now am Governor of Malta; true.
> But Malta hates me, and in hating me
> My life's in danger; and what boots it thee,
> Poor Barabas, to be the Governor,
> When as thy life shall be at their command?
> No, Barabas, this must be look'd into;
> And, since by wrong thou got'st authority,
> Maintain it bravely by firm policy;
> At least, unprofitably lose it not.   (V.ii.28–36)

but as he regains control the lines become less broken and the *enjambement* increases.

Shakespeare's early tragedies and the histories take the soliloquy little if any further. Juliet's soliloquy in III.ii. introduces the paradox of the tedious day and the wished-for night, since Romeo is *day in night*. Such complexities as this will develop into the difficult and distorted syntax of the later plays, where the heroine both is and is not Cressid and nothing is but what is not. Juliet needs to summon all her courage to swallow the Friar's potion, and the technique of rapid questions and self-answers gradually gives way to that of the description of the horrors of waking from her sleep shut within the Capulet family vault. Yet even there the parentheses and sudden changes of direction recreate the sheer terror she feels at what she is proposing to do:

> Or, if I live, is it not very like
> The horrible conceit of death and night,
> Together with the terror of the place –
> As in a vault, an ancient receptacle
> Where for this many hundred years the bones
> Of all my buried ancestors are packed;
> Where bloody Tybalt, yet but green in earth,
> Lies festering in his shroud; where, as they say,
> At some hours in the night spirits resort –
> Alack, alack, is it not like that I,
> So early waking – what with loathsome smells,
> And shrieks like mandrakes torn out of the earth,
> That living mortals, hearing them, run mad –
> O, if I wake, shall I not be distraught,
> Environed with all these hideous fears?   (IV.iii.36–50)

Romeo's dying soliloquy is, I think, less impressive. Once more it opens with a series of questions, but they are questions which no longer matter, and Romeo is easily diverted into a conceit:

The literary language of Shakespeare

> For here lies Juliet, and her beauty makes
> This vault a feasting presence full of light.
> Death, lie thou there, by a dead man interred. (V.iii.85–7)

His elaboration of further conceits, however moving (Death, with his pale flag, keeps Juliet here in dark to be his paramour), is not so convincing as Juliet's own earlier fears. In Romeo's mind, the star-crossed lovers and their quarrelling families struggle with an as yet undeveloped sense of personal responsibility for Juliet's death. The business of moral responsibility for one's actions will become matter for later soliloquies.

In *King John*, the Bastard's soliloquies mimic the falseness of *worshipful society* and the all-conquering power of commodity. The very smoothness of such hypocrisy must be mirrored in the syntax. Although circumstances drive him out of his detached cynicism and force him to take sides, we do not share in his perturbation: it is simply stated:

> I am amazed, methinks, and lose my way
> Among the thorns and dangers of this world. (IV.iii.140–1)

The death of young Arthur rouses his anger, and anger, characteristically with him, shows itself not in reflection but in action and a surge of patriotism. Bolingbroke never soliloquises, and does not even seem to confide in his associates. As Henry IV he cannot sleep, but his single soliloquy refuses to face the real reason, his guilt over the way he came by the crown. Richard II's only soliloquy – one of the longest Shakespeare wrote – takes place in prison. He momentarily admits his fault ('I wasted time and now doth time waste me'), but his mind immediately diverts itself with yet another conceit and the syntax reveals little of his anxiety. Falstaff's prose soliloquies, syntactically quite complex, are simply wilful evasions of his own responsibilities. He is fully capable of seeing through the posturings of honour or the boasting of Shallow, but it does not suit him to admit this publicly.

It is Brutus who first articulates the psychological condition which gives rise to the best of the later Shakespearean soliloquies:

> Between the acting of a dreadful thing
> And the first motion, all the interim is
> Like a phantasma or a hideous dream:
> The genius and the mortal instruments
> Are then in council; and the state of man,

> Like to a little kingdom, suffers then
> The nature of an insurrection. (II.i.62–9)

In the early seventeenth century there was a growing interest in psychology, and this, coupled with the development of satire in the later sixteenth century, most probably fostered the use of the soliloquy as a convention for the expression of a disturbed mental state. Brutus, of course, is not emotionally unbalanced, although Hamlet seems to have moments of being fascinated by what he condemns. For almost the first time in Shakespeare, Brutus makes a deliberate moral choice, visualising the consequences of what he will do before he commits himself. This in turn necessitates a means of making the audience aware of his mental conflict. His first soliloquy, 'It must be by his death . . .', is therefore uncharacteristic, not in its diction since the whole play contains remarkably few obvious Latinisms, nor in its syntax which, as usual with Brutus, is composed of fairly short, coordinate phrases, but in the three analogies he uses: the adder, ambition's ladder and the serpent's egg. Although Brutus has occasional metaphors elsewhere – the tide in the affairs of men, for example – such a grouping of images is unusual with him and is perhaps indicative of his overwhelming need to prove to himself at this point that with Caesar's murder the end would justify the means.[8] As yet, however, we are not fully admitted to the recesses of his mind. He argues with Cassius rather than with himself. We see the philosophical conclusions of his deliberations rather than the deliberations themselves:

> There is a tide in the affairs of men,
> Which, taken at the flood, leads on to fortune;
> Omitted, all the voyage of their life
> Is bound in shallows and in miseries.
> On such a full sea are we now afloat. (IV.iii.216–20)

Twice (II.i.229, IV.iii.265) as the boy Lucius falls asleep, we are prepared for Brutus to reveal his innermost thoughts, but each time his reverie is interrupted, first by Portia and later by Caesar's ghost, before it has properly begun. In the noblest Roman of them all, the instinctive desire not to kill Caesar conflicts with his regard for the good of the state – but publicly, not privately. Later tragedies reverse this procedure: the passions of the individual cause upheavals in the state, rather than, as earlier, the public situation giving rise to private passions. Plutarch's interest in personality might be another feature leading to the development of the soliloquy after Julius Caesar.[9]

And so (inevitably) to *Hamlet*, with its seven soliloquies from the hero, plus one from Claudius. Should anyone doubt what the soliloquies contribute to *Hamlet*, let him read Marston's *Antonio's Revenge* (probably 1600 and therefore almost exactly contemporary). Antonio's father, too, has been poisoned and his mother is about to marry the murderer; the ghost of his dead father reveals the crime and calls upon his son to revenge it. Whether one play borrowed from the other or each borrowed independently from the *Ur-Hamlet*, need not concern us here. There are differences: Pandulpho is not Polonius, nor Mellida Ophelia. Although Antonio delays his revenge, there is little of the subtlety of *Hamlet*. His first response is to stab the murderer's little son Julio whose flesh is later served as a dish to Antonio's adversaries (shades of *Titus Andronicus*!). He often seems too concerned with the nicely-turned phrase (e.g. IV.i.38–59) or the show of grief (IV.ii.78–81). And, as J. W. Lever points out,[10] Antonio is not alone: the isolation of Hamlet is exceptional in revenge tragedy. Whether or not Marston tempered his approach to the abilities of his child actors, we are not shown the psychological pressures upon Antonio; his hysteria fails to convince. At the close of Act I, Hamlet sees the need 'to put an antic disposition on'. Everybody notices the change in him, and hence the greater need of the soliloquy to inform us of the true state of affairs. In *Hamlet* the soliloquies punctuate the play at significant points. The first establishes Hamlet's immediate reaction to his father's death and his mother's o'er-hasty marriage; the second occurs after the Ghost has told him that the death was in fact murder; the third follows the Player's recital of Aeneas' Tale to Dido and concludes the second act; the fourth ('To be or not to be?') comes very early in Act III and is unusual in that it is pure meditation with no direct application to Hamlet's own circumstances[11]; the fifth and shortest separates the confirmation of Claudius' guilt in the play scene and Hamlet's visit to his mother in her bedroom; in the sixth, Hamlet has stumbled upon Claudius vainly trying to pray; the last, again more philosophical and less violent than usual in its language, is occasioned by the news of Fortinbras' expedition to Poland. There are no soliloquies in Act V in which the play hastens to its bloody ending. What have they in common? First of all, Hamlet is naturally introspective, so that it seems fitting for him to soliloquise and indeed to philosophise and generalise, for, like Timon, he always reasons from the particular to the universal. Secondly, the pace may vary considerably within a soliloquy, and with it the kind of syntax employed.

Perhaps this is best illustrated by a closer examination of the first and the third soliloquies. The exclamations and curses of the first simply show Hamlet's anger and disgust, but what it is that disgusts him emerges gradually through the repetitions: 'But two months dead, nay, not so much, not two.... within a month... A little month... Within a month.' The parentheses, on the other hand, both reveal his habit of generalisation and, more important, show the confused thoughts bubbling to the surface of his mind, thus giving the illusion of natural, disordered mental activity, especially under stress:

> And yet *within a month* –
> Let me not think on't. Frailty, thy name is woman.
> A little month, or e'er those shoes were old
> With which she followed my poor father's body
> Like Niobe, all tears, why *she*, even she –
> O God, a beast that wants discourse of reason
> Would have mourned longer – *married with my uncle*,
> My father's brother, but no more like my father
> Than I to Hercules. (I.ii.145–53)

The third soliloquy uses different techniques. As in the final *Faustus* soliloquy, there are short lines which allow pause for reflection but which also carry the burden of the argument: 'For Hecuba' (the Player's feigned passion), 'Yet I' (what do *I* do?), 'O vengeance' (what I *should* do), 'A scullion'[12] (what I seem to be). A series of stressed nouns (*slave, player, fiction, passion, soul, conceit, tears, distraction, voice, function*) relate to comparatively weak verbs (*am, is, force, wanned, suiting* – the last two not finite verbs but participles). After the first short line, however, the verbs dominate: *weep, do, drown, cleave, make mad, appal, confound, amaze* – the player *does* something. A series of quick-fire questions:

> Am I a coward?
> Who calls me villain? Breaks my pate across?
> Plucks off my beard and blows it in my face?
> Tweaks me by the nose? Gives me the lie i' th' throat
> As deep as to the lungs? Who does me this? (II.ii.568–72)

gives way to two lines of curses:

> Bloody, bawdy villain!
> Remorseless, treacherous, lecherous, kindless villain! (577–8)

culminating in the next short line. Thereafter the ranting and cursing slow to a normal, far less broken syntax, in which Hamlet, with logical reasoning, decides on the next step, the use of the play to test Claudius' guilt. We can follow Hamlet's reaction to a changing situation (changing as his knowledge increases) through the soliloquies, because the soliloquy has now developed sufficiently to allow both character and audience to verbalise, in Daniel Seltzer's words, 'the thoughts and feelings of the moment', that is, how much information both can be expected to be aware of at that point in the play. No longer do characters describe themselves 'as though they knew the end of the plot of the play in which they were acting'.[13] Through the developed syntax of the soliloquies, Hamlet is able to convey to us what he asked of the actors, 'the very age and body of the time his form and pressure'.

Unlike Hamlet, Macbeth is not alone. Lady Macbeth carries on where the Witches leave off. The Witches do not mention murder to Macbeth; they prophecy the ends but they do not will the means. It is left to Lady Macbeth to show him that to achieve the throne of Scotland he must change his own nature. As McElroy puts it, Macbeth and his wife are complementary:

> Macbeth and his lady have the makings of one murderer between them. She is capable of contemplating the crime with something that borders upon exaltation, but is not, it turns out, capable of dealing the fatal stroke herself. He is quite capable of doing that, but cannot even think of the moral quality of the act without horror and aversion. He would, no doubt, be capable of resisting the temptation to strike were it not for the devastating attack she launches against the foundation of his world-view, his concept of what it means to be a man. Thus, the great confrontation between them in Act 1, scene vii, presents the disconcerting picture of two people inciting each other to crime, for the presence of each makes crime possible for the other.[14]

Possible, but not easy, for his doubts remain. She seemingly has no doubts, for the sharp interrogatives and imperatives of her plain style contrast with his agonising: '*What* do you mean?', '*Who* was it that thus cried?', and the directives:

> *Go, get* some water,
> And *wash* this filthy witness from your hand.
> *Why* did you bring these daggers from the place?
> They must lie there. *Go, carry them* and *smear*
> The sleepy grooms with blood.   (II.ii.46–50)

> *Retire we* to our chamber.
> A little water clears us of this deed;
> How easy is it then! Your constancy
> Hath left you unattended. *Hark!* more knocking.
> *Get on* your nightgown, lest occasion call us

And show us to be watchers. *Be not lost*
So poorly in your thoughts.   (II.ii.66–72)

and, seemingly conclusively:

Things without all remedy
Should be without regard; what's done is done.   (III.ii.11–12)

Later on, when the ghost of Banquo appears to Macbeth, she needs to be the perfect hostess, shepherding her guests away from disquieting thoughts and reminding him of his social obligations. Once more she is short with him:

Shame itself!
Why do you make such faces? When all's done
You look but on a stool.   (III.iv.65–7)

Her characteristic mode of utterance (especially in the first part of the play) is one composed, as here, of short syntactic units. Only to herself, as she receives the double news of the witches' appearance to Macbeth and Duncan's visit to the castle, will she admit to any *compunctious visitings of nature*: the high style is not for her.

She continually urges him on against what he sees as his better judgement. The opposition, following the killing of Duncan (Banquo, Malcolm, Macduff) is not particularly impressive and is within itself geographically divided. These two facts result in Macbeth being, in a very real sense, his own worst enemy. His moral convictions, originally firmly based, have been shattered by the Witches' promises and his own evident ability to follow them and murder Duncan. Henceforth, to quote McElroy once more, he is 'forced to judge himself and his deeds by a set of values from which his own actions have estranged him'.[15] Late in the play, Mentieth, more psychologically aware than his associates, recognises what has been Macbeth's dilemma throughout:

Who then shall blame
His pestered senses to recoil and start,
When all that is within him does condemn
Itself for being there?   (V.ii.22–5)

In this sort of situation the soliloquy comes into its own.

Macbeth's first 'soliloquy' is really an aside, but the distinction is unimportant. It at once introduces a type of syntax characteristic of the play, a kind of see-saw movement between opposites:

> This supernatural soliciting
> Cannot be ill, cannot be good. (I.iii.129–30)

The speech proceeds to consider each proposition logically: 'If ill . . .
If good . . .', and the antithesis runs throughout ('Present fears / Are
less than horrible imaginings'). It concludes with a paradox, 'nothing
is but what is not'. Paradox is perhaps more strongly marked in
Macbeth than in any other play.[16] Macbeth's very first words are pa-
radoxical:

> So foul and fair a day I have not seen. (I.iii.37)

and almost his last utterance realises the true paradox of the Witches'
promises:

> And be these juggling fiends no more believed
> That palter with us in a double sense,
> That keep the word of promise to our ear
> And break it to our hope. (V.vi.58–61)

As ever, Lady Macbeth is his best commentator, and, in her soliloquy as she reads the letter with the news of her husband's advancement, she significantly adopts 'his' syntax:

> What thou wouldst highly
> That wouldst thou holily, wouldst not play false,
> And yet wouldst wrongly win. (I.v.18–20)

and again, as she sees the danger posed by Banquo:

> Naught's had, all's spent,
> Where our desire is got without content. (III.ii.4–5)

And one paradox at least is finally proved true, as Birnam Wood
does indeed come to Dunsinane.

In the meantime, the same rhythm continues in Macbeth's second
soliloquy:

> If it were done when 'tis done, then 'twere well
> It were done quickly. If the assassination
> Could trammel up the consequence, and catch
> With his surcease success – that but this blow
> Might be the be-all and the end-all! – here,
> But here, upon this bank and shoal of time,
> We'd jump the life to come. (I.vii.1–7)

The rhetorical structure is once more taut: *If... then...*, and the logic equally firm: *But in these cases... He's here in double trust: / First... then... Besides...* Only with the mention of the *angels trumpet-tongued* does the soliloquy begin to slip out of control. Macbeth's vivid imagination is seen in the images of the naked newborn babe, heaven's cherubin, and the tears drowning the wind; only the entrance of Lady Macbeth interrupts the mounting hysteria. The dagger, at the beginning of the next soliloquy, very soon afterwards, is another manifestation of his mental torment. Again he swings between thinking of it as *palpable* and a dagger 'Proceeding from the heat-oppressed brain'. Repetition ('I see thee yet... I see thee still') helps to bind together the first half of the soliloquy, but once more logic gives way to imagination: the wolf arouses withered murder which, thus personified, stalks, ghostlike, its destined prey. In his soliloquies then, Macbeth drifts off into middle style generalities and personifications. It is his way of evading the consequences of reality, '*Words* to the heat of deeds' or, as his wife disdainfully calls it, 'the very painting of your fear'.

Once the deed is done, the tone alters. The simplicity of Banquo's 'Thou hast it now', which begins Act III, signals the change. Macbeth's 'To be thus is nothing, but to be safely thus...' appears to continue the probing syntax of his previous soliloquies, but most of the speech simply rehearses the Witches' prophecies. There follows immediately the scene with the assassins, in which Macbeth refuses to speak of murder but instead talks of *that business, his fall, the business* (again), *it, the work, absence, the fate of that dark hour.* He has caught an earlier trick of Lady Macbeth's: *that which rather thou dost fear to do, This night's great business, this enterprise, the deed.* But for her, what's done is done; for him the snake is merely scotched. He needs to articulate his fears, and so he turns to euphemism.[17] G. R. Hibbard reminds us that Macbeth tells his wife of the plot to murder Banquo only after all the arrangements have been made.[18] Even then, he does not speak directly, and her reply 'What's to be done?' (III.ii.44), lacking the decision of her earlier imperatives, perhaps begins the gradual process of isolation and resignation which ends in her suicide. Together with all this goes his decreasing grasp of present reality. Stones have been known to move and trees to speak. Macbeth appears only in the first scene of the fourth act and Lady Macbeth not at all. (Ironically she disappears commending to him 'the season of all natures, sleep' and reappears in V.i. sleep-walking.) Time must elapse for Lennox, 'another Lord', Ross, and also Malcolm and Macduff to signify, in the high style of affairs of state, the condition of Scotland under the usurper.

In Acts IV and V, flashes of the old antithetical style linger: 'From this moment / The very firstlings of my heart shall be / The firstlings of my hand'; 'This push / Will chair me ever or disseat me now'; and, most clearly:

> *If thou speak'st false,*
> Upon the next tree shalt thou hang alive
> Till famine cling thee. *If thy speech be sooth,*
> I care not if thou dost for me as much. (V.v.38–41)

but the resignation of *the sear and yellow leaf* and *tomorrow and tomorrow and tomorrow* increasingly take their place. The early violent images of the naked babe and the wolf give way to the walking shadow, the poor player, and the bear tethered to his stake. Macbeth has done his best to make himself into an automaton. He cannot quite sustain the role: he has *almost* supped full of horrors, is uneasily aware of the loss of sustaining honour and friendship, unwilling to fight with Macduff whose family he has murdered, conscious of the response his wife's death ought to – but no longer can – elicit ('There would have been a time for such a word'). But essentially Macbeth and his Lady have changed places. For her now 'All the perfumes of Arabia will not sweeten this little hand' ('A little water clears us of this deed') and she is troubled with *thick-coming fancies*. For him life has been pared down to plain style 'reality'. There remains only 'her' recipe of action, Bellona's bridegroom but no longer fighting the same enemy. Foul cannot, after all, be made fair. O come in, equivocator.[19]

Some of the techniques which Shakespeare had developed within the form of the soliloquy are employed in contemporary and later plays, but never, I think, so impressively as in *Hamlet* and *Macbeth*. Antony's soliloquies are primarily informative, but at the same time he reveals the tug-of-war between his duty to Rome and the delights of Cleopatra. The news of Fulvia's death, the marriage to Octavia, his belief that Cleopatra has betrayed him by surrendering her fleet to Caesar, his preparations for suicide after he supposes Cleopatra to be dead – all these soliloquies confirm a decision already made. But all are short, perhaps because the decision was never really in doubt. Enobarbus, too, soliloquises, but for a different reason. He is the keeper of Antony's conscience, the commentator on Antony's declining fortunes, but he is too loyal to reveal his true feelings publicly.

In *Othello*, the divided state of the hero's mind is conveyed by the same rhythm as in *Macbeth*:

> I think my wife be honest, and think she is not;
> I think that thou art just, and think thou art not.
> I'll have some proof. (III.iii.381−3)

and these lines occur at practically the dead centre of the play. Othello's control at the beginning of the action, both in Venice and in Cyprus ('Keep up your bright swords, for the dew will rust them'; 'He that stirs next to carve for his own rage / Holds his soul light: he dies upon his motion') contrasts sharply with the incoherence which, by Act IV, Iago's insinuations have produced. (To all intents this is a soliloquy, for Othello is not really conscious of Iago's presence.):

> Lie with her? Lie on her? − We say lie on her when they belie her. Lie with her! Zounds, that's fulsome! − Handkerchief − confession − handkerchief! To confess and be hanged for his labour. First to be hanged and then to confess! I tremble at it. Nature would not invest herself in such shadowing passion without some instruction. It is not words that shakes me thus! Pish! Noses, ears, and lips! Is't possible? − Confess? Handkerchief! O devil! (IV.i.35−43)

It communicates practically nothing directly because the normal syntactic connectors which make isolated words into sentences are absent. It is also in the prose often typical of a character temporarily deranged, and it has affinities with the broken, choking syntax of the soliloquy beside Desdemona's death-bed, just before Emilia enters:

> Yes, 'tis Emilia. − By and by. − She's dead.
> 'Tis like she comes to speak of Cassio's death:
> The noise was high. Ha! No more moving?
> Still as the grave. Shall she come in? Were't good?
> I think she stirs again. No. What's best to do?
> If she come in, she'll sure speak to my wife −
> My wife! My wife! What wife? I have no wife.
> O insupportable! O heavy hour!
> Methinks it should be now a huge eclipse
> Of sun and moon, and that th'affrighted globe
> Should yawn at alteration. (V.ii.92−102)

In the light of outbursts like these, we are encouraged to think again about Othello's earlier calm language: was it, after all, an imposed control, something the soldier had trained himself to show? Even in these earlier expressions there seems to lurk a sort of suppressed passion and poeticism: the *bright* swords may be rusted by

the *dew*. 'Rude am I in my speech', says Othello, but I doubt
whether he really believes it. He is more to the point five lines later:

> And little of this great world can I speak
> More than pertains to feats of broil and battle;
> And therefore little shall I grace my cause
> In speaking for myself. (I.iii.86–9)

since, as we have already seen, Iago can run rings round him philosophically and dialectically. For a professional soldier, Othello seems
oddly romantic about the pride, pomp and circumstance of glorious
war and we hear no mention of any private life until he met Desdemona. In his soliloquy which begins V.ii ('It is the cause...') the
syntax is straightforward enough, but he feels the need of figurative
language to represent Desdemona's purity: *smooth as monumental ala-
baster, that Promethean heat / That can thy light relume, thy rose, balmy
breath*. In the last few lines of the soliloquy just quoted, after the deed
is done and Emilia bangs on the door for entry, he thinks the whole
world, not simply *his* world, should end with the act. Yet I cannot
believe that all this is simply self-dramatisation, flamboyance, a delight in observing – or at least imagining – his own reactions. We
must allow for the rhetoric thought appropriate by the Elizabethans
for the description of heroes, and, at the other extreme, for our modern distaste for the heroic in drama, so that twentieth-century
tragedies are apt to be about the little man lost in a world wholly
alien to him. No one in the play accuses Othello of histrionics and he
does not seem to be striking a pose in the manner of Richard II.
Othello's grand manner never becomes ridiculous; it is part of his
make-up, to love expansively and to act immediately. The pity of it
is that he acts on insufficient evidence, really on no evidence at all.
The soliloquies show up the cracks in the facade.

Iago, too, has his soliloquies, but they are essentially in the manner of Richard III's, explaining how he delights to make the puppets
dance. There is certainly an air of spontaneity ('Let me see now...
How? How? Let's see... I have't') but there is practically no self-
questioning, for the *how* of the deed is all that matters to him. He is,
in fact, surprisingly opportunist, giving an impression of energy (by
a liberal use of compounds and colloquial idiom) and making clear
the general direction of his thought, but leaving the execution until
the last moment: ''Tis here, but yet confused' (II.i.302).[20] His
motivation is various and unclear – Cassio's advancement? Othello's
fancied adultery with Emilia? He is simply a master tactician.

Edmund, who has three soliloquies in the same scene (I.ii), has something of Iago's verve ('Now gods stand up for bastards.') but rather firmer logic ('Wherefore?... Why?... Well, then... Well...') and he has the detachment to view his own position philosophically ('This is the excellent foppery of the world').

One might expect Lear to soliloquise, but, as McElroy points out, the whole structure of the play differs from that of *Hamlet* and *Othello:*

> From his earliest plays onward, Shakespeare usually constructed characterizations sequentially; that is, the character unfolds before our eyes gradually, and we get to know a fair amount about him before he performs his most crucial actions. Thus, Hamlet soliloquizes, philosophizes, and discourses upon a variety of subjects, including himself, before he confronts the Ghost. We see Othello before he is jealous, and are shown Iago's plot developing gradually in his mind from its first inception. Nothing of the kind occurs in *King Lear.* The old monarch walks out, sits down on the throne, and without preliminaries proceeds to commit several of the most astounding blunders anywhere in world drama. At this point in the play, we know nothing of what is going on inside his mind... Lear's world makes sense to him, but we do not find out what kind of sense until by his own actions he has undermined its foundations.[21]

So we follow laboriously the progress of Lear's self-discovery. Technically there are no soliloquies; often it is difficult to be sure whether or not the other characters are meant to overhear him. Increasingly, Lear inhabits a world of his own creation and in it carries on a conversation with all kinds of characters, some real, some imagined. As E. A. J. Honigmann has perceptively observed:

> And when things go badly for him he retires into the inner self, where no one can follow – we hear him talking to himself but feel shut out from his inwardness, a retreat more impenetrable than Hamlet's or Othello's, because we hear only a part of a continuing private dialogue, Lear answering himself:
>
> > No, I will be the pattern of all patience;
> > I will say nothing.   (III.ii.37–8)
>
> > No, they cannot touch me for coining; I am the King himself.
> >   (IV.vi.83–4)
>
> Torn open by grief and rage, pitifully exposed by madness, the quintessential Lear shrinks into a secret place and wards off the prying world with his characteristic verbal gesture, negation, which is psychologically necessary to him as he tries to maintain his identity.[22]

The repeated *No* gives the illusion of a dialogue, but it is often difficult to identify Lear's *they.*

The 'problem' comedies have their soliloquies too, but, with one exception, they seem undeveloped in comparison with those of *Hamlet* and *Macbeth*. *Troilus and Cressida* uses soliloquies to punctuate the development of the love-affair: Troilus' opening realisation that he needs Pandarus to win Cressida's love dissolves in a conceit. Her decision ('Yet hold I off') and Troilus' fear that achievement cannot possibly measure up to expectation, are both short and neither is really argued. What might have been the exploration of a paradox in the manner of *Macbeth*, Troilus' refusal in V.ii to admit that Cressida can be false ('This is, and is not, Cressid'), is not, in fact, a soliloquy at all. The Duke in *Measure for Measure* has two expository soliloquies, and Isabella's resolve to ask Claudio to sacrifice himself for her ('More than our brother is our chastity') shows that the decision has really been arrived at before the soliloquy is begun. The exception to all this is Angelo's inability to pray (at the opening of II.iv). The effect is achieved by the regular clash of antitheses in stressed positions: *words / invention* ('imagination'), *mouth / heart, gravity / plume, place / seeming*. Once more we see the mind divided against itself. Yet, in my view, the two final images, the crowd around a fainting man whom they deprive of air and the multitude who flatter and distract a king, blur rather than reinforce the effect already made which is better achieved by the irony of Isabella's immediate entrance: 'I am come to know your pleasure'.

It is sometimes said that, in the final plays, soliloquies are reduced in number and that exploration of character gives way to complexity of plot,[23] as fathers rediscover lost children, and husbands wives, and themselves in the process. This is only partly true. *Cymbeline* is full of soliloquies. The Queen, Imogen, Iachimo, Cloten, Posthumus, Pisanio, Belarius – in fact, almost everyone except Cymbeline himself – soliloquises. For the most part, however, these soliloquies are of the earlier expository kind which reveal to the audience either the situation or the character's future intentions and which recall most the early histories and tragedies. Perhaps the intricacy of the plots makes some of these necessary to the audience's comprehension. Wolsey, that arch-politician, seems a likely figure to soliloquise, and he has two soliloquies in *Henry VIII* III.ii. The first shows his mind racing to find explanations for his apparent sudden fall from grace and a possible *new device* to regain royal favour; it is full of rapid self-questions to which, alas, he sees no sure answers. The second, 'A long farewell to all my greatness', is metaphorical, somewhat in the manner of Richard II in prison, but without the self-pity. Posthumus, wrongly believing Imogen to be unfaithful, acts not unlike

Hamlet. Extravagant praise jostles with curses and heaped-up questions:

> O, vengeance, vengeance!
> Me of my lawful pleasure she restrained
> And prayed me oft forbearance – did it with
> A pudency so rosy, the sweet view on't
> Might well have warmed old Saturn – that I thought her
> As chaste as unsunned snow. O, all the devils!
> This yellow Iachimo in an hour, was't not?
> Or less? At first?

Like Hamlet, he generalises: Imogen is false, so must all women be. Copious lexis 'proves' his case:

> Be it lying, note it,
> The woman's; flattering, hers; deceiving, hers;
> Ambitions, covetings, change of prides, disdain,
> Nice longing, slanders, mutability,
> All faults that have a name . . .   (II.v.8–15, 22–7)

I have earlier analysed the kind of syntax which reveals Leontes' extreme perturbation.[24]

Yet it remains true that, in the last plays, Shakespeare seems less concerned to show the mind turned against itself and more interested in – what? The language which suggests true pathos or the serenity of reconcilement? The true pastoral of the Welsh mountains or of Bohemia (with its rogue Autolycus but no melancholy Jaques)? Whatever it was, there are signs of yet further experimentation with language, a willingness to revive old techniques occasionally but a refusal to stand pat on what had already been achieved. If the final style often appears diminuendo, this is no more than rhetorical decorum, but that need not be restrictive. Man had always been infinite in his faculties, in form and moving express and admirable. There was still so much to do.

But perhaps I am wrong about this, and it might be instructive, even if fanciful, to imagine Shakespeare taking another view of his writing around 1612–13. The final plays work through a relative simplicity of lexis to the alternation of colloquial and deliberately complex syntax. The peal of ordnance which set fire to the Globe in 1613 and burnt down the theatre might have had its linguistic counterpart. Perhaps Shakespeare not altogether unwillingly put off the amazing technicolour dreamcoat of literary language to return to Stratford, to at least semi-retirement, to just about the best house in the town (with its second-best bed). The time is free. He can pass his days once more in speaking that 'real' language which, in the last resort, we can never really know.

NOTES AND REFERENCES

1. Bradbrook (1951), p.83.
2. Bennett (1976).
3. Examples of the first kind are *1 Hen VI* III.i.189–203, V.iii.24–9, *2 Hen VI* IV.x.74–82, *3 Hen VI* I.iv.1–26, and of the second, *1 Hen VI*, I.i.173–7, V.v.103–8, *2 Hen VI* I.i.212–57, *3 Hen VI* III.iii.256–65.
4. Saccio (1977), p.159. Hibbard (1981); p.96 interestingly sees Petruchio as the comic counterpart of Richard III: a consummate actor-manager and a master of rhetoric.
5. Turner (1964), p.257.
6. *The Spanish Tragedy* is quoted from *Minor Elizabethan Tragedies*, ed. T. W. Craik, Dent (1974), and Marlowe from *Complete Plays and Poems*, ed. E. D. Pendry, Dent (1976).
7. Clemen (1961), p.50. See also Palmer (1964).
8. Palmer (1970).
9. Whitaker (1965), p.97 and Heilman (1964).
10. Lever (1971), pp. 18–26; *Antonio's Revenge* is edited by G. K. Hunter, Arnold (1968).
11. Clemen (1972), p.160.
12. So F1; Q2, followed by New Penguin, reads *stallion*.
13. Seltzer (1977).
14. McElroy (1973), p.221.
15. McElroy (1973), p.228.
16. Burrell (1954).
17. Jorgensen (1971), p.49.
18. Hibbard (1981), p.29.
19. *Equivocation* is rare in Shakespeare outside *Macbeth*.
20. This chapter was already in draft when I read the discussion in Evans (1979), pp. 128–32.
21. McElroy (1973), p. 164.
22. Honigmann (1976), p.136.
23. Ewbank (1980), p.115.
24. pp. 101–2

Select bibliography

I have made most use of the following reference books:

The Oxford English Dictionary (OED), ed. J. A. H. Murray, H. Bradley, W. A. Craigie and C. T. Onions, Clarendon Press, Oxford (1933)

ONIONS, C. T. The Oxford Dictionary of English Etymology, Clarendon Press, Oxford (1966)

SPEVACK, M. The Harvard Concordance to Shakespeare, Belknap-Harvard, Cambridge, Mass. (1973)

BULLOUGH, G. Narrative and Dramatic Sources of Shakespeare, I–VIII, Routledge & Kegan Paul (1957–75)

BEVINGTON, D. Shakespeare, Goldentree Bibliographies, AHM Publishing, Arlington Heights, Illinois (1978)

WELLS, S. Shakespeare, Oxford Select Bibliographical Guides, OUP (1973)

TRAVERSI, D, Renaissance Drama, Macmillan (1980)

Abbreviations

CQ	Critical Quarterly
E & S	Essays and Studies by Members of the English Association
EC	Essays in Criticism
ELH	ELH, A Journal of English Literary History
Eng. St.	English Studies
PBA	Publications of the British Academy
REL	Review of English Literature
SEL	Studies in English Literature
SQ	Shakespeare Quarterly
S on A St.	Stratford on Avon Studies

S St.   Shakespeare Studies
SS   Shakespeare Survey
TPS   Transactions of the Philological Society

Books are cited by author, title, publisher, place of publication (if other than London) and date. Secondary sources are cited in full in the Notes.

ANDERSON, J. J. 'The morality of *Love's Labour's Lost*', *SS*, **24** (1971), pp. 55–62

BARBER, C. *Early Modern English*, André Deutsch (1976)

BARISH, J. A. *Ben Jonson and the Language of Prose Comedy*, Harvard University Press, Harvard (1960)

BARISH, J. A. 'Shakespeare's prose', Ch. 16. pp. 245–63 in N. Rabkin (ed.), *Approaches to Shakespeare*, McGraw-Hill, New York (1964)

BARISH, J.A. '*The Spanish Tragedy* or the pleasures and perils of rhetoric', Ch. 3, pp. 59–86, in *Elizabethan Theatre*, *S on A St.*,**9** (1966)

BARISH, J.A. 'Pattern and purpose in the prose of *Much Ado About Nothing, Rice University Studies*, **60**, (1974), pp. 19–30

BAXTER, J. *Shakespeare's Poetic Styles*, Routledge & Kegan Paul (1980)

BENNETT, R. B. 'The reform of the malcontent: Jaques and the meaning of *As You Like It*', *S. St.*, **9**, (1976), pp. 183–204

BERRY, R. *The Shakespearean Metaphor*, Rowman (1978)

BLAKE, N. F. *Caxton's Own Prose*, André Deutsch (1973)

BOOTH, S. *An Essay on Shakespeare's Sonnets*, Yale University Press, New Haven and London (1969)

BOOTH, S. 'Syntax and rhetoric in *Richard II*', *Mosaic,* **10** (1977), pp. 87–103

BRADBROOK, M. C. *Shakespeare and Elizabethan Poetry*, Chatto & Windus (1951)

BRADBROOK, M. C. *Shakespeare: The Poet in His World*, Weidenfeld & Nicolson (1978)

BROOK, G. L. *The Language of Shakespeare*, André Deutsch (1976)

BROOKE, N. *Shakespeare's Early Tragedies*, Methuen (1978)

BROOKS, H.F. *A Midsummer Night's Dream*, New Arden edition, Methuen (1979)

BROWN, J. R. *The White Devil*, Methuen (1960)

BULLOUGH, G. *Narrative and Dramatic Sources of Shakespeare*, **I–VIII**, Routledge & Kegan Paul (1957–75)

BURCKHARDT, S. *Shakespearean Meanings*, Princeton University Press, Princeton (1968)

BURRELL, M. D. '*Macbeth*: a study in paradox', *Shakespeare Jahrbuch*, **90** (1954), pp. 167–90

BURTON, D. M. *Shakespeare's Grammatical Style*, University of Texas Press, Austin and London (1968)

CALDERWOOD, J. L. '*Love's Labour's Lost*: a wantoning with words', *SEL*, **5** (1965), pp. 317–32

CALDERWOOD, J. L. '*Coriolanus*: wordless meanings and meaningless words', *SEL*, **6** (1966), pp. 211–24

CALDERWOOD, J. L. *Metadrama in Shakespeare's Henriad*, University of California Press, Berkeley and Los Angeles (1979)

CAREY, J. 'Sixteenth and seventeenth century prose', Ch. 12, pp. 339–431 in C. Ricks (ed.) *English Poetry and Prose, 1570–1674*. Sphere (1970)

CARROLL, W. C. *The Great Feast of Languages in 'Love's Labour's Lost'*, Princeton University Press, Princeton (1976)

CHAMPION, L. *Shakespeare's Tragic Perspective*, University of Georgia Press, Athens, Georgia (1976)

CLEMEN, W. *English Tragedy before Shakespeare*, Methuen (1961)

CLEMEN, W. *Shakespeare's Dramatic Art*, Methuen (1972)

CLEMEN, W. *The Development of Shakespeare's Imagery*, 2nd edn, Methuen (1977)

CLEMEN, W. 'Some aspects of style in the *Henry VI* plays', pp. 9–24 in P. Edwards, I-S. Ewbank, and G. K. Hunter, (eds), *Shakespeare's Styles, Essays in Honour of Kenneth Muir*, CUP (1980)

COLMAN, E. A. M. *The Dramatic Use of Bawdy in Shakespeare*, Longman (1974)

COOK, A. J. 'The audience of Shakespeare's plays: a reconsideration', *Sh.St.*, **7** (1974) pp. 283–305

COOK, A. J. *The Privileged Playgoers of Shakespeare's London*, Princeton University Press, Princeton (1981)

COPLEY, J. *Shift of Meaning*, OUP (1961)

COULTHARD, M. *An Introduction to Discourse Analysis*, Longman (1977)

CRUTWELL, P. *The Shakespearean Moment*, Chatto and Windus (1954)

CUSACK, B. 'Shakespeare and the tune of the time', *SS*, **23** (1970), pp. 1–12

DANBY, J. *Shakespeare's Doctrine of Nature*, Faber & Faber (1949)

DANSON, L. P. *Tragic Alphabet, Shakespeare's Drama of Language*, Yale University Press, New Haven and London (1974)

DANSON, L. P. *The Harmonies of the Merchant of Venice*, Yale University Press, New Haven and London (1978)

DE GRAZIA, M. 'Shakespeare's view of language: an historical perspective', *SQ*, **29** (1978) pp. 374–88

DIXON, P. *Rhetoric*, Methuen (1971)

DONNER, M. 'Derived words in Chaucer's language', *Chaucer Review*, **13** (1978), pp. 1–15

DORAN, M. *Shakespeare's Dramatic Language*, University of Wisconsin Press, Madison and London (1976)

EBIN, L. 'Lydgate's views on poetry', *Annuale Mediaevale*, **18** (1977), pp. 76–105

ELIOT, T. S. *Selected Essays*, Faber & Faber (1951)

EVANS, B. *Shakespeare's Tragic Practice*, Clarendon Press, Oxford (1979)

EWBANK, I-S. '"Were man but constant, he were perfect": constancy and consistency in *The Two Gentlemen of Verona*', Ch. 2, pp. 31–57, in *Shakespearean Comedy*, S on A St. **14** (1972)

EWBANK, I-S. '"My name is Marina": the language of recognition', pp. 111–30 in P. Edwards, I-S. Ewbank, and G. K. Hunter (eds), *Sheakespeare's Styles, Essays in Honour of Kenneth Muir*, CUP (1980)

FOWLER, R. *Style and Structure in Literature*, Basil Blackwell, Oxford (1975)

GILBERT, A. J. *Literary Language from Chaucer to Johnson*, Macmillan (1979)

GILBERT, A. J. 'Techniques of focus in Shakespeare's sonnets', *Language and Style*, **12** (1979), pp. 245–67

GREENE, G. 'Language and value in Shakespeare's *Troilus and Cressida*', *SEL*, **21** (1981), pp. 271–85

HALL, A. D. 'Tudor prose style: English humanists and the problem of a standard', *English Literary Renaissance*, **7** (1977), pp. 267–96

HARRIS, D. J. *Elizabethan Prose*, Longman (1968)

HART, A. 'Vocabularies of Shakespeare's plays', *Review of English Studies*, **19** (1943), pp. 128–40

HEILMAN, R. B. '"To know himself": an aspect of tragic structure', *REL*, **5** (1964), pp. 36–57

HENIGER, S. K. 'The pattern of *Love's Labour's Lost*', *S. St.*, **7** (1974), pp. 25–33

HIBBARD, G. R. 'The forced gait of a shuffling nag', pp. 76–88, in C. Leech, and J. M. R. Margeson (eds), *Shakespeare 1971*, University of Toronto Press, Toronto (1972)

HIBBARD, G. R. *The Making of Shakespeare's Dramatic Poetry*, University of Toronto Press, Toronto and London (1981)

HILL, R. F. 'Dramatic techniques and interpretation in *Richard II*', Ch. 5, pp. 101–22 in *Early Shakespeare*, S on A St., **3** (1961)

HILL, R. F. '*Coriolanus*: violentest contrariety', *E & S*, **17** (1964) pp. 12–23

HOCKEY, D. C. 'A world of rhetoric in *Richard II, SQ,* **15** (1964), pp. 179–91

HOLMES, E. *Aspects of Elizabethan Imagery,* Basil Blackwell, Oxford (1929)

HONIGMANN, E. A. J. *Shakespeare: Seven Tragedies,* New York, Barnes and Noble (1976)

HULME, H. M. *Explorations in Shakespeare's Language,* Longman (1962)

HUME, R. D. 'Individuation and development of character through language in *Antony and Cleopatra',* *SQ,* **24** (1973), pp. 280–300

HUNTER, G. K. 'The dramatic technique of Shakespeare's sonnets', *EC,* **3** (1953) pp. 152–64

HUNTER, G. K. *All's Well That Ends Well,* New Arden, Methuen (1959)

HUNTER, G. K. *John Lyly: The Humanist as Courtier,* Routledge & Kegan Paul (1962)

INGLEDEW, J. *Antony and Cleopatra,* New Swan Advanced series, Longman (1971)

INGLEDEW, J. *Coriolanus,* New Swan Advanced series, Longman (1973)

JONES, R.F. *The Triumph of the English Language,* Stanford University Press, Stanford (1953)

JORGENSEN, P. *Redeeming Shakespeare's Words,* University of California Press, Berkeley and Los Angeles (1962)

JORGENSEN, P. *Our Naked Frailties: Sensational Art and Meaning in Macbeth,* University of California Press, Berkeley and Los Angeles (1971)

JOSEPH, M. *Shakespeare's Use of the Arts of Language,* Columbia University Press, New York (1947)

JUMP, J. 'Shakespeare and history', *CQ,* **17** (1975), pp. 223–44.

KERNAN, A. 'The plays and the playwrights', Ch. 4, pp. 269–99, particularly pp. 288–99, in C. Leech and T. W. Craik (eds) *The Revels History of Drama in English,* III, Methuen (1975)

KERNAN, A. *The Playwright as Magician,* Yale University Press, New Haven and London (1979)

KING A. H. *The language of Satirized Characters in Poetaster, Lund Studies in English,* **10**, Gleerup, Lund (1941)

LANHAM, R. A. *The Motives of Eloquence,* Yale University Press, New Haven and London (1976)

LEIDER, E. W. 'Plainness of style in *King Lear',* *SQ,* **21** (1970), pp. 45–53

LEVER, J. W. *The Tragedy of State,* Methuen (1971)

LLOYD, M. 'The Roman tongue', *SQ,* **10** (1959), pp. 461–8

MacALINDON, T. P. 'Language, style and meaning in *Troilus and Cressida', Publications of the Modern Language Association of America*, **84** (1969), pp. 29–43

MCELROY, B. *Shakespeare's Mature Tragedies*, Princeton University Press, Princeton (1973)

MCINTOSH, A. '*As You Like It*: a grammatical clue to character', *REL*, **4** (1963), pp. 68–79

MAHOOD, M. M. *Shakespeare's Wordplay*, Methuen (1957)

MATTHEWS, W. 'Language in *Love's Labour's Lost', E & S*, **17** (1964), pp. 1–11

MILLWARD, C. 'Pronominal case in Shakespearean imperatives', *Language*, **42** (1966), pp. 10–17

MUIR, K. *Shakespeare's Sonnets*, Unwin (1979)

MUIR, K. AND SCHOENBAUM, S. *A New Companion to Shakespeare Studies*, CUP (1971)

MULHOLLAND, J. '"Thou" and "You" in Shakespeare: a study in the second person pronoun', *Eng. St.*, **48** (1967), pp. 34–43

MULRYNE, J. R. '*The White Devil* and *The Duchess of Malfi*', Ch. 9, pp. 201–25, in *Jacobean Shakespeare, S on A St.*, **1** (1960)

NEELY, C. T. '*The Winter's Tale*: the triumph of speech', *SEL,* **15** (1975), pp. 321–38

NOWOTTNY, W. 'Formal elements in Shakespeare's sonnets', *EC*, **2** (1952), pp. 76–84

NOWOTTNY, W. *The Language Poets Use*, Athlone Press (1962)

OLIVER, H. J. *The Merry Wives of Windsor*, New Arden edition, Methuen (1971)

OWEN, C. A. 'Comic awareness, style and dramatic technique in *Much Ado About Nothing', Boston University Studies in English*, **5** (1961), pp. 193–207

PALMER, D. J. 'Magic and poetry in *Doctor Faustus', CQ*, **6** (1964), pp. 56–67

PALMER, D. J. 'Elizabethan tragic heroes', Ch. 1., pp. 11–36 in *Elizabethan Theatre, S on A St.*, **9** (1966)

PALMER, D. J. 'Tragic error in *Julius Caesar', SQ,* **21** (1970), pp. 399–410

PARTRIDGE, A. C. *Orthography in Shakespeare and Elizabethan Drama*, Edwin Arnold (1964)

PARTRIDGE, A. C. *The Language of Renaissance Poetry*, André Deutsch (1971)

PARTRIDGE, A. C. *A Substantive Grammar of Shakespeare's Non-Dramatic Texts*, University of Virginia Press, Charlottesville, Virginia (1976)

PARTRIDGE, E. *Shakespeare's Bawdy,* Routledge & Kegan Paul (1947)

PEARSALL, D. A. *John Lydgate,* Routledge & Kegan Paul (1970)

PEET, D. 'The rhetoric of *Tamburlaine*', *ELH,* **26** (1959), pp. 137–55

POTTER, L. 'The antic disposition of Richard II', *SS,* **27** (1974), pp. 33–41

QUIRK, R. 'Shakespeare and the English language', Ch. 5, pp. 67–82 in K. Muir and S. Schoenbaum (eds), *A New Companion to Shakespeare Studies,* CUP (1971)

REES, J. *Shakespeare and the Story,* Athlone Press (1978)

REPLOGLE, C. 'Not parody, not burlesque: the play within the play in Hamlet', *Modern Philology,* **67** (1969), pp. 150–9

REIBETANZ, J. *The Lear World,* Heinemann (1977)

SACCIO, P. *Shakespeare's English Kings,* OUP (1977)

SALMON, V. 'Sentence structures in colloquial Shakespearean English', *TPS* (1965), pp. 105–40

SALMON, V. 'Elizabethan colloquial English in the Falstaff plays', *Leeds Studies in English,* new series, **1** (1967), pp. 37–70

SALMON, V. 'Some functions of Shakespearean word-formation', *SS,* **23** (1970), pp. 13–26

SAMUELS, M. I. 'The role of functional selection in the history of English', *TPS,* pp. 15–40 (1965), reprinted in R. Lass *Approaches to English Historical Linguistics,* pp. 325–44 (1969)

SAMUELS, M. L. *Linguistic Evolution,* CUP (1972)

SELTZER, D. 'Prince Hal and the tragic style', *SS,* **30** (1977), pp. 13–27

SHERBO, A. *English Poetic Diction from Chaucer to Wordsworth,* Michigan State University Press, East Lansing (1975)

SICHERMAN, C. M. '*Coriolanus*: the failure of words', *ELH,* **39** (1972), pp. 189–207

SMITH, J. 'The language of Leontes', *SQ,* **19** (1968), pp. 317–27

STARNES, D. T. AND NOYES, G. E. *The English Dictionary from Cawdrey to Johnson, 1604–1755,* North Carolina University Press, Chapel Hill (1946)

SUTHERLAND, J. R. 'How the characters talk', Ch. 6, pp. 116–35 in J. R. Sutherland and J. Hurtsfield (eds), *Shakespeare's World,* Arnold (1964)

TAYLOR, E. W. 'Shakespeare's use of –*eth* and –*es* endings of verbs in the First Folio', *CLA Journal,* **19** (1976), pp. 437–57

THOMSON, P. 'Rant and cant in *Troilus and Cressida*', *E & S* **22** (1976), pp. 33–56

THORNE, J. P. 'The grammar of jealousy: a note on the character of Leontes', pp. 55–65 in A. J. Aitken, A. McIntosh and H. Palsson (eds) *Edinburgh Studies in English and Scots*, Longman (1971)

TURNER, R. Y. 'Characterization in Shakespeare's early history plays', *ELH*, **31** (1964), pp. 241–58

VAN DYKE, J. 'Making a scene: language and gesture in *Coriolanus*', *SS*, **30** (1977), pp. 135–46

VICKERS, B. *The Artistry of Shakespeare's Prose*, Methuen (1968)

VICKERS, B. *Seventeenth Century Prose*, Longman (1969)

VICKERS, B. 'Shakespeare's use of rhetoric', Ch. 6, pp. 83–98 in K. Muir and S. Schoenbaum (eds) *A New Companion to Shakespeare Studies*, CUP (1971)

VICKERS, B. *Shakespeare: The Critical Heritage*, Routledge & Kegan Paul (1974)

VICKERS, B. *Shakespeare: Coriolanus*, Edwin Arnold (1976)

WALDRON, R. A. *Sense and Sense-Development*, André Deutsch (1967)

WALES, K. 'An aspect of Shakespeare's dynamic language', *Eng. St.*, **59** (1978), pp. 395–404

WALL, S. 'Shakespeare: his later plays', Ch. 4, pp. 253–73 in C. Ricks (ed.), *English Drama to 1710*, Sphere (1971)

WATKINS, W. B. C. *Shakespeare and Spenser*, Princeton University Press, Princeton (1950)

WHITAKER, V. K. *The Mirror Up to Nature*, Huntington Library, San Marino (1965)

WILLCOCK, G. D. 'Language and poetry in Shakespeare's early plays', *PBA*, **40** (1954), pp. 103–17

WILLIAMSON, G. 'Senecan style in the seventeenth century', *Philological Quarterly*, **15** (1936), pp. 321–51, reprinted in S. Fish (ed.), *Seventeenth Century Prose*, OUP (1971)

WILSON, F. P. 'Shakespeare and the diction of common life', *PBA*, **27** (1941), pp. 167–97, reprinted in H. Gardner (ed.), *Shakespearean and Other Studies*, Clarendon Press, Oxford (1969)

Index

211

List of words